TOP F

attrac

CW00432675

DISNEY'S ANIMAL KINGDOM® T

At Walt Disney World this latest theme park brings together more than 1,000 exotic animals and birds, exciting colorful shows and the world's largest sculpted tree. Disney's Animal Kingdom is part zoo, part fantasy and is unlike anywhere else in Walt Disney World.

DISNEY-MGM STUDIOS

Lose yourself in film land for a day. There are one or two rides, plus The Twilight Zone™ Tower of Terror which could be the ultimate in terror rides.

Epcot®

Two themes in one: Future World which has ten major exhibits/attractions and World Showcase which features eleven national pavilions. There are no thrill rides here.

MAGIC KINGDOM® PARK

The best of all the theme parks. Disney magic and Mickey Mouse plus lots of glitz, mainstreet America as it could have been and enough entertainment for children of all ages.

SEA WORLD OF FLORIDA

If you are into marine life and manatees, this is for you. Journey to Atlantis is the park's major thrill ride. Sea World features Shamu the killer whale.

UNIVERSAL STUDIOS FLORIDA

More film land, with family shows and where popular hell-fire terror rides are an art form.

BUSCH GARDENS

A zoological garden set mainly in Africa with thrills galore on several rides. In Tampa, an hour's drive from Orlando.

KENNEDY SPACE VISITORS COMPLEX

The best family value in Florida. Free admission. The only ride here is on a bus! You pay for the IMAX theaters and the bus rides only.

For a family of four, a day's entrance and carpark fee at some attractions can be about $165, even with discounts. See pages 10-11 for details.

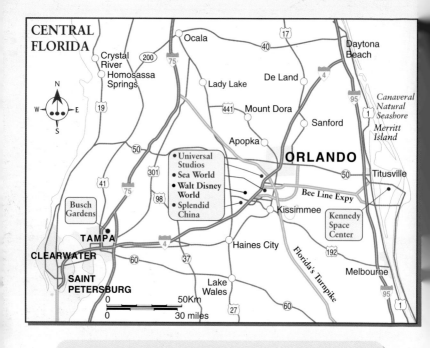

MAPS

- Walt Disney World® Resort — 19
- Magic Kingdom® Park — 30/31
- Epcot® — 50
- Disney's Animal Kingdom® Theme Park — 70
- Disney – MGM Studios — 78
- Sea World — 91
- Universal Studios — 107
- Splendid China — 115
- Greater Orlando: Other Attractions — 122
- International Drive Resort Area — 126
- Kissimmee – St Cloud Attractions — 130
- Ideas for days out — 143
- Central Gulf Coast — 159
- Busch Gardens — 162
- Ybor City — 173
- The Space Coast — 198
- Greater Orlando: Accommodation — 218

Orlando
& Central Florida

Don Philpott

LANDMARK VISITORS GUIDE

Contents

1 WELCOME TO ORLANDO & CENTRAL FLORIDA 6

Flora and Fauna 7
History 8
Major Attractions
Price Guide 10
Planning Your Holiday 12
Getting Around 15
Questions & Answers 17

2 WALT DISNEY WORLD® RESORT 18

The Theme Parks 21
Planning your visit 23

THE MAGIC KINGDOM® PARK 29
Shows 29
Main Street USA 31
Cinderella Castle 33
Adventureland 34
Frontierland 35
Liberty Square 37
Fantasyland 41
Mickey's Toontown Fair 43
Tomorrowland 44

Epcot® 48
Getting there 48
Attractions, entertain-
ments and tours 48
Essential Information 49
Getting around Epcot 51
Future World 51
World Showcase 60

DISNEY'S ANIMAL KINGDOM® THEME PARK 68
The Oasis 69
Safari Village 69

Camp Minnie-Mickey 72
Africa 72
Conservation Station 72
Asia 73
DinoLand USA 73
Disney's Animal
Kingdom Shows 73

DISNEY-MGM STUDIOS 75
Getting there 75
Arrival 75
Essential Information 76
Entertainment 76
Park Attractions 80

OTHER DISNEY ATTRACTIONS 86

3 SEA WORLD, UNIVERSAL STUDIOS AND SPLENDID CHINA 90

SEA WORLD OF FLORIDA 90
Planning your day 91
Essential Information 92
Shows and Stadiums 93
Making the most
of your day 94
Park Attractions 96

UNIVERSAL STUDIOS FLORIDA 104
Getting there 104
Getting around 104
Essential Information 105
Main attractions 106

SPLENDID CHINA 114
Major exhibits 117

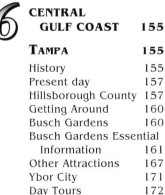

4 **OTHER ATTRACTIONS** **119**

Orlando 119
Kissimmee and
St Cloud 130

5 **IDEAS FOR DAYS OUT** **138**

Bok Tower Gardens 138
Cypress Gardens 139
Silver Springs 141
Seminole County 143
Lake County 147

STATE NATIONAL PARKS, HISTORIC SITES & RECREATION AREAS 152

6 **CENTRAL GULF COAST** **155**

TAMPA **155**

History 155
Present day 157
Hillsborough County 157
Getting Around 160
Busch Gardens 160
Busch Gardens Essential
Information 161
Other Attractions 167
Ybor City 171
Day Tours 172

ST PETERSBURG & CLEARWATER 180

Tarpon Springs
and the Pinellas
Suncoast 182
Attractions 185
South of Tampa Bay 191

STATE NATIONAL PARKS, HISTORIC SITES & RECREATION AREAS 193

7 **THE SPACE COAST 199**

Kennedy Space
Visitor Center 200
Watching The
Orbiter Lift Off 202
Touring KSC 204
Canaveral National
Seashore & Merritt
Island National
Wildllfe Refuge 206
Cocoa Beach
and Beyond 210

STATE NATIONAL PARKS, HISTORIC SITES & RECREATION AREAS 217

FACTFILE **218**
Eating Out 227
Information for
Overseas Visitors 235
INDEX **252**

SHOPPING

Orlando 124
Kissimmee & St Cloud 137
St Petersburg
& Clearwater 189

CALENDARS

Orlando 121
Kissimmee & St Cloud 132
Lake County 150
Central Gulf Coast 184
Space Coast 215

WELCOME TO ORLANDO & CENTRAL FLORIDA

1

'Once you get the Florida sand in your shoes, you will always want to return.'

Central Florida is the world's top tourist destination and is set to stay that way. Its success is a result of a number of factors including year-round sunshine, world class attractions, relaxed atmosphere, superb beaches, great service, good food, fascinating wildlife and spectacular value. The popularity of Central Florida is best illustrated by the millions of people who go back year after year. There is always something new or different to see, and you would have to spend a lifetime of holidays there to fully experience everything that Central Florida has to offer.

Florida covers an area of almost 58,665 sq miles (152,066 sq km) and is mostly a peninsula jutting out from the south-east corner of the continent separating the Atlantic Ocean and the

Above: *You are guaranteed a wonderful day out at Universal Studios (© Universal Studios Florida)*

Gulf of Mexico. It is the most southerly mainland state of the USA. Its most northerly point is still 100 miles (161km) south of the most southerly point in California, and more than 1,000 miles (1,610km) further south than the French Riviera. It borders only two states — Georgia and Alabama in the north — and its capital Tallahassee is in the north-west area known as the Panhandle.

The resident population is just under 13 million although this mushrooms every year as around 45 million holidaymakers are drawn to the 'Sunshine State'.

The average summer temperature tops 80°F (27°C) throughout the state and winter temperatures in the south average 68.5°F (20°C). There are more than 30,000 lakes, 105 State Parks, 7 National Parks, 3 National Forests, around 1,000 golf courses, 17 greyhound tracks, 6 horse racing venues, and of course, some of the world's top tourist attractions such as Walt Disney World® Resort, Sea World, Busch Gardens and Cape Canaveral. It is no wonder that Florida is the world's number one tourist destination.

The highest point in the state is in the far north, just south of the border with Alabama, and at 345ft (105m) above sea level it is in Florida terms a veritable mountain. Most of the land is less than 100ft (30m) above sea level. Underneath the topsoil lies a limestone bed, and erosion of this has carved out the thousands of lakes, caves and springs for which the state is so famous.

Flora and Fauna

More than half of Florida is covered by forests and more than 300 types of trees have been identified together with over 3,500 other plants. The hardwood forests of the north give way to the tropical forests and mangrove swamps of the south, but everywhere there is lush vegetation. In the north beech, sweet gum, red maple, hickory and magnolia predominate, while in the south it is oaks, pine, cypresses, palms and mangroves. In Central Florida the two types of habitat merge. The State tree is the **Sabal Palm** and the State flower the **Orange Blossom.**

Florida also has a rich and diverse wildlife and many of the rarer animals, such as panther and crocodile are protected. There are about 100 species of mammals including black bear, boar and puma. The delightful manatee needs all the protection it can get, while porpoises and dolphins are plentiful and can be found in inland and coastal waters. There are about 420 species of birds (the State bird being the **Mocking Bird**),

700 species of fish, 40 species of snake — the four poisonous types are rattlesnake, coral, cottonmouth moccasin and copperhead — and many other reptiles of which the alligator is the most celebrated. You are quite likely to see armadillos or porcupines shuffling along roadsides late at night.

History

There were many Indian tribes occupying different parts of Florida when the first European explorers arrived; the Apalachees, Tocobagas and Timucuans in the west, the fierce nomadic Calusas, allegedly 7ft (2m) tall, who were masters of the Everglades and a number of smaller tribes, mostly on the move to avoid the others. By 1750, however, imported diseases, slavery and war had wiped out almost all the Indians.

The first permanent Spanish settlement, and the oldest European settlement anywhere in the USA, was established by Pedro Menéndez de Áviles at St Augustine in 1565. A year earlier, and about 50 miles (80km) away, a group of Protestant Huguenots under René Goulaine de Laudonniér built Fort Caroline at the mouth of the St Johns River, but it was overrun by Menéndez in 1565 and renamed San Mateo. The Spanish colonisation then

Juan Ponce de León

Florida was named by Juan Ponce de León who landed on the Atlantic Coast, somewhere near present-day St Augustine on Easter Monday, 1513. He thought he had discovered a new island in the Bahamas and claimed it for Spain. The discovery was named Florida after **Pascua Florida**, the traditional Spanish Feast of Flowers held during Easter. He returned with another expedition in 1521 intending to establish a settlement, but Indian attacks forced him to withdraw.

spread through northern Florida with a chain of forts and they dominated the region for the next 150 years.

By the early eighteenth century English colonists from Georgia and South Carolina started to move south attacking the Spanish settlements in their path. At the same time the French were attacking Spanish settlements in the west and in 1719 they captured Pensacola. In 1763 after the Seven Years War, a deal was struck between England and Spain, and Florida was ceded to the English in return for Cuba.

Florida was divided into two territories each with its

own capital — East Florida administered from St Augustine and West Florida with its headquarters in Pensacola. But plans to colonise them were disrupted by the American War of Independence. Although both territories remained loyal to the English crown their remoteness and the confusion caused by the war, allowed the Spanish to return and they reclaimed Florida for themselves.

The Indians

A period of intense colonisation started but the new settlers were in almost constant conflict with the Indians who had also moved in from the north to populate the region. This was the time of the Indian Wars. Creek Indians and other tribes became known as Seminoles, from the Spanish word for 'wanderers'. The **First Seminole War** started in 1817 and ended 4 years later when Spain sold the territory to the USA. East and West Florida were united and a new capital was declared in Tallahassee.

The Seminoles who had survived the war were ordered to leave Florida for the Indian Territory but the refusal of their chief Osceola to agree to this precipitated President Andrew Jackson into launching the **Second Seminole War** in 1835. The bloody Seven Years War left most of the Indians dead, a few hundred escaped

into the Everglades and the rest were herded on to the Indian Territory hundreds of miles away to the north-west.

Today there are 2,000 Indians living in and around the Everglades, about three-quarters of them descendants of the Seminoles and the rest Miccosukees. It was only in 1962 that official relations between the Indians and the US Government were resumed.

Three years after the end of the Second Seminole War, Florida, with a population of about 55,000, became the twenty-seventh State in the USA. The population was concentrated in the north and the economy relied almost entirely on the agricultural plantations.

Development

In the 1880s tourism came to Florida. A railroad was driven down the east coast and then another down the west, and resorts and industry developed.

Marshland and swamps were drained for farming, roads built and new communities developed. Spanish and Cuban settlers established themselves around Tampa, Greek immigrants moved into Tarpon Springs, Jewish émigrés to Miami, Slovaks into Masaryktown, and many other nationalities moved in.

The property boom lasted until the Depression and was not rejuvenated until the United

MAJOR ATTRACTIONS PRICE GUIDE

ADMISSION CHARGES			CAR PARK CHARGES
$	=	under $10	< = under $5
$$	=	$10-19	> = $5 or more
$$$	=	$20-28	
$$$$	=	$29-35	These are not discount
$$$$$	=	over $35	prices and are correct at time of going to press.

ATTRACTION	TELEPHONE NUMBER	CAR PARK CHARGE	ADMISSION
A World of Orchids	(407) 396 1887	free	Adult/children $
Alligatorland Safari Zoo	(407) 396 1012	free	Adult $ Children $
Arabian Nights Dinner Attraction	(407) 239 9223	free	Adult $$$$$ 3-11yrs $$$ performing horses/dinner
Bok Tower Gardens	(813) 676 1408	free	Adult/children $
Busch Gardens	(813) 987 5171	<	Adult $$$$ 3-9yrs $$$
Cypress Gardens	(813) 324 2111	<	Adult $$$ 3-9yrs $$
Disney's Animal Kingdom® Theme Park	(407) 824 4321		Adult $$$$$ 3-9yrs $$$$
Epcot®	(407) 824 4321	>	Adult $$$$$ 3-9yrs $$$$
Disney-MGM Studios	(407) 824 4321	>	Adult $$$$$ 3-9yrs $$$$
Downtown Disney Pleasure Island	(407) 934 7781	free	Adults only $$ No charge for diners
The Magic Kingdom® Park	(407) 824 4321	>	Adult $$$$$ 3-9yrs $$$

Flying Tigers Warbird Air Museum	(407) 933 1942	free	Adult/Children $
Fun 'N Wheels Orlando	(407) 351 5651	free	Adult/children $
Fun 'N Wheels Kissimmee	(407) 239 8038	free	Adult/children $
Gatorland	(407) 855 5496	free	Adult $$ 3-11yrs $
Kennedy Space Visitor Complex	(407) 452 2121	free	free - charge for bus tours/IMAX theaters
King Henry's Feast	(407) 351 5151	free	Adult $$$$ 3-11yrs $$$ dinner/show
Medieval Life	(800) 229 8300	free	Adult/Children $
Medieval Times Dinner & Tournament	(800) 229 8300	free	Adult $$$$ 3-12yrs $$$ dinner/show
Polynesian Luau, Sea World of Florida	(800) 227 8048	free	Adult $$$$ 8-12yrs $$$ 3-7yrs $$ Dinner/ Polynesian show
Sea World of Florida	(407) 351 3600	>	Adult $$$$ 3-9yrs $$$$
Silver Springs	(800) 234 7458	free	Adult $$$ 3-10yrs $$
Splendid China	(800) 244 6226	free	Adult $$$ 5-12yrs $$
Typhoon Lagoon	(407) 824 4321	free	Adult $$$ 3-9yrs $$
Universal Studios Florida	(407) 363 8000	>	Adult $$$$$ 3-9yrs $$$$
Water Mania	(407) 239 8448	free	Adult $$$ 3-12yrs $$
Weeki Wachee Springs	(800) 678 9335	free	Adult/children $$
Wet 'N Wild	(407) 351 3200	free	Adult $$$ 3-9yrs $$

States entered the World War II and needed a reliable good weather training ground. Florida was chosen, the property market took off again and things have not looked back since.

Present day

Tourism plays the most important role in the State's economy, but agriculture, mining and industry are all key players. Today, the population of Florida is expanding faster than in any other State, and the property boom continues at a frantic pace.

It is a staggering thought that in 1970, before Walt Disney World® Resort opened, Central Florida attracted fewer than 10 million visitors a year — around 800,000 a month — with most of them going to the coast for sea, sun and sand. By the end of 1999, tourism to Central Florida is likely to top 50 million visitors a year, almost a million a week, with the attractions the big draw for most.

Central Florida has no intention of relinquishing its position as the world's top tourist destination. Walt Disney World and the other major attractions have already embarked on major expansion programmes, some of them spanning well into the twenty-first century. The others are constantly introducing new entertainments and others are being attracted to the area. The number of hotels, restaurants, shopping malls and so on, continues to expand, as do the sporting facilities ranging from world class golf courses and floodlit tennis, to jet boats and scuba-diving.

Yet you only have to stray a little off the tourist routes to find the real Florida, the cattle and horse ranches and citrus groves, and many of Central Florida's main attractions — the sea, the countryside and the spectacular wildlife — are free.

The sprawling urban mass of Greater Orlando plays host to many of the world's top tourist attractions, the most famous of which is, of course, **Walt Disney World**. It is difficult to imagine the transformation that has taken place in little more than 25 years, when the surrounding countryside was mostly citrus groves, cattle ranches and woodlands. The fine year-round weather which made it so suitable for agriculture, however, is also the magic ingredient sought by tourists from around the world.

Planning Your Holiday

If flying into Florida, especially from abroad, you are probably going to land in the late afternoon or during the evening, and after a long flight you are likely to be tired and wanting your bed. The best thing to do is to pick up your rental car, shuttle

The Orlando Magicard and Super Pass

You can save hundreds of dollars with the **Orlando Magicard**, an area wide discount card that looks like a credit card and works like a coupon book. The FREE card provides savings of between 10 and 50 per cent at 110 area attractions, hotels, restaurants, auto and RV rental firms and retail outlets. Visitors can order the card by calling 1-800-551-0181, or stopping at the Official Visitor Information Center at Mercado Village on International Drive any day between 8am and 8pm.

The Mears Transportation Group also offers an **Orlando Super Pass,** designed to offer travelers with a safe, efficient shuttle service for their entire stay in the area. The Super Pass entitles visitors to unlimited round trip travel between Orlando International Airport, most major hotels and all the main attractions. The Super Pass is available at tourist offices and from hotels.

bus or taxi and get to your destination as quickly as possible to unpack and unwind. Many hotels offer a free coach shuttle to and from the airport.

If staying in a rented home, it might be a good idea to stop off at a 7-11 store and buy milk, orange juice and other soft drinks, and perhaps some other basics like tea and coffee. If you are very tired, it is a good idea to postpone a long drive and stay overnight at an airport hotel.

When you wake the next morning, it is time to start drawing up your holiday time-table. Even in 2 weeks, it is impossible to see and do every-thing that Central Florida has to offer, so you must decide what your priorities are. You really do need 3 or 4 days to do

Walt Disney World (including the new Disney's Animal King-dom® Theme Park) full justice. Sea World and Universal Studios of Florida need a full day, then there are supper shows to see, trips to Kennedy Space Center, Tampa and the Gulf Coast, the sunbathing, shopping and all the other attractions and sightseeing.

It is important to plan care-fully. It is quite easy to be among the first people to arrive at Walt Disney World in the morning, and be among the last to leave late at night, but while your day will be packed with excitement it can also be exhausting, especially if you have young children. That is why it is a good idea to alternate day trips to the attractions with less action-packed days, otherwise you might need another holiday to recover! You should spend the first 2 or 3 days acclimatizing to the sun. Do not spend too long in the sun, especially at the hottest times of the day, and wear sun screen, hat and sunglasses.

It is worth at least one trip each to the Gulf and Atlantic Coasts. From Greater Orlando, the Atlantic Coast is around an hour's drive, while the Gulf can

be reached in about 75 minutes. If heading for the Atlantic Coast, you can take in the famous Cocoa Beach, and visit the Kennedy Space Center. If heading west and to the Gulf, there is Tampa with its own attractions, notably Busch Gardens, St Petersburg and

Top right: Lorikeets in the avery at Busch Gardens®, Tampa Bay

Above: Meet an astronaut at Kennedy Space Visitor Complex

Right: Adventure Island is situated adjacent to Busch Gardens®

Ticket Brokers

It is also a good idea to get your attraction tickets from a licensed ticket broker because you can save hundreds of dollars if you do it right. Beware of people offering tickets who are really trying to sell time-shares. If you have a steel will and are prepared to give up an hour or so, to look round a time-share operation, you can end up with free tickets to major attractions worth hundreds of dollars, but time-share sales staff are very skilled at selling their product, and you could end up buying something you had not bargained for.

Licensed ticket brokers are attached to most hotels and many have deals with management companies looking after rental homes. The advantages of using these ticket brokers are that if they come to you, you can buy all your tickets in one go, usually at substantial discounts, and you by-pass the pay booth queues at the attractions. Also, if you do not use all your tickets, the brokers will usually buy them back from you.

Clearwater, and the coastal resorts south of this conurbation.

Greater Orlando takes in the cities of **Orlando, Kissimmee** to the south and **St Cloud** to the south-east, and a host of satellite towns and suburbs, notably **Winter Park, Maitland** and **Altamonte Springs** to the north. The skyscraper skyline of Downtown Orlando contrasts sharply with the mostly single-storey buildings in the surrounding area, a sign that land has been traditionally cheap so people could build out rather than up. As you drive around Central Florida you can see just how much open land there still is, and you only have to drive off the main tourist roads to see old Floridian homesteads and ranches.

Getting Around

Interstate 4 snakes its way from north-east to south-west through the area, and is the fastest route from the north and Downtown Orlando to Walt Disney World® Resort. Off I-4 are other major attractions such as **Sea World, Universal Studios** and **Wet N'Wild**.

Highway 192 intersects with I-4 and runs east to west. If you turn off I-4 and head west on 192, you reach Walt Disney World. If you turn off on 192 East, you drive along the main road through Kissimmee. At night, the road, often eight lanes wide, is a blaze of neon lights and advertising hoardings. For mile after mile, the road is flanked by restaurants, hotels, motels, attractions and shopping malls. It is just over 20 miles (32km) from Walt Disney World® Resort to Downtown Orlando, and about 10 miles (16km) from Walt Disney World to Kissimmee.

The most popular tourist route in Orlando is **International Drive**, which runs parallel and to the east of I-4 for a few miles. It is a more upmarket version of Kissimmee's 192, and the hotels, restaurants and shops tend to be more expensive. It too, is packed with attractions and entertainments, and its popularity often leads to traffic jams. From Kissimmee, highway 441 runs north to Orlando, and this area between I-4 and highways 192 and 441, is known as the 'Tourist Triangle'.

Another area bordered by I-4, highway 192, and highway 27 in the west, is known as the 'Golden Triangle'. This is where much of Walt Disney World's expansion is taking place, and it will be the home of many other new attractions and developments over the next few years. There is even talk of a Japanese style 'bullet train' which will speed visitors into Walt Disney World from Tampa and the Miami area.

Orlando is a sprawling city with a fast-growing downtown area and some spectacular skyscrapers which most people see only as they drive along I-4. Most of the major tourist attractions are concentrated on or around International Drive, which is a bustling, busy area throughout the day and into the early hours.

Many hotels provide shuttle buses to transport visitors to and from the major attractions, but transport to other areas can be a problem which is why most people use rental cars or taxis.

There is now a shuttle service operating on International Drive. Fifteen 30ft (9m) buses run up and down International Drive every 5 minutes between Sea World on the south end to American Way on the north.

Take Care

There are areas of Orlando, as in all major cities, where care must be exercised. As a general rule, if you have to drive into a strange area plan your route in advance, and if you suspect anything at all is wrong, keep on driving. It must be stressed, however, that the crime rate of Central Florida, especially violent crime, is very low particularly when one considers just how many visitors pass through every week. In most tourist areas, there is no need at all for concern but be careful. If you are, you will have a great time.

QUESTIONS
and answers

Q: Which is the best studio park?

A: Neither, you need to go to both Disney-MGM Studios and Universal Studios Florida

Q: Where are the inexpensive attractions?

A: Try the State Parks and recreational areas, plus Canaveral National Coastline and Merritt Island National Wildlife Refuge. They are free and often very attractive. Also Bok Tower Gardens.

Q: Where are the best shopping bargains?

A: Try your luck at Belz Shopping Mall complex with 160 factory shops where you can find such names as Levi, Reebok, Van Heusen, Bally, etc.

Q: Are there facilities for disabled visitors?

A: Yes. The major theme parks cater for disabled visitors but remember they can get very busy.

Q: What do you do if you have forgotten your camera?

A: Do not worry, cameras can be rented at most parks.

Q: Where is the best eating out?

A: This is very subjective, but it can be expensive. However there are plenty of offers, so shop around. For a listing refer to the FactFile.

Q: When in Florida, how do you get further information?

A: For **Walt Disney World Information**:
   ☎ (407) W-DISNEY (934 7639)

   For **Central Florida**:
   Central Florida Convention and Visitors Bureau,
   PO Box 1839, Bartow FL 33830 ☎ (813) 534-4375

   For **Orlando and Orange County**:
   Orlando/Orange County Convention and Visitors Bureau,
   7208 Sand Lake Road, Suite 300, Orlando FL 32819
   ☎ (407) 363-5800

2 WALT DISNEY WORLD® RESORT

Walt Disney World Resort, comprising the Magic Kingdom® Park, Epcot®, Disney's Animal Kingdom® Theme Park and Disney-MGM Studios, is located at Lake Buena Vista, 20 miles (32km) south-west of Orlando off Interstate 4 and highway 192. Walt Disney World Resort occupies a 28,000-acre (11,200-hectare) site of which only 7,500 acres (3,000 hectares) are currently developed. More than 8,000 acres (3,200 hectares) are set aside as a designated wilderness preserve. Walt Disney World Resort employs 35,000 people and is open daily year-round.

The Walt Disney World Resort just keeps on growing. It covers 43sq miles (111sq km) and has its own road and integrated transport system. There are now 25 deluxe hotels built around spectacular lakes, golf-courses and luxuriant landscapes. The resort hotels offer a wide range of activities

Above: *Mulan: The Parade, Disney-MGM Studios*
(© Disney Enterprises, Inc)

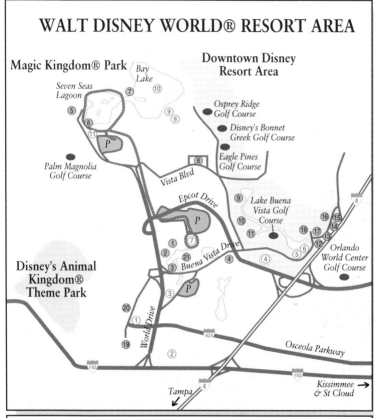

WALT DISNEY WORLD® RESORT AREA

Magic Kingdom® Park

Bay Lake

Seven Seas Lagoon

Downtown Disney Resort Area

Osprey Ridge Golf Course

Disney's Bonnet Greek Golf Course

Eagle Pines Golf Course

Palm Magnolia Golf Course

Vista Blvd

Epcot Drive

Lake Buena Vista Golf Course

Orlando World Center Golf Course

Disney's Animal Kingdom® Theme Park

Buena Vista Drive

World Drive

Osceola Parkway

Tampa

Kissimmee & St Cloud

KEY TO MAIN ATTRACTIONS, RESORTS & HOTELS

① Disney's Blizzard Beach Water Park
② Disney's Wide World of Sports
③ Disney – MGM Studios
④ Disney's Typhoon Lagoon Water Park
⑤ Planet Hollywood
⑥ Downtown Disney Market Place
⑦ Epcot®
⑧ Fort Wilderness Campground
⑨ River Country
⑩ Disney's Discovery Island
⑪ Walt Disney World Speedway

① Disney's Yacht & Beach Club Resorts
② Walt Disney World Dolphin
③ Walt Disney World Swan
④ Disney's Caribbean Beach Resort
⑤ Disney's Grand Floridian Resort & Spa
⑥ Disney's Polynesian Resort
⑦ Disney's Contemporary Resort
⑧ Disney's Wilderness Lodge Resort & Campground
⑨ Disney's Dixie Landings Resort
⑩ Disney's Port Orleans Resort

⑪ Disney's Vacation Club
⑫ The Hilton
⑬ Courtyard by Marriott
⑭ Hotel Royal Plaza
⑮ Doubletree Guest Suite Resort
⑯ Travelodge Hotel
⑰ Grosvenor Resort
⑱ Wyndham Palace
⑲ All Star Resorts
⑳ Coronado Springs Resort
㉑ BoadWalk Resort

as well as speedy access by road, water and even monorail to the theme parks.

Epcot® resort hotels include Walt Disney World Swan and Walt Disney World Dolphin, each easily identified by the huge rooftop statues; Disney's Yacht and Beach Club Resorts and Disney's Caribbean Beach Resort.

As part of the Magic Kingdom® Park, there are the Disney's Grand Floridian Resort and Spa, Disney's Contemporary Resort and Disney's Polynesian Resort. In addition, there are the Downtown Disney Resort Area Hotels, including Disney's Port Orleans Resort and Disney's Dixie Landings Resort, and Disney's 780-acre (312-hectare) Wilderness Lodge Resort and Campground. New theme resorts include Disney's All-Star Sports Resort, All-Star Music Resort and Disney's BoardWalk Inn and Villas.

If that was not enough, there are a further seven hotels in the Disney Village Hotel Plaza. The hotels occupy a special position as they are the only ones not owned by Walt Disney allowed to operate within Walt Disney World. The hotels are the Wyndham Palace, Courtyard by Marriott, Grosvenor Resort, Doubletree Guest Suite Resort, The Hilton Hotel, Hotel Royal Plaza and the Travelodge.

Parking at Walt Disney World

There is an all-day car park fee, so do not lose your ticket if you plan to leave the park and return later the same day. The car parks are so huge that transport is then laid on to take you from a suitable pick up point near your car to the park entrance. It is absolutely essential to remember where you parked your car. It is no good thinking you will spot it because, if it is a rental car, it will be one of thousands all looking the same. Take a note of the parking area you are in — the row and row number. The different parking areas are named after Disney characters — Daisy, Donald, Sneezy, Bashful, Grumpy, Happy, Goofy, Pluto, Chip and Dale, Minnie, Sleepy and Dopey. Special parking is available for handicapped visitors.

All the hotels within Walt Disney World Resort offer a wide range of activities and recreational facilities as well as wining and dining to suit all tastes. Worthy of special mention is the **Contemporary Resort**, a 15 storey, 1,050 room hotel, through the center of which the monorail travels giving stunning views over the impressive Grand Canyon Concourse. You do not have to be staying at one of the resort hotels to take advantage of the facilities, although reservations are usually required if you want to dine or take in one of the special shows.

The **California Grill** restaurant on the fifteenth floor of Contemporary Resort, for instance, has an award-winning critically acclaimed menu with stunning panoramic views, while Victoria and Albert's in the Grand Floridian Resort and Spa offers superb dining although reservations are essential.

The Resort boasts five championship golf courses, tennis, volleyball, biking, jogging and horse riding trails, lakes with artificial beaches, boating, swimming and all manner of water sports.

If you cannot start your car or have locked your keys inside, one of the mobile patrols will come to your aid.

If you really like the water, visit **Disney's Typhoon Lagoon Water Park** or **Disney's Blizzard Beach Water Park** where man-made waves are powerful enough for body-surfing, or spend time at River Country near **Fort Wilderness Resort and Campground**. It is a water park with slides, white water rapids, a gigantic swimming pool and beach area.

Downtown Disney Marketplace offers Disney memorabilia and Florida gifts, and when you have done all your shopping you can let your hair down at Downtown Disney Pleasure Island. You can choose from six different clubs each offering a different style of music and entertainment, and every evening finishes with a New Year's Celebration. Children under the age of 18 must be accompanied by an adult.

The Company has also developed a resort at Vero Beach on Central Florida's Atlantic Coast and now has its own cruise line.

The Theme Parks

The Magic Kingdom® Park

Forty-five major attractions on 100 acres (40 hectares), the Magic Kingdom is divided into seven 'lands' — Adventureland, Fantasyland, Frontierland, Liberty Square, Main Street, USA, Tomorrowland and Mickey's Toontown Fair. Most popular attractions include Splash Mountain, Pirates of the Caribbean, Big Thunder Mountain Railroad, Haunted Mansion and Space Mountain.

Epcot®

The Experimental Prototype Community of Tomorrow opened as Epcot Center on 1 October 1982. It is now a permanent international showplace covering 260 acres (104 hectares), and featuring Future World and World Showcase. Future World is a theme area focusing on discovery and scientific achievements with a wide range of major attractions. World Showcase currently features pavilions representing different nations.

Disney's Animal Kingdom® Theme Park

This billion dollar theme park is Disney's latest attraction and is centered around animals — real, imaginary and extinct. Lots of opportunities for close encounters with exotic animals and birds, plus rides, an African Safari and DinoLand USA.

Disney-MGM Studios

A working TV and film studio as well as a theme park. Production facilities opened in the summer of 1988. Attractions include movie backlots, rides, theater performances, a production tour, an Indiana Jones™ Stunt Spectacular and much more!

Downtown Disney

The place for shopping, dining and fun. Consisting of:

Downtown Disney Pleasure Island — where every night is New Year's Eve, and as popular with the locals as tourists. A 6-acre (2-hectare) area that comes to life after dark, although it is open during the day and the restaurants offer a very relaxing haven for lunch.

The island is connected to Downtown Disney Market Place by three footbridges, and has a selection of restaurants and shops. After 7pm a single admission fee gives access to all the Downtown Disney Pleasure Island clubs and the nightly New Year's Eve spectacular and fireworks.

Downtown Disney Market Place — shops, restaurant, cafes.

Downtown Disney West Side — a lively dining and entertainment district.

Disney's Typhoon Lagoon Water Park

A 56-acre (22-hectare) water park with the main swimming area designed to resemble a Caribbean lagoon complete with waves up to 4ft (1m) high which are ideal for body surfing. You can drift on an inflatable tube along Castaway Creek, crash down one of the whitewater rides, hurtle down one of the many slides, or snorkel around a coral reef with sharks as companions (non man-eaters thankfully!) There are two restaurants, restrooms and changing facilities.

Disney's Blizzard Beach Water Park

Popular water park featuring Summit Plummet and children's area, restaurants, restrooms and changing facilities.

River Country

The first of Disney's water parks, with a more relaxed atmosphere than Blizzard Beach and Typhoon Lagoon. The huge concrete-lined pool offers good swimming, and there are areas where you can swing out over the water on ropes and shoot the white water rapids on inner tubes. For the adventurous there are the two huge slides, the longest more than 250ft (76m) long. There are two eating places: Pop's Place which is open year round offering snacks, and the Waterin' Hole, only open in peak season.

Disney's Discovery Island

A wildlife refuge and a member of the American Association of Zoological Parks and Aquariums. The 1.5 acres (half-hectare) are home to more than 100 different species of animals and birds, with one of the world's largest walk through aviaries, as well as a fascinating mixture of tropical plants and trees. There is a bird show in the open-air theater, and the best way to see the island is to pick up a map and explore it on foot. If you are interested in wildlife you can easily spend all day here.

Planning your visit

If you plan your visit in advance you will get maximum enjoyment from your stay. Before you enter your chosen theme park for the day, you have to get there. If you are staying at one of the hotels within Walt Disney World Resort, or have a multi-day ticket, you can catch either the monorail or take the bus.

If you are taking a shuttle bus from a hotel outside Walt Disney World Resort, you will be dropped close to the ticket booths near the entrance. If you are driving you will be directed, along with tens of thousands of other drivers, to the car parks which cover hundreds of acres.

Decide where you want to go, what you want to see and in what order. A full day in any of the Walt Disney World theme parks is great fun but it can be very exhausting, especially if you have young children.

Remember to wear sensible clothing. Wear lightweight, loose-fitting casual clothes and comfortable footwear as, over the course of a day, you can walk a good few miles. Sunglasses and hats are also a good idea, especially if you are not used to the Florida sun. The only exception to this is if you plan to dine in one of the restaurants which have a dress code, usually requiring men to wear jackets.

23

Plan to get to the theme parks early so that you are ready to go as soon as they open. If you would like a mid-day rest or want to pop out for a swim, make sure you have your hand stamped so that you can return to spend the rest of the day and evening in one of the parks.

It is fair to say that Walt Disney World is always busy, but some times more so than others. The crowds, and queues, tend to build up during school holidays, both summer holidays and spring and fall (autumn) half terms, as well as Christmas, New Year and Easter. If you want to avoid the crowds, the best times to plan your visit are from early January to early February and between September and Christmas.

Christmas and Easter are great times to visit Walt Disney World but the parks are very busy. There is, however, an even more special atmosphere at these times of the year with decorations, carols and nativity plays over Christmas, and an Easter parade that is televised nationwide.

According to Walt Disney World, Mondays, Tuesdays and Wednesdays attract the biggest crowds in the Magic Kingdom Park, Tuesdays and Wednesdays at Epcot and Thursdays and Fridays at Disney-MGM Studios. Sundays tend to be the least

Walt Disney World Hotels

Twenty-five hotels, a campground, vacation villas and vacation club providing accommodation for more than 26,000 people.

Magic Kingdom® Resort Area includes Disney's Contemporary Resort (1,053 rooms), Disney's Polynesian Resort (855 rooms), Disney's Grand Floridian Resort and Spa (901 rooms), Disney's Fort Wilderness Resort and Campground (1,192 campsites and vacation trailers, plus group camping area) and Disney's Wilderness Lodge.

Epcot® Resort Area includes Disney's Yacht Club Resort (635 rooms), Disney's Beach Club Resort (580 rooms), Walt Disney World Swan (758 rooms), Walt Disney World Dolphin (1,514 rooms), and Disney's Caribbean Beach Resort (2,112 rooms).

Downtown Disney Village Resort Area includes Disney's Old Key West Resort (585 family villa units), Disney's Port Orleans Resort (1,008 rooms), Disney's Dixie Landings Resort (2,048 rooms), Disney Vacation Club Resort (197 units), plus Official Hotels of Walt Disney World (3,744 rooms in Wyndham Palace, Grosvenor Resort, Doubletree Guest Suite Resort, The Hilton, Courtyard by Marriott, Hotel Royal Plaza and Travelodge Hotel).

Newest hotels are the 729-room deluxe Disney's Wilderness Lodge set among giant forests and a geyser field on the shores of Lake Bay, Disney's All Star Sports, Music and Movies Resorts with 1,920 themed rooms. The 378-room Disney's BoardWalk Inn and Villas is a deluxe waterfront resort and entertainment area beside Crescent Lake and Disney's Coronado Springs Resort with 1,900 rooms aimed at the convention market, and located just north of Disney-MGM Studios, opened in 1996.

crowded at all the theme parks.

All the parks have coin-operated lockers where you can stow items you do not want to carry around, and all parks have facilities for families with very young children who may need feeding or changing. Strollers can be rented for a small charge, and if you plan to visit a second theme park in the same day, keep your receipt as the rental fee covers you for the whole day.

If you have young adventurous children, it is a good idea to pick up a name tag from City Hall in Magic Kingdom, Earth Station at Epcot or at Guest Services at Disney-MGM Studios and Disney's Animal Kingdom® Theme Park, just in case they decide to go exploring on their own. All staff at the parks are well trained to be on the alert for lost children, and if you do lose a child report it at once to a member of staff.

If you are a member of a group and want to split up, arrange a time and place where you can all meet up, and make sure you all know where it is. If you lose anything, report it to City Hall in Magic Kingdom Park or Guest Relations at Epcot, Disney-MGM Studios and Disney's Animal Kingdom Theme Park. To encourage people to hand in lost property, all items not claimed by the owner after a certain period are offered to the finder.

Disney's Wilderness Lodge (© Disney Enterprises, Inc)

Disabled visitors are well catered for throughout the Resort area and in all the theme parks. Wheelchairs are available for rent and assistance is always available if necessary.

If you want to eat in comfort, reserve a table in one of the Magic Kingdom® Park or Epcot® restaurants. Remember that most people eat between 11am and 1pm and between 6-8pm so expect crowds or eat outside these times.

You can now be married at any of the Walt Disney World attractions, with Mickey Mouse as Best Man, with a wedding breakfast afterwards in Cinderella Castle with Cinderella as a guest. Disney has even built a number of honey-moon cottages.

The Disney Institute also offers all-inclusive activity holidays, ranging from keep fit to film making, and Cordon Bleu cookery to wine appreciation.

Finally, visiting Walt Disney World Resort is meant to be fun, not an assault course. Plan your time carefully in order to enjoy your holiday to the full. However, do not rush around too much during the hottest parts of the day and make sure you drink enough liquid to prevent dehydration. Above all, have a great time.

Tickets

One day tickets are available which allow you access to one park only. They are worth buying if you are desperately pressed for time but to do full justice to all the parks you really do need several days. The Seven Day All-In-One Hopper Pass, and the even better value Five Day All-In-One Hopper Pass should allow you to see most things with a bit of careful planning.

These passes allow unlimited access to all four Disney theme parks, three water parks and Downtown Disney Pleasure Island. You can visit as many attractions and parks as you like each day and days do not have to run consecutively to allow maximum flexibility.

There is no time limit on the tickets. If you do not manage to use up all the days during your visit, the remaining days are still valid if you ever return.

There is now the unlimited Magic Passport for guests staying at selected Walt Disney Resort Hotels. On arrival, the guests receive a special resort identification pass which allows unlimited access to all Disney attractions for the duration of their stay.

THE MAGIC KINGDOM PARK

This is a place where everyone can be a child again, no matter what their age. The Magic Kingdom is real Walt Disney make believe, it is the kingdom of our dreams, our fantasies and our childhood, and that is the way to enjoy it to its full.

Once you are through the turnstiles, you enter a different world. Everything is clean and tidy, there is no litter to be seen, and everyone is out to have a good time. You have a choice as to how to get to the Magic Kingdom; you can catch the ferry boat which takes about 5 minutes, or take the monorail which is quicker if there are not long queues. Both take you to Town Square where you can get information about the day's events and attractions from the City Hall. There is also a lost and found office and the Walt Disney World Railroad Station. The 1.5 mile (2.5km) circuit takes you right round the park in about 20 minutes (including stops), or you can use the railway to travel to the next part of the Magic Kingdom to be explored. The railroad has four locomotives, all built in the USA around the beginning of the twentieth century or in the 1920s, and were being used to pull freight in the Yucatan, Mexico when found by Disney scouts in 1969. All have been lovingly restored and converted to use diesel.

HOT TIP

If you want to get ahead of the early morning crowds, take the first train from the Main Street Station to Frontierland and that should mean you are one of the first in the queues for Splash Mountain or Big Thunder Mountain Railroad.

As you enter the Town Square you may be greeted by Disney characters, and there might be a jazz band or other forms of entertainment helping to maintain the party atmosphere. If you are any good at bearings, it may be useful to remember that if you look up Main Street towards Cinderella Castle, you are looking almost due north.

Shows

You can come across Disney characters and street entertainments at any time throughout the Magic Kingdom. There are the Dapper Dans (the barber

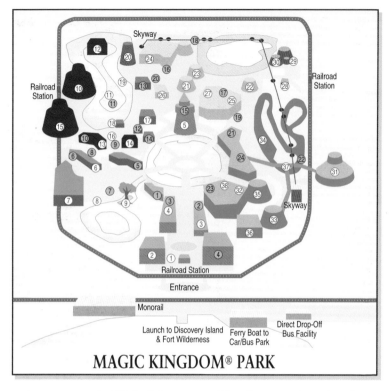

MAGIC KINGDOM® PARK

shop quartet), Walt Disney World® Band which gives concerts every morning in Town Square and during the summer, college marching bands are featured.

To help you plan your day it is worth noting the following:

Mickey's Magical Moments Parade (floats, dancers, and Disney characters) takes place every afternoon at 3pm finishing at Main Street, USA. One visiting family is picked out to be VIP's in the parade and children can take part, dancing with the performers.

Flag Retreat takes place just after 5pm each day when a small band and color guard take down the American flag flying in Town Square. A flock of snow white doves is released and they fly off to Cinderella Castle where they live.

SpectroMagic was created to celebrate Walt Disney World twentieth anniversary celebrations and is now a firm favorite at night time. It is a light parade the like of which you will never have seen before, with lasers, fibre optics, holographs and every other high tech device that can be used. There are two

MAIN STREET, USA

① Main Street Vehicles
② City Hall
③ Main Street Cinema
④ Penny Arcade
⑤ Cinderella Castle

Refreshments
① The Crystal Palace
② Main Street Bake Shop
   The Plaza Restaurant
   Plaza Ice Cream Parlor
③ Casey's Corner
④ Tony's Town Square Restaurant

ADVENTURELAND

⑥ The Enchanted Tiki Room
   Under New Management
⑦ Pirates of the Caribbean
⑧ Jungle Cruise
⑨ Swiss Family Treehouse

Refreshments
⑤ Aloha Isle
⑥ El Pirata Y el Perico Restaurant
⑦ The Oasis
⑧ Sunshine Tree Terrace

FRONTIERLAND

⑩ Big Thunder Mountain Railroad
⑪ Tom Sawyer Island
⑫ Fort Sam Clemens
⑬ Country Bear Jamboree
⑭ "The Diamond Horseshoe
   Saloon Revue"
⑮ Splash Mountain
⑯ Frontierland Shootin' Arcade

Refreshments
⑨ Diamond Horseshoe Jamboree
⑩ Pecos Bill Cafe
⑪ Aunt Polly's Dockside Inn

LIBERTY SQUARE

⑰ The Hall of Presidents
⑱ Liberty Square Riverboat
⑲ Mike Fink Keel Boats
⑳ The Haunted Mansion

Refreshments
⑫ Liberty Tree Tavern
⑬ Columbia Harbour House
⑭ Sleepy Hollow

FANTASYLAND

㉑ Cinderella's Golden Carrousel
㉒ Mad Tea Party
㉓ Dumbo, The Flying Elephant
㉔ It's A Small World
㉕ The Many Adventures of
   Winnie the Pooh
㉖ Peter Pan's Flight
㉗ Snow White's Adventures

Refreshments
⑮ Cinderella's Royal Table
⑯ The Pinocchio Village Haus
⑰ Lumiere's Kitchen
⑱ Scuttle's Langing
⑲ Enchanted Grove
⑳ Hook's Tavern

MICKEY'S TOON-TOWN FAIR

㉘ The Barnstormer at Goofy's
   Wiseacre Farm
㉙ Mickey's Country House
㉚ Mickey's Toontown Hall of Fame

TOMORROWLAND

㉛ Space Mountain
㉜ Carousel of Progress
㉝ Buzz Lightyear's
   Space Ranger Spin
㉞ Tomorrowland Speedway
㉟ Astro Orbiter
㊱ Galaxy Palace Theatre
㊲ The Tomorrowland
   Transit Authority
㊳ The Time Keeper

㉑ Refreshments
㉒ Cosmic Ray's Starlight Cafe
   Auntie Gravity's
㉓ Galactice Goodies
㉔ The Plaza Pavilion
   The Lunching Pad
   at Rockettower Plaza

MAGIC KINGDOM® PARK

SpectroMagic parades nightly during busy seasons (9pm and 11pm), and the best place to see it is on the elevated waiting area in front of the Walt Disney Railroad Station in Town Square.

Fantasy in the Sky is an impressive firework display presented nightly when the park is open until 10pm or later. One rocket or star burst is fired every two seconds over a four minute period.

Disneymania — Mickey and his friends appear in a musical revue in front of Cinderella Castle.

Main Street, USA

This street runs from Town Square to Cinderella Castle which is at the heart of Magic Kingdom. In front of the castle is the Hub or Central Plaza, surrounded by canals over which bridges radiate to take you to the seven 'lands' in the Magic Kingdom® Park — Main Street, USA, Adventureland, Frontierland, Liberty Square, Fantasyland, Mickey's Toontown Fair and Tomorrowland. Main Street, USA, is one of the 'lands' in Magic Kingdom, although many people do not realize this. It is modelled on a typical small town main street at the end of the nineteenth century, and the buildings house a wide range of shops, entertainments and eating rooms. Apart from all the buildings being in perfect condition and looking as if they have just had a fresh coat of paint, it is worth inspecting them from inside as well as out. Every building is different not only because of what it sells, but also because of the way each one has been furnished and decorated. In this way, virtually every style of turn-of-the-century decor can be seen somewhere in the street. Outside horse drawn trolleys, open top buses and vintage cars are available for visitors who want to sightsee in comfort.

Main Street, USA at night is even more attractive as the tens of thousands of little white lights around the roofs are illuminated while street 'gas' lamps are lit. As there is so much to see and do, it is almost impossible to take it all in

Getting hungry?

Crystal Palace — entrées, salads, desserts, and a great place for full breakfasts, open all day, cafeteria service.

Main Street Bake Shop — tearooms offering pastries and pies, cookies and soft drinks.

Plaza Ice Cream Parlor — cool decor with a wide range of flavours.

The Plaza Restaurant — table service. Lots of windows, mirrors and art nouveau. Hot dishes, salads, sandwiches and burgers, and the biggest sundae in the Magic Kingdom.

Refreshment Corner — enjoy a hot dog or brownies (for overseas visitors — chewy chocolate biscuits) and listen to the pianist.

Tony's Town Square Restaurant — table service for Italian specialties. Fresh pasta, salads, steaks, seafood, pizza, burgers, deli platters and fresh fruit plates. Enjoy breakfast, lunch and dinner.

during a single visit. Even the names painted on the second storey windows advertising various services are genuine. They are all former or current Disney executives.

If you want to see **The Diamond Horseshow Saloon Revue**, a live show in Frontierland, you should book your seats as early as possible at **Disneyana Collectibles** on **Main Street, USA**. The seats are allocated on a first come basis.

There are all sorts of fascinating shops to explore, you can watch magic being performed at the **House of Magic**, or sweets being made at the Confectionery. There is the **Penny Arcade**, with its machines old and new, and **Main Street Cinema**, with its multiple screens, which shows vintage Disney cartoons, including *Steamboat Willie*. Made in 1928 it was the first sound cartoon and featured a mouse called Mickey. The rest is history.

You can find out how *Steamboat Willie* came to be made and learn more about the man behind the legend by watching the *Walt Disney Story*, which is shown in the cinema on the east side of Town Square. It is worth spending a few minutes looking round the various exhibits on display which tell you more about Walt Disney, his life and achievements. You can even have a haircut in the **Harmony Barber Shop**, which is just off Main Street, at the end of a pretty, flower-filled alley.

Cinderella Castle

This dominates the Magic Kingdom. The multi-turreted castle stands 180ft (55m) tall and is based on a number of ideas taken from twelfth-century French architecture and the mad King Ludwig of Bavaria's castle at Neuschwanstein, together with a large input from Disney's own designers. Reservations at the second-floor **Cinderella's Royal Table Restaurant** are essential for breakfast with Disney characters as well as for lunch and dinner.

Most of its eighteen floors, however, are private and house a broadcasting studio, security offices and even an apartment originally built for the Disney family.

Beneath the Castle there is a maze of service tunnels which allow the day to day running of the Magic Kingdom. Have you ever wondered where all the litter goes, or how the shops and restaurants are kept supplied? The answer is that almost everything is transported along subterranean roads.

Around the Castle's entrance are the massive murals which tell the story of Cinderella. There are more than a million pieces of Italian glass and real silver and gold was used by creator Dorothea Redmond and Hanns-Joachim who was responsible for the mosaics.

The coat-of-arms on the north wall is the Disney crest, while all the others belong to other Disney executives.

Most people like to make their way methodically through the Magic Kingdom so as not to miss anything and most people do this by travelling through the various lands in a clockwise direction, which is why, after walking up **Main Street, USA**, they turn into **Adventureland**.

Adventureland

This make-believe exotically-landscaped area offers adventure and excitement for young children. Adults can also have a great time here, and can also appreciate the lush vegetation and beautiful flowers and plants.

The Enchanted Tiki Room Under New Management was the first of the Audio-Animatronics® attractions, first introduced in Disneyland in 1963. The charming show, featuring animated birds, flowers and Tiki god statues, allows you to catch your breath, in air-conditioned comfort, before going on one of the Adventureland cruises.

Pirates of the Caribbean is one of the most popular attractions in Magic Kingdom for children and adults alike. The cruise travels through a number of sets showing a pirate raid on a Caribbean port. At one stage you pass between the pirate ship firing broadsides at the fortress guarding the port. There is so much to see as you travel through the attraction, that a second trip is really necessary to spot all those things missed first time round. Apart from the imagination involved in conceiving such sets, the detail and skill required to convert that into reality is amazing.

Jungle Cruise is another water-borne journey round the world visiting Amazon rain forests, the Mekong river as it runs through Cambodian jungle, the Nile Valley and the Congo as it meanders through African plains and jungle. The sets are stunning and many of the exotic flowers and plants are real, although the skill of the designers is such that it is often difficult to tell nature's own from man-made. There are the appropriate computer controlled animals for each habitat, and each cruise boat is skippered by a guide who, despite delivering the same speech numerous times a day, still manages to entertain and amuse.

The other hugely popular attraction in Adventureland is the **Swiss Family Treehouse**. The gigantic artificial tree with massive concrete roots, is draped with real Spanish moss, and all ages love to clamber through the branches exploring the different levels and rooms, all beautifully furnished with patchwork quilts, mahogany dressers and tables. The attention to detail is remarkable. Note the huge clam that acts as the kitchen sink, and the very elaborate water supply provided by a network of bamboo canes. The tree is around 90ft (27m) in diameter, has more than 600 branches and around 800,000 vinyl leaves, each of which had to be attached separately.

Getting hungry?

Aloha Isle — refreshment stand offering Dole Whip soft serve ice-cream and pineapple spears.

El Pirata Y el Perico Restaurante — enjoy tacos, taco salads, nachos, sandwiches. Counter service.

The Oasis — snacks and soft drinks.

Sunshine Tree Terrace — citrus specialities, non-fat frozen yoghurt shakes, soft drinks.

As you make your way to the next 'land', you might be entertained by **J. P. and the Silver Stars**, the steel drum band.

Frontierland

Relive the days of the Wild West and do not be surprised at anything that happens. You can be walking along the street and suddenly find yourself in the middle of a shoot out — but the good guy always wins! The most popular attraction in Frontierland is the 'runaway' roller coaster on the **Big Thunder Mountain Railroad**. The ride actually passes through a near 200ft (61m) tall redstone mountain, and the track twists and turns its way through a variety of scenes depicting gold rush days, each with their own Audio-Animatronics® actors and animals. Almost all the old mining equipment is the real thing, however.

The mountain took 15 years to plan, more than 2 years to build and contains around 650 tons of steel, more than 4,600 tons of cement and 16,000 gallons of paint. The parts of the mountain that the ride does not pass through, house much of the machinery needed to make the roller coaster work, as well as the computers which control it and the many Audio-Animatronicsc figures seen along the way. The ride takes between 3 and 4 minutes and almost everyone says it is better experienced at night because you cannot see the bends coming! It is very popular and there can be long lines, but it is worth the wait.

Big Thunder Mountain Railroad, like many of the rides in the Magic Kingdom has a height restriction for safety reasons, and youngsters are not allowed on board if they are not tall enough.

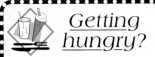

Getting hungry?

The Diamond Horseshoe Saloon Revue — enjoy a high-kicking dancing and singing Wild West revue and enjoy potato and corn chips, home baked pies, and sandwiches. Reservations essential.

Pecos Bill Cafe — salads, chicken sandwiches, burgers. Eat in or out, counter service. The bar offers Tex-Mex dishes.

Aunt Polly's Dockside Inn — on Tom Sawyer Island and a great place for a quiet drink of old-fashioned lemonade while the children go exploring. Picnic baskets and ice cream available.

The youngsters may prefer to raft over and explore **Tom Sawyer Island** with its fort, winding paths through the trees, hills and caves. The island is really two islands connected by a rocking swing bridge. On the main island there are caves to explore and hide in, including an almost black cavern with lots of twists and turns, an old fashioned mill and playground.

Fort Sam Clemens is on the second island where children can fire very loud 'air' guns (the guns pump out air, not pellets!), and if you do not want to explore, you can sit and enjoy a soft drink at Aunt Polly's Dockside Inn.

Then, when you have all met up again, head for the mainland and enjoy the show at the popular **Country Bear Jamboree**, and **The Diamond Horseshoe Saloon Revue**. The first is a foot-tapping musical extravaganza where you are introduced to a group of larger than life bears (lasts 15 to 17 minutes), and the second whisks you back to a western dance hall saloon, with real life high-kicking dancing girls, comedians and a host of other entertainers. The show lasts 30 minutes. Reservations are necessary for **The Diamond Horseshoe Saloon Revue** and these should be made as early as possible on Main Street, USA.

Splash Mountain is the other

major attraction in Frontier-land, and a great way of cooling down! The ride, a giant water flume, is based on Disney's film, *Song of the South*, released in 1946, and features its animated stars Brer Rabbit, Brer Fox and Brer Bear, all of whom appear as the water borne log 'canoes' which snake through lily ponds and swamps, gradually climbing for their final plunge into the water below. The boats drop just over 50ft (15m) at an angle of 45 degrees at a speed of 40mph (64kph) and make a massive splash. In the hot Florida sun you quickly dry off, however, and on those rare days when it rains it does not matter if you get a little wetter.

For those who want to stay dry but enjoy seeing others get soaked, there is an excellent vantage point from the footbridge between **Splash Mountain** and **Thunder Mountain**, and you can get great photographs from here as well. After the big splash, you can test your skills as a sharp-shooter at the **Frontierland Shootin' Arcade**.

The Walt Disney World Railroad stops in Frontierland if you want to alight or catch a ride.

Liberty Square

Journey back to the hey day of the Mississippi riverboats and the birth of the nation. Liberty Square hugs the lake shore-line and commemorates life around the time of the Founding Fathers, and has a very relaxed atmos-phere. It is best known for **The Hall of Presidents**, and the stunningly life-like performances of the Audio-Animatronics® figures. The presentation starts with a short film about the American Constitution and how it has withstood various threats over the years, then features all the Presidents who in turn acknowledge their presence, before Abraham Lincoln's famous address.

The attention to detail is remarkable and all the Presidents' costumes are made in the styles and materials of their day. Some cloths even had to be specially woven to provide the right fabrics. The show is fascinating both for the level of patriotism generated, and for the sheer brilliance of the technology involved. The theater is air conditioned so also makes an excellent retreat during the hottest parts of the day.

Liberty Square is a charming area of brightly painted red brick and clapboard houses, with colorful window boxes, ornate weather vanes, and attractive flower-laden gardens. The architecture reflects Georgian and Federal styles, and there is a delightful shaded and secluded area with benches and tables, behind

The fantastic Big Thunder Mountain Railroad, one of Magic Kingdom's best thrill rides (© Disney Enterprises, Inc)

the Silversmith Shop where you can sit and relax for a few moments.

The Liberty Tree is festooned with thirteen lanterns, one for each of the thirteen original states. The massive oak tree, at least 125 years old, was growing on the southern edge of Walt Disney World, and was lifted by crane to its present site.

You can get another taste of history by taking a relaxing ride on the **Liberty Square Riverboat,** the *Richard F. Irvine,* which was actually built in a dry dock at Walt Disney World. Although the boiler converts water to steam to drive the paddle wheel, the riverboat is actually 'steered' along its half-mile (1km) route on an underwater rail. If you sit at the front or the back of the boat you can see both river banks at the same time. The **Mike Fink Keel Boats** ply the same stretch of water, but are much smaller and you are packed in. The two squat little boats are named after a Missouri riverboat captain and a friend of Davy Crockett. The round trip takes about 15 minutes and it is best to do the **Liberty Square Riverboat** one day, and the Keel Boats another.

After a gentle trip on the water, it is back to the attractions and a visit to **The Haunted Mansion**, although it is more thrilling than chilling for the sake of the many young visitors. Based on a typical Dutch home found in the Hudson River valley in the eighteenth century, the attraction uses all the high tech gadgetry at its disposal to conjure up ghosts, eerie noises and special effects from the moment you step inside. You walk the first part

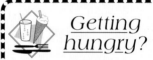

Getting hungry?

Liberty Tree Tavern — eat in eighteenth-century splendour surrounded by pewter and copper utensils and even a large fireplace. Lunch offers sandwiches and salads, while dinner offers fish, seafood and steaks. Try the oysters or clam chowder served at both meals. Full table service. Reservations recommended and taken at the door.

Columbia Harbour House — a fast food shrimp house also offering salads, sandwiches, fish, chowder and chicken. Counter service.

Sleepy Hollow — for soft drinks, hot dogs, cookies and Disney 'Handwiches'.

of the attraction taking in the portrait gallery with its moving walls and floors, avoiding the sprayed on cobwebs and layers of dust. You then board your car for the final part of the ride which culminates in there always being one more 'body' than when you set off. The ride is very popular because of the thrills, and many people take it over and over again in order to spot every detail. Read the humorous epitaphs on the tombstones for instance.

It is worth pointing out that this is the only attraction where the staff try to keep a straight face and not smile, and the only one where you are likely to see any sign of dust. The dust which coats the hundreds of objects in the attic is specially brought in.

Fantasyland

Walt Disney set out to create this as a 'timeless land of enchantment', and he and his successors have certainly done that. It is a land plucked straight from the fairy tale books, where favorite children's characters come to life, and whose main aim is to enthral. No matter how old you are, it is difficult to stop yourself singing along to **It's A Small World**, and humming it to yourself days after you have left the park. **Cinderella's Golden Carrousel** dominates the courtyard inside Cinderella Castle and is surrounded by many other rides, especially popular with younger children.

The Carrousel was rescued from a New Jersey fairground, although the roundabout, built by Italian wood carvers working for the Philadelphia Toboggan Company in 1917, was originally destined for the Detroit Palace Garden Park. It originally had seventy-two prancing horses but during renovation by Walt Disney World craftsmen, another eighteen were added, and each is unique. A good way of spending the time while waiting for your ride, is to try to spot all the differences. Also, spend some time appreciating the hand-painted scenes on the inside of the wooden canopy above the horses. The paintings, each measuring about 2ft by 3ft (0.5m by 1m), depict scenes from the Disney's 1950 film of *Cinderella*.

The Mad Tea Party is not for the very young, especially as you can use the wheel in the center of each giant tea cup, in which you sit, to spin yourself around even faster. Again, the ride is based on a Disney film, this time the 1951 release of *Alice in Wonderland*. At the end of each ride, if you are in a fit state to notice, the doormouse pops up out of the teapot in the center of the attraction.

Dumbo, The Flying Elephant is definitely for the young, although a good number of adults like it too! Based on Disney's classic 1941 animated film, the ride features lots of Dumbo's with big ears, and each has a control column so that you can go gently up and down as the ride revolves.

"It's A Small World" is a musical boat ride round the world to the accompaniment of a very catchy little number that once heard, is almost impossible to get out of your head. It is a delightful attraction which gently moves around various sets, each depicting different countries and dolls dressed in the appropriate national costumes. You have got to be really hard-hearted not to enjoy it. The children love it.

Peter Pan's Flight based on Barrie's story about the boy who would not grow up, allows you to take off for Never Land over the streets of London, aboard your flying sailing ship. In fact the 'sailing ships' are suspended from a rail as they travel round the attraction which offers wonderful starlit views over London before you meet Wendy, Tinker Bell, Captain Hook, the 'ticking' crocodile and the rest of the gang. A very popular attraction which only lasts for around 3 minutes.

Snow White's Adventures

is based on the classic fairytale but it may prove a little scary for younger visitors because of some of the special effects. The attraction concentrates on the wicked witch who keeps swooping at you out of nowhere, and there are

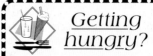

Getting hungry?

Cinderella's Royal Table — eat in medieval splendour in Cinderella Castle. The waitresses are dressed in 13th century style gowns and Cinderella mingles with the diners. Same day reservations taken at the door.

The Pinocchio Village Haus — a maze of rooms decorated with cuckoo clocks and murals provide ample space to enjoy hot dogs, burgers, sandwiches and pasta salads. Counter service.

Lumière's Kitchen — counter service offering children's meals and adults menu.

Scuttle's Landing — for soft drinks and milk shakes.

Enchanted Grove — for throat numbing iced-lemonade slushes and ice cream.

Hook's Tavern — for snacks.

skeletons and lots of spooky noises and effects.

"The Legend of the Lion King", is performed daily on the giant stage of Fantasyland's Theatre by a cast of Disney 'Humanimals'. Music is by Elton John and Tim Rice.

The Skyway will transport you in the skies to Tomorrow-land if you have finished exploring Fantasyland. The aerial cab takes 5 minutes and gives marvellous views over Fantasyland, especially the huge aquamarine tank that houses Captain Nemo's submarines. Most people agree, however, that the ride is better done the other way, from Tomorrowland to Fantasyland so that you get an aerial taste of what is to come, as much of Tomorrowland is actually under cover.

Mickey's Toontown Fair

Mickey's Toontown Fair was opened in 1988 as Mickey's Starland to celebrate Mickey's sixtieth birthday. The 3-acre (1-hectare) site is a great favorite with young children because most things are their size, like the miniature brightly-colored houses set in their manicured gardens.

The best way to arrive in Mickey's Toontown Fair is to catch the train at Walt Disney Railroad Station in Main

H O T   T I P

As the line to meet Mickey is moved along quite briskly, it is a good idea to have your camera ready before you reach him.

The children can let off steam climbing Mickey's Treehouse and try and find their way out of the not-too-difficult Mouskamaze.

Street, USA, and then you can explore **Mickey's Country House**, see what his favorite foods are from the shopping list on the fridge and inspect his car with its enormous wheels, and see where Pluto lives when he is in the doghouse. The radio naturally plays Disney song favorites, and the television screens the '*Mickey Mouse Club*'. It is a nice touch that Mickey's room is always a bit of a mess, very reassuring to all the visiting children.

You can also explore **Minnie's Country House**, Donald Duck's houseboat and Goofy's home. After walking through Mickey's house, you find yourself at the entrance to **The Judge's Tent**, where Mickey Mouse awaits your arrival. **The Toontown Hall of Fame** located inside a large striped tent contains a wide selection of your favorite Disney characters who are all delighted to have their pictures taken. Also awaiting is the **Barnstormer at Goofy's Wiseacre Farm** — a biplane themed, scaled down roller-coaster perfect for youngsters.

Tomorrowland

Space Mountain dominates Tomorrowland and still has a futuristic look and this is helped by the rocket pointing skywards from the center of Star Jets, and the strangely manicured trees and shrubs that abound.

Space Mountain itself is just over 180ft (55m) high, and the steel and concrete dome with its spiked turrets and aerials, like a large flying saucer, has a diameter of about 300ft (91m). The ride itself is a combination of roller coaster and light show, and although it only lasts a little over 150 seconds, it will imprint itself on your memory. For many people it is the most exciting ride, not only because it has all the thrills of a roller coaster but also because of the tricks played on your senses which add enormously to the experience.

The atmosphere builds up even before you climb into one of the three passenger 'rockets' because of the flashing lights and strobe effects as you wait, and the screams from passengers ahead of you as they hurtle round in space. As the line snakes its way forward, you catch glimpses of the rockets hurtling past, and if you think it might all be too much for you, you can still make a graceful exit before it is too late. Even while standing in the strange blue half-light, you get the impression of being in space and if you look up, all you can see are the pinpoints of lights from thousands of distant stars.

Once aboard your rocket, things start gently enough as the rockets slowly climb to the top of the dome. By the time you have arrived, you are in pitch darkness, and it is this that dramatically heightens the effect of the ride because you cannot see the twists and turns until you are actually doing them, and your stomach seems to get the message first!

Speeds of 28mph (45kph) are reached although you get the impression that you are moving very much faster. There is a height restriction on the ride and pregnant women and those who suffer from motion sickness, heart, back or neck problems are advised against going on this ride. However it is great fun, and knees do stop shaking after a couple of minutes back on terra firma. It is a good idea to secure your possessions before setting off as sun glasses, wallets, hats and the like can get thrown off.

It is a good idea to ride **Space Mountain** before lunch or a good while after.

The moving walkway which takes you out of Space Mountain transports you past **Dream of a New World**, a series of scenes which illustrate the role the electronic media will play in all our lives in the future.

The Time Keeper is a 21 minute journey through time in Circlevision 360 which constantly has you turning your head to watch the images displayed all round you on the bank of giant 20ft by 30ft (6m by 9m) screens. Disney Imagineers combined with Audio-Animatronics® figures and special effects create the illusion that you are flying back in time, during which you meet famous inventors and visionaries. The theater can handle more than 3,000 visitors an hour, so even if the lines look long, they go down quickly.

Walt Disney's Carousel of Progress moved to Walt Disney World in 1975 after being first seen at the 1964 World Fair hosted by New York. The revolving theater features an Audio-Animatronics family who tell the story of electricity from the pioneering days of Edison who invented the electric light bulb (in Florida) in the 1880s, up to the present day, and then gives a glimpse of the future, in the 22 minute presentation.

Buzz Lightyear's Space Ranger Spin is a new interactive attraction in which you must help Buzz defeat the Evil Emperor Zurg.

Tomorrowland Speedway is a firm favorite with the older children who get the chance to drive their own cars

Getting hungry?

Cosmic Ray's Starlight Cafe — hot and cold sandwiches, salads and soups.

Auntie Gravity's Galactic Goodies — ice cream, smoothies, fruit juice.

The Plaza Pavilion — pizzas, Italian speciality sandwiches and pasta salads, counter service.

The Lunching Pad at Rockettower Plaza — natural foods, frozen yoghurt and fruit juices.

around the winding track. Adults who do not want to have a go, can watch from the grandstand. The gas (petrol) powered sports cars have rack and pinion steering, although the vehicles actually run along a 2,260ft (689m) long track. They do have to be steered, however, to keep them going in the right direction. Always popular, so expect to wait.

Astro Orbiter is a good old-fashioned fairground ride despite its appearance and the Saturn-rocket look-alike around which it is built. You sit in a two-man open space craft and simply relax while enjoying the views over the park. You can add excitement by 'steering' your craft so that its movements are more pronounced.

The Galaxy Palace Theater alongside the **Walt Disney's Carousel of Progress** presents live productions featuring Disney characters

and performers. Another hi-tech attraction is **The Extra TERROR-estrial Alien Encounter** — frighteningly thrilling, which has replaced the "Mission to Mars" attraction.

The Tomorrowland Transit Authority offers a gentle 5 to 6 minute trip around and through Tomorrowland, and it is a good way to get an overview of what is on offer. The five car trains travel at 10mph (8kph) along the 1 mile (1.5km) track and actually travels through Space Mountain where the screams of those on the ride echo around you! The TTA could well become a popular form of transport in the years to come. It is driven by a linear induction motor which has no moving parts, is silent, uses minimum power and emits no pollutants.

If you have not already taken the **Skyway**, take the cable car for an aerial ride to Fantasyland.

Opposite: The Parade, Magic Kingdom® Park
(© Disney Enterprises, Inc)

Epcot®

The massive eighteen-storey-high **Spaceship Earth**, looking like a giant silver golf ball, dominates Epcot and the surrounding area. It stands at the entrance to what has to be the world's most successful educational theme park, and the enormous success of Epcot is that it entertains and expands your mind at the same time.

Walt Disney first conceived the idea of Epcot (Experimental Prototype Community of Tomorrow) in the 1960s. In October, 1966 he wrote that he wanted to create this experimental prototype community of tomorrow using the very latest ideas and know-how in science and technology from the creative centers of American industry. It was to be 'a showcase to the world for the ingenuity and imagination of American free enterprise.' On 1 October 1982, Epcot Center was opened as part of Walt Disney World.

Epcot, covers 230 acres (93 hectares) and consists of two areas — **Future World**, which has ten major exhibits/attractions presented by leading American companies, and **World Showcase**, which features eleven national pavilions, giving an insight into their culture, traditions, art and cuisine.

Getting there

By car take the special exit from I-4 which leads directly into Epcot or take the main Walt Disney World entrance just after highway 192 west turn off from I-4 and follow the very clearly signposted route. Epcot has its own car park for 9,000 vehicles and there is a parking fee (free for guests staying at Walt Disney World Resorts). Guests should carry their ID Card issued to them when checking in. Make a note of your parking line and bay number, and then catch one of the trams to take you to the main entrance.

By bus or **Walt Disney World Monorail** to and from the Magic Kingdom and Walt Disney World Resort hotels. There is a shuttle bus service between Epcot and Disney-MGM Studios.

Attractions, entertainments and tours

Disney characters now mingle with the crowds throughout Epcot, and you can often find them wearing the national costumes of the pavilion they are visiting. At lunchtime, Mickey and friends can normally be seen at Plaza Towers

Epcot®
Essential Information

- **Opening times**: Epcot is open from 10am to 9pm year round, but opens earlier and stays open later during Easter and summer, and during special holiday times such as Washington's Birthday week.

- Tickets are available for 1, 4, 5, 6 and 7 days. One day tickets can be used at one theme park only, while 4, 5 and 6 day passes allow access to all the theme parks and use of the connecting transportation.

- Visit **Earth Station** at the base of Spaceship Earth for up-to-the-minute information, especially on entertainment schedules and guided tours. Table reservations for lunch and dinner can be made using the World Key interactive terminals. Earth Station also provides information about lost children and can supply personal translator units in Spanish, French or German, information for guests with disabilities, taped narrations for guests with sight impairments, and written descriptions for guests with hearing difficulties. There is also information about behind-the-scenes educational and professional development schemes.

- There are baby changing and nursing facilities in the **Odyssey Complex** in Future World. Baby strollers are available for rent on the east side of Spaceship Earth and at International Gateway, where trams arrive from a number of Epcot Resort hotels.

- Cameras and videocamcorders can be rented at the **Kodak Camera Center**. You can drop film in for 2-hour processing, anywhere you see the Photo Express sign; pick your prints up at the Camera Center. Film is readily available and Kodak have identified the best 'photo spots' around the park so that you can get the best pictures. Lockers are available for rent on the west side of Spaceship Earth.

- Wheelchairs are available for rent on the east side of Spaceship Earth or at International Gateway.

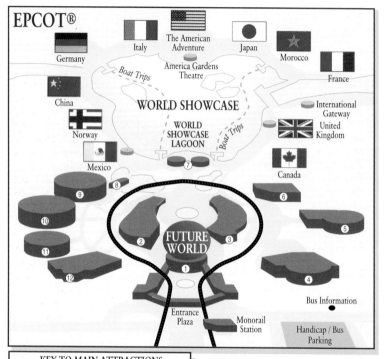

KEY TO MAIN ATTRACTIONS

① Spaceship Earth
② Innoventions East
③ Innoventions West
④ The Living Seas
⑤ The I and
⑥ Journey Into Imagination
⑦ Showcase Plaza
⑧ Odyssey Center
⑨ GM Test Track
⑩ Horizons
⑪ Wonders of Life
⑫ Universe of Energy

in front of the lake. You can also have breakfast with Disney characters every day in the Stargate Restaurant. In addition, there are strolling entertainers and musicians.

The main show/attraction is IllumiNations, an after-dark laser show combining music, fireworks and dancing water fountains which takes place at closing time each night.

Dinner entertainments include joining in an Oktoberfest celebration at the Biergarten in the Germany Pavilion, and being serenaded by strolling musicians at Alfredo's in the Italy Pavilion.

There are two behind the scenes morning tours, both lasting about 4 hours. They are for people aged 16 and over, are excellent value and very popular, so early reservations are essential (several weeks in advance if planning to visit at very busy periods).

Getting around Epcot

Epcot is shaped like a figure eight, with the top circle, World Showcase, about three times larger than the bottom one, Future World. Arriving by the main entrance, you enter Future World with Spaceship Earth at its heart and with the other attractions arranged around it. The national pavilions in World Showcase are built around World Showcase Lagoon.

The best way to get around is by foot, so wear sensible footwear, but if you want to ride, catch one of the sedate double decker buses that cruise around World Showcase stopping outside most of the pavilions, or catch one of the five 'Friend-Ship' water taxis that ply between Showcase Plaza and docks in front of either the Germany or Morocco Pavilion. It is quicker to walk than taking either the bus or boat.

Future World

Most of the pavilions contain rides which transport you around the exhibit and most have areas where you can spend time afterwards, discovering more about them, and often getting hands-on experience. You should allow at least 30 minutes for each pavilion, and some require far longer than this in order to do them justice.

Spaceship Earth

The huge silver ball is 180ft (55m) high, 164ft (50m) in diameter and rests on six giant legs supported by pylons driven 100ft (30m) into the ground. The structure encloses an area of more than 2 million cubic feet, and is so large that on a clear day, it is clearly visible from aircraft flying down either Florida's Atlantic or Gulf coastlines.

At the base of Spaceship Earth is **Earth Station**, the visitor information center, and the sphere itself contains the ever popular **Spaceship Earth** ride, a journey through time and space telling the story of communications from the dawn of civilisation to the present and then looking ahead to predict what the future holds.

The journey tells how communication developed from cave paintings and hieroglyphics to the first alphabets and the written word, and the remarkable advances and achievements of the past few decades. The detail of each scene and the special effects are incredible. The 15 minute trip ends as if you were in space with a spectacular view of earth photographed by astronauts on one of the Apollo

Planning your visit

You can whiz through Epcot in a day, spending half your time in **Future World** and the remainder in **World Showcase**, but you really do need more time than this to see and do everything. However long you plan to spend at Epcot, get there early. If you plan to eat at one of the full service restaurants you must reserve your table as soon as possible.

On arrival visit **Earth Station** to get the latest information about what is on and show times, and make your meal reservations, then head straight for **World Showcase**, working your way around the national pavilions methodically in either a clockwise or anticlockwise direction. In this way, you will get ahead of the crowds who normally descend in a rush on **Spaceship Earth** as soon as they arrive and then proceed to spend the next few hours visting the other attractions in **Future World**, and not arriving in **World Showcase** until lunchtime.

If you have only one day, you can spend the morning touring **World Showcase** and the afternoon and early evening visiting **Future World**, when the queues for many of the attractions are lower than in the morning. If you are planning to spend 2 days at the center, spend the first morning in **World Showcase** and the afternoon in **Future World**. Spend the second morning taking in the remaining attractions to be seen in **Future World** and any others that you want to do again, then the afternoon in **World Showcase** taking in the shows you missed the first day.

moonshots. The attraction is always popular but the lines tend to be longest in the mornings and shortest in the evening.

The bands **Future World Brass** and **Future Corps** perform daily outside **Spaceship Earth**.

Innoventions

Innoventions, one of Disney's most popular attractions, with its combination of innova-tion and invention, really does give visitors a hands-on glimpse of the future. It is an ever-changing, interactive technology attraction which fascinates people of all ages. Experience at first hand how products like voice-activated appliances, high definition televisions, electric vehicles, home electronics and comput-ers will impact on and improve our lives in the years ahead.

Opened in 1994, Innoventions was created to help ease a technology wary public into the information age and judging by the thousands of people who spend many hours in the pavilions, the experiment has obviously worked. It is now one of the most popular attractions at Epcot. Highlights include:

AT&T Innoventions. Lots of hands-on and interactive displays of leading-edge services and technologies such as Internet access, digital satellite entertainment and real-time language translation for more than 140 languages through a single phone call.

Bill Nye, the Science Guy features U.S. TV's popular science teacher in a light-hearted multimedia presentation which shows how the wildest ideas grow from laboratory to market place.

Family PC enables families to explore and learn about the world of computers with themed activity areas and the latest hardware and software available for testing.

The GE TechnoLab is a multimedia exhibit featuring the TechnoLab Science Theater. Using the latest technology, visitors can see inside the human body, test the strength of different materials and star in some of America's most popular television programs.

General Motors Corp huge facility stars its latest electric vehicle which can be 'test driven' thanks to the latest simulator technology.

The Ultimate House of the Future is presented by Honeywell and features the most innovative and advanced home comfort technology available now — or soon to be. There are also hands-on interactive areas.

IBM Corporation's new exhibit features ground-breaking innovative and interactive demonstrations of the company's latest products such as animated video pets who respond to spoken commands, and the latest software for pre-school learning and playtime.

Motorola displays a look ahead into the future of information and communication technology with **Sky Cyberguy** as the master of ceremonies. Visitors can interact with many innovative products and glimpse into the company's future in space and have a virtual reality experience with computers powered with semiconductors.

SEGA offers visitors the opportunity to play more than 140 of the latest, hottest videogames, including getting behind the wheel of a 200 mile an hour racing car, or battling a T-Rex in your own Lost World Adventure.

Finally, Silicon Graphics' **Inspired By Vision** exhibit allows visitors to discover how visualization technology

Spaceship Earth
& Monorail Mark VI, Epcot®
(© Disney Enterprises, Inc)

is responsible for many of the ordinary and extraordinary things around us, from putting the crunch in cornflakes to building a jet fighter.

Universe of Energy

Ellen's Energy Adventure is an attraction featuring cars powered by solar energy gathered from panels mounted on the roof of the pavilion, as you explore the world of energy. This attraction is what Epcot is all about, technically complicated, very informative and above all, hugely entertaining and enjoyable.

Follow your host Ellen round the attraction consisting of three films and a ride which really moves you. The first film, which lasts about 10 minutes, looks at energy resources today. It is screened on a wall made up of 100 separate computerised and synchronised moving monitors. You then make your way into the second screening area where there are bench seats arranged in blocks.

The second 5 minute film, on a massive screen 155ft (47m) long and 32ft (10m) high, tells how today's fossil fuels were created during the days of the dinosaurs, and then you realize that all the blocks of seats are slowly turning. You are transported back into time as you travel through a prehistoric world

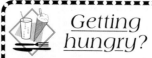

Getting hungry?

Stargate Restaurant — offers breakfast with Disney characters every day between 9-10am. You can also get chicken sandwiches, burgers and salads throughout the day. Counter service.

Beverage Base — offers frozen yoghurt, shakes and soft drinks.

Sunrise Terrace — offers pizza, pasta and is open for lunch and dinner. Counter service.

of dinosaurs, monster insects and remarkable primeval vegetation. Smells, smoke and eerie lighting all add to the effect. The various dinosaurs are the largest Audio-Animatronics® ever made.

The presentation concludes with a 12 minute film showing where today's energy comes from, including stunning footage from North Sea oil rigs and the Alaskan oil fields, and ends with a space shuttle blast off reinforcing the message that this perhaps, is where our future lies. There are usually lines but just under 600 people are admitted each time, so you do not normally have too long to wait.

Wonders of Life

A whole galaxy of things to keep the children amused for hours if you do not keep an eye on the time. The pavilion is devoted to health, fitness and modern lifestyles although it gets its message across in a highly entertaining and often hilarious way.

Body Wars was Epcot's first real thrill ride. You take your seat in the capsule, which is then 'miniaturised' and injected into a human body. The ride combines a flight simulator and audio visual effects on the screen, so that you actually do feel as if you are hurtling around. Because of this it is not recommended for pregnant women and people with heart, neck or back problems. Children under the age of 3 are not allowed to board, and children under the age of 7 must be accompanied by an adult.

Having been shaken up by Body Wars, relax and enjoy a good laugh at *Cranium Command* which attempts to fathom out the mind of a typical 12-year-old boy. The presentation combines theater set, Audio-Animatronics figures, special effects and screens to explain how the body's organs work and what they do, and how emotions and actions are controlled by the different sides of the brain. It is educational and very funny, especially for parents who have lived with a 12-year-old boy.

There are three theater presentations. *Goofy About Health* is one way of getting the good health message. The 8 minute multi-screen cartoon presentation shows how Goofy transforms himself from being an unhealthy wreck into a clean-living healthy guy. All the improvised sketches are to do with health and fitness. *The Making of Me* is a 14 minute film which tells the story of a man who travels back in time to find out where he comes from. It includes scenes of a birth, and while it is very sensitively done, parental discretion is recommended.

At the **MetLifestyle Revue**, if you punch in various personal details like age, weight, height and so on, the computer

Getting hungry?

Pure and Simple — offers, as you might expect, a selection of healthy foods such as salads, sandwiches, oat bran waffles and frozen yoghurts. Counter service.
Odyssey Center — has baby care facilities and the Odyssey Restaurant on three spacious levels. Offers hotdogs, burgers and other snacks. Counter Service.

will tell you what you are doing wrong and what you should do to lead a healthier and more stress free life. Finally **Frontiers of Medicine** features a frequently-changing exhibition which looks at the latest scientific and medical breakthroughs.

Horizons

Board your four-man cars for a journey which first traces man's visions of the future over the centuries, then looks at science today on the huge wrap around screen, and then transports you into what it may be like several years from now. Watch the space shuttle blast off on a giant screen, or see how crystals grow, before your trip into the future. The suspended cars take you on a futuristic journey to see what city life will be like, whether it is a city on the ocean bed or in space. The ride lasts about 15 minutes.

GM Test Track

Epcot's latest attraction and the longest and fastest Disney theme park attraction. Presented by General Motors, Test Track highlights the rigorous tests GM puts its vehicles through, including a highway speed test reaching 65 mph.

Honey, I Shrunk The Audience

A highly popular 3D special effects presentation.

The Land

A pavilion dedicated to food, growing it, developing new technologies for the future and eating it, either in the bright **Sunshine Season Food Fair** or revolving Garden Grill

Getting hungry?

The Garden Grill Restaurant — offers full table service in this plush revolving restaurant which takes in scenes from the Listen to the Land ride. Breakfast, lunch and dinner are served and reservations for midday and evening meals are recommended. The lunch menu offers sample-size portions of the dinner entrées so that you can taste more than one dish, while dinner offers lobster, shrimp, steaks and chicken.

Sunshine Season Food Fair — in the food court. Has a number of separate counter-service booths each with their own menus, and offering a huge range of dishes from New England chowder to freshly baked bagels, and smoked sausages to blueberry muffins.

Restaurant. The pavilion covers 6 acres (2 hectares) and includes experimental growing areas and greenhouses. Take a boat ride to look at food production methods of the past and those of the future, or take one of the guided walking tours to learn more about the experimental techniques now being used and developed to produce the food needed to feed the fast expanding global population.

Living with the Land is a 13.5 minute boat ride from the past into the agricultural technologies of the future. It features prairie agriculture at the turn of the century and shows how deserts can be farmed to produce food, how crops can be grown without soil, and how plant science can produce new crops to survive the harshest of environments. There are guided tours every half hour which follow the same route as the boat ride, yet on foot and in far more detail with a guide who can answer all your questions.

All the guides have agricultural degrees and are members of agricultural operations staff. The tours normally last about 45 minutes, but longer if there are a lot of questions! It is advisable to book your place on the tour as early as possible, and it is recommended you take the boat ride first.

The Harvest Theater presents the 19 minute film *The*

Circle of Life which looks at the delicate balance between man and land, and farming and the damage it can cause. It is well worth seeing and despite some of the film's early soundings of gloom and doom, it does finish with some reassuring messages.

The Living Seas

A favorite with young and old alike, and even the rock garden at the entrance, with waves crashing over, is a source of fascination. As you enter the pavilion you pass a number of exhibits, illustrations and old photographs showing man's early attempts at undersea exploration, as you make your way to **Caribbean Coral Reef**.

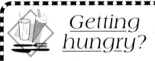

Getting hungry?

Coral Reef — restaurant serving mainly fresh seafood and offering wonderful underwater views of the coral reef of **The Living Seas** exhibit. The dining room is built on several floors so all diners have views of the water through the 8ft (2m) high windows. The menu varies according to the season. Reservations for lunch and dinner are recommended. Full table service.

Your journey starts when you enter the 'hydrolators' which dive down beneath the sea. It is the floor vibrating that gives the impression that you are descending and, in fact, you only go down 2 inches. When the doors open, however, you are in another world as you board the two-man cars for the trip round the coral reef. The man-made coral reef is housed in a 5.7 million gallon round tank, the home of more than 200 species of fish and marine life, including brightly colored tropical fish, sea lions, dolphins and diamond rays.

The trip ends at **Sea Base Alpha,** a mock-up of a prototype underseas research facility, on two levels connected by escalators and with six modules, each focusing on a different aspect of marine life or exploration. Here you can look down into another tank housing fish, moray eels, sharks and barracuda.

World Showcase

It is only 1.3 miles (2km) around the Lagoon on World Showcase Promenade, but in that short space you will cross time zones, experience new cultures and traditions, and gain a new insight into the country and the people whose pavilions you visit.

One of the reasons that World Showcase is so successful is the enormous care that is taken to make each pavilion area as realistic as possible, even down to landscaping them with the trees and plants that would be found in each country represented. Each exhibit is designed to give a taste of the country and this is enhanced by exhibitions, film shows or presentations. Wherever possible, nationals are recruited to work in the pavilion of the country where they were born. Traditional craftsmen can often be seen at work.

In addition, all the goods sold in the pavilion shops are genuine, the entertainment is authentic and the food offered is the same as that served back home, although occasionally it has been altered slightly to make it more acceptable to the American palate.

Even the walk around the promenade is a gardener's delight with scores of different plants to identify if you can. There are plots full of flowering rose bushes, and the camphor trees which line the path will provide more shade as they grow taller.

HOT TIP

As most people spend the first few hours in Future World, follow our suggested itinerary, and head straight for World Showcase to avoid the crowds.

Following a clockwise route, the pavilions are as follows:

Mexico

Sail through the rivers of time in **El Rio del Tiempo**, a gentle 6 minute boat ride which explores Mexico's history and traditions, and tourism opportunities. The ride entrance is inside the pavilion topped by a reconstruction of a third-century Mayan pyramid. The charming interior is designed to look like a small Mexican plaza (town square) at dusk, with a fountain surrounded by brightly-colored flowers and stalls packed with Mexican crafts and goods. Mexican bands play traditional music both inside the pavilion and outside. A gallery houses **Art of Mexico** with exhibits from Mexican culture from the earliest days to the present.

Norway

The pavilion is modelled on Akershus, the fourteenth-century fortress which guards Oslo harbour, and alongside is a reconstruction of a twelfth-century wooden Stave church, which would have been built at the time of the Vikings. Inside is 'To the ends of the Earth', an exhibit which records Norway's considerable achievements in polar exploration.

The **Maelstrom** is a 'Viking' long boat ride which takes you on a journey through a Viking coastal village and finishes up in the turbulent North Sea, past oil rigs and into the treacherous Maelstrom. Do not let the name of the ride fool you, it is very tame, but still fun. As you leave the ride you are ushered into a theater for a film on Norway's stunning scenery. Traditional entertainment is provided by folk singers and dancers.

China

The recreation of the red and gold **Temple of Heaven** in Beijing's Hidden City houses the China pavilion. There is a very tranquil atmosphere inside, helped by the gentle Chinese music played softly in the background.

The star exhibit is _Wonders of China_, a spectacular 20 minute film shown on Circle-Vision 360, which takes you to every corner of this vast country. Few people realize just how huge China is and the diversity of landscapes it offers. There are lean rails (not seats), however, which are useful because you do get the impression on occasions, because of the way the film is shot, that you are actually moving.

Visit the **Hall of Prayer for Good Harvest**, where everything (building materials and dimensions) was dictated by astrological associations, and take time for the exhibition of Chinese art and artifacts, which changes every 6 months or so.

Entertainment is provided by oriental musicians and the incredible Pu Yang acrobats.

Germany

A collection of quaint architectural styles drawn from many German towns and dominated by the turreted Eltz Castle, north of the Mosel Valley or a close likeness to it. A strolling accordianist entertains along with other musicians, the hourly chimes from the clock tower's glockenspiel, and cuckoo clocks which are everywhere.

The main draw is the lively **Oktoberfest Muskanten**, which nightly echoes to the music and revels of a traditional Bavarian beer festival. It is held in the Biergarten, which offers food and beer during the day accompanied by a Bavarian brass band.

The pavilion is packed with shops offering a wide range of goods from books to beer steins, cuckoo clocks to Christmas decorations, and woodcarvings to fine wine. The toy shop with its animated cuddly animals, and the sweet (candy) shop are a must.

Italy

Enormous attention to detail has been lavished here as you stroll through the Piazza San Marco in Venice, past the Doge's Palace with its gold covered angel on top of the 100ft (30m) high bell tower, and beside the tethered gondolas. There are lots of statues and architectural examples to remind you of Italy's impressive history.

Mexico Pavillion, World Showcase, Epcot®
(© Disney Enterprises, Inc)

Getting hungry? World Showcase

Mexico

San Angel Inn — offers full table service and a traditional Mexican menu. For those not used to Mexican food, there is a combi-platter which allows you to try a little of everything. You dine in very subdued lighting, alongside the lagoon which is part of the El Rio del Tiempo ride. Unless you want to eat early, reservations are recommended.

Cantina de San Angel — offers counter service for burritos and other Mexican snacks.

Norway

Restaurant Akershus — offers a traditional Norwegian 'Royal' buffet with hot and cold dishes and Norwegian beer if you wish. Buffet service.

Kringla Bakeri og Kafé — offers open sandwiches and pastries with Norwegian beer. Counter service.

China

Nine Dragons Restaurant — offers a number of different Chinese styles of cooking. Full table service.

Lotus Blossom Cafe — egg rolls, stir fry dishes and other Chinese fast-foods with Chinese beer. Counter service.

Germany

Biergarten — offers full table service for lunch and dinner, and reservations are necessary for the evening festivities.

Sommerfest — counter service for *bratwurst*, pretzels, desserts and soft drinks.

Italy

L'Originale Alfredo di Roma Ristorante — famous for its home-made pasta dishes and almost life-like murals. Full table service for lunch and dinner. Reservations necessary.

The American Adventure

Liberty Inn — enjoy burgers, hot dogs, chicken and apple pie and other American fare. Counter service.

Japan

Teppanyaki Dining Rooms — for grilled meats, seafood, Japanese beer. You sit at counters and your chef prepares your meal in front of you. Reservations for lunch and dinner recommended. Table service.

Tempura Kiku Sushi — offers a wide range of *tempura* (fried in batter) dishes for lunch and dinner. Table service.

Matsu No Ma Lounge — serves sushi and other appetisers.
Counter service.

Yakitori House — Japanese fast food, broiled chicken, *teriyaki* sandwiches.
Counter service.

Morocco

Restaurant Marrakesh — traditional and very tasty Moroccan dishes. If you cannot make up your mind, try a sample platter which offers a taste of several dishes. Reservations recommended. Table service.

France

Chefs de France — a gastronomic experience. The restaurant is run by three of France's most famous and most proficient chefs. Traditional French food, using the finest, freshest ingredients and served *à la nouvelle* cuisine. Open for lunch and dinner. Table service. Reservations essential.

Boulangerie Pâtisserie — find this by following your nose! Enjoy freshly baked croissants, cakes and pastries. Counter Service.

United Kingdom

Rose and Crown Dining Room — offers traditional British pub grub for lunch — fish and chips, steak and kidney pie, Scotch eggs and so on. There is a wide choice for dinner. Reservations recommended. It also offers afternoon teas.

Rose and Crown Pub — serves real ale, beer and spirits in a traditional British pub. Enjoy your pint inside or on the terrace overlooking the lagoon. The beer mats here disappear like hot cakes!

Canada

Le Cellier — offers hearty Canadian specialities, buffet-style.

Items on sale in the shops and little outdoor market include leather goods, jewelry, fine glassware and delicious chocolates. Entertainment includes an Italian quartet which performs in the courtyard, and Rondo Veneziano, classical music performances.

The American Adventure

This half-hour, not to be missed, presentation stands at the top of the Lagoon and is the center piece of World Showcase. The 110,000 red clay bricks for the Colonial-style **Philadelphia Liberty Hall** were all hand-made, and the attention to detail is even more acute inside.

The American Adventure is one of the most technologically advanced and complex shows of its kind ever put together. It uses elaborate moving sets, almost life-like Audio-Animatronic figures, incredible sound systems and the world's largest rear-projection screen, to celebrate the spirit of America from its earliest beginnings with the arrival of the Pilgrim Fathers, to the present day. The presenters are Ben Franklin and Mark Twain who talk you through all the great moments in American history. It is difficult at the time to remember that these are not actors but Audio-Animatronics, albeit some of the most sophisticated ever made.

The **America Gardens Theatre** by the Shore stages a variety of shows, including international folk dances and songs.

Japan

The quiet and peaceful atmosphere of the Japanese pavilion and its lovely gardens is shattered several times a day by the magnificent Matsurizu drummers, whose pounding rhythm echoes round World Showcase. Apart from making incredible music, it is clearly an excellent way of keeping one's weight down.

The pagoda which dominates the pavilion is modelled on an eighth-century one in Nara. Each of its five storeys represents one of the elements in the Buddhist faith. The huge bright red *torii* gate which stands by the water's edge was copied from the one at the Itsukushima shrine on Hiroshima Bay.

The Japanese gardens with their use of rocks, streams and pools are a delight. The **Bijutsu-kan Gallery** displays Japanese cultural items — the exhibition is changed periodically — and you can watch craftsmen at work demonstrating traditional skills such as kite making or making elaborate shapes from rice toffee.

Morocco

Entering the intricately carved wooden gate, it is easy to

imagine that you really are in Morocco, the atmosphere is so well created. There are replicas of Marrakesh's famous **Koutoubia Minaret**, and the **Nejjarine fountain** in Fez at the center of a flower-filled courtyard with lots of intriguing alleyways housing carpet vendors and craftsmen offering silver, gold and brass ware, and other traditional goods.

Moroccan art and artifacts are displayed in the **Gallery of Arts and History** and the exhibits are changed regularly. Entertainment includes belly-dancing daily in the restaurant, and the Festival Marrakesh in the courtyard, a programme of music, song and dance.

France

The Eiffel Tower, accordian players, street kiosks and pavement cafés leave you under no illusions that you are now in France. Treasures include the charming La Petite Rue, modelled on a typical French lane around 1600. *Impressions de France* is an 18 minute long journey through France in the Palais du Cinema, an air-conditioned theater with seats and a 200 degree screen, accompanied by a splendid musical sound track featuring French classical composers.

Outside, you come across strolling musicians. There are Parisian-style shops offering perfume, jewelry and other luxury goods, but above all this pavilion is about good food and wine. There are excellent home made cakes and pastries, biscuits and chocolates on sale, wines to be tried and bought, and a string of eateries.

United Kingdom

The whole gamut of architecture to be found in Britain is represented here, from graceful Georgian mansions in a plane-tree lined London Square, to thatched cottages and Tudor buildings. There is a traditional herb garden and maze and for entertainment there are the strolling 60's band *"The British Invasion"*. The shops offer for sale luxury goods which Britain is famous for, such as china, crystal, tartan and woollens.

Canada

The Canadian pavilion is dominated by the **Gothic Hotel du Canada**, modelled on Quebec's Château Frontenac and Ontario's Château Laurier. Stroll round the rushing streams, rock canyons and formal flower gardens, inspired by the Butchart Gardens in Victoria, before taking in *O Canada*, a 17 minute CircleVision 360 spectacular, featuring Canada's breathtaking scenery. The lean rails are for when you feel a little dizzy after zooming over a waterfall, or soaring over the Rockies.

DISNEY'S ANIMAL KINGDOM

Walt Disney World's newest theme park took four years to create and brings together more than 1,000 exotic animals and birds, exciting, colorful shows and the world's largest sculpted tree. Disney's Animal Kingdom is part zoo, part fantasy and is unlike anywhere else in Walt Disney World.

The first thing you notice when you enter Disney's Animal Kingdom, Disney's first new theme park for ten years, is the lack of noise and bustle which is ever present in the Magic Kingdom® Park, Disney-MGM Studios and Epcot®.

As you enter the park you wander along a quiet botanical path which winds through lush vegetation to the center of Disney's Animal Kingdom and the spectacular 145-foot tall **Tree of Life**.

Apart from the animals, there is DinoLand USA where children can become amateur archaeologists and uncover dinosaur bones and learn about these extinct monsters and the ever present threat to other species. **Countdown to Extinction** is the Disney's Animal Kingdom's only thrill ride although there are many other shows and a daily parade of truly bizarre creatures.

The 500-acre (223-hectare) Disney's Animal Kingdom, built at a cost of $800 million, starts at the entrance plaza and the Rainforest Cafe. You then walk through the Oasis Garden to the Safari Village, the first of the five main areas of the park that radiate out around the Tree of Life. You can take a boat ride or walk to the other four 'lands': **Africa**, with its safari ride and wildlife exploration trail; **Camp Minnie-Mickey** with its stage shows; **DinoLand USA**; and **Asia**

Getting around Disney's Animal Kingdom

Walk, take the Kilimanjaro Safari ride or hop aboard the Wildlife Express train.

As you walk, you can spot tree kangaroos and two-toed sloth and a wealth of exotic birdlife. Then, you can take a Safari ride aboard an open vehicle for an even closer look at the wildlife on the 110-acre (44-hectare) savanna. The ride culminates in a thrilling chase after poachers and you realize that this is all part of the Disney Magic.

which is still being expanded.

During the construction, more than 40,000 mature trees were planted to complement the 40 acres (16 hectares) of Florida oaks on the park's eastern edge. In addition, hundreds of thousands of plants and shrubs were used to create a truly exotic landscape. There are more plants in Disney's Animal Kingdom than in the three other Disney parks combined.

Artists from Bali spent three years carving the animal figures on the exteriors of the buildings and Zulus were flown in to build the thatched-roof huts in Harambe Village. The animals, however, are the chief attraction. There are more than 1,000 animals from 200 species and visitors really can have close encounters with most of them. Because the animals are up and about just after dawn, the park opens daily at 7am and it shuts at 8pm shortly before the animals are rounded up for the night.

The Oasis

This area is the quietest in the park and acts as a buffer zone between the bustle and rush of Florida and the lush, tropical greenery and exotic wildlife of the Disney's Animal Kingdom. It is here that you start to spot the huge array of tropical birds and animals from around the world, although some are more difficult to see than others. There are two paths and it is best to walk them both as each has different animal displays. Both paths meet at the border of The Oasis by the stone bridge that crosses **Discovery River** into **Safari Village**. It is from this point that you also get your first full view of the Tree of Life.

Safari Village

This is the equivalent of Main Street, USA in Magic Kingdom. There are shops and restaurants, street performers and a host of brightly colored buildings, all decorated with paintings and sculptures of animals. It is the venue of the zany **March of the ARTimals** and if you look around, you will see animals everywhere. Every building has a different animal theme, carved elephants act as the bases of lamp-posts and dragonflies are carved into window shutters. Altogether there are more than 2,500 animal carvings in Safari Village.

Dominating both the village and the park is the **Tree of Life**. It took two years to create, is as tall as a 14-storey building and has a 50 foot wide trunk. The canopy spreads more than 160 feet and its 8,000 branches contain 103,000 leaves. Beneath the boughs is housed a 430-seat theater which shows a 3-D film about insects, *It's Tough To Be*

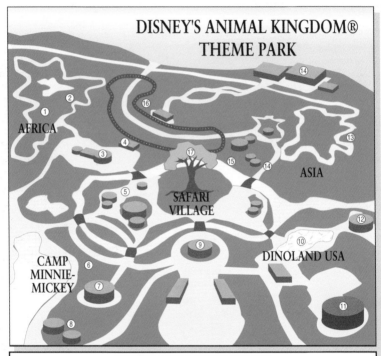

DISNEY'S ANIMAL KINGDOM® THEME PARK

KEY TO MAIN ATTRACTIONS

1. Africa
2. Kılımanjaro Safaris
3. Harambe Village
4. Pangani Forest Exploration Trail
5. Safari Village
6. Camp Minnie - Mickey
7. Festival of the Lion King
8. Colors of the Wind
9. The Oasis
10. The Boneyard
11. Countdown to Extinction
12. The Journey Into The Junglebook
13. Kali River Rapids
14. Conservation Station
15. Flights of Wonder at Caravan Stage
16. Wildlife Express
17. The Tree of Life

Opposite: Digging up dinosaur bones in Dinoland USA, Disney's Animal Kingdom® Park (© Disney Enterprises, Inc)

A Bug. See how many of the 325 animal carvings you can spot on the trunk and don't forget the many live animals that live between the gnarled roots

Camp Minnie-Mickey

You can find most of Disney's best loved creations as you follow the four short trails in Camp Minnie-Mickey. **Mickey Trail** leads to Mickey's House; **Arbor Trail** takes you to visit Minnie, Goofy and other Disney favorites; **Jungle Trail** introduces you to characters from *The Jungle Book* and *The Lion King*; and the **Forest Trail** takes you to meet Winnie The Pooh and friends.

There are two shows to see: *Festival of the Lion King* and *"Colors of the Wind, Friends from the Animal Forest"*.

Africa

Harambe Village with its outdoor bazaars and restaurants, is modelled on a typical East African coastal port village. The architecture switches from Arabian to Zulu and Swahili as you pass through the village, as it would as you travel deeper into Africa. It is here that you can take the Kilimanjaro Safaris. Riding in open vehicles, the safari allows you to view at close quarters the animals roaming the savanna. Towards the end of the journey poachers are spotted and the ride switches from a gentle safari to a chase as you race to apprehend them. It is all part of Disney's Disney's Animal Kingdom philosophy of mixing animal experiences with the thrill of a ride.

Other things to do are walk the **Pangani Forest Exploration Trail** and catch the **Wildlife Express** to ride to Conservation Station.

Conservation Station

This 'land' is a mix of education, hi-tech and close animal encounters. The whole aim of Conservation Station is to alert visitors to the ecological and environmental problems facing the planet and its population, both human and animal.

There are lots of hi-tech displays with conservation stories being told electronically on touch-screen computers. You can learn about animal migration in the **Wildlife Tracking Center**, or visit **EcoWeb** where you can research conservation projects around the world. You can watch a baby gorilla being fed or pop into the petting zoo known as the **Affection Section**.

The park's animal hospital is also here and you can watch vets and researchers at work through the large windows of the treatment center.

Asia

This land is still being developed and is scheduled to be fully open in 1999 when it will feature animals of Asia. One of the star attractions will be a thrill ride, combining white water rafting and lessons in habitat conservation. In the meantime, you can enjoy the **Flights of Wonder Bird show**.

DinoLand USA

Fact and fantasy get a little blurred in DinoLand USA. You can sift through the sand in the Boneyard looking for fake dinosaur bones, take the **Countdown to Extinction** thrill ride and learn more about the huge reptiles that used to roam the earth. If you are interested in plants, take the **Cretaceous Trail** which includes the palms, ferns and cycads that dinosaurs used to feed on.

At the **Fossil Preparation Lab** you can see the bones of

HOT TIP

The animals are most active in the morning so take the Kilimanjaro Safari as early as possible. Although the safaris run throughout the day, the animals will be napping by mid-afternoon.

a 65 million year-old T-Rex being prepared for assembly. DinoLand USA is also the home of the *Journey Into Jungle Book* stage show.

Disney's Animal Kingdom Shows

Real animals rub shoulders with make believe creatures in many of the shows staged several times each day in the park. There are four main shows plus the twice-daily parade of zany creatures and street performers.

Festival of the Lion King is a song and dance celebration based loosely on the hugely successful Broadway hit *The Lion King* and the Disney animated film of the same name.

"Colors of the Wind, Friends from the Animal Forest" is based on the Disney film *Pocahontas* and incorporates live animals ranging from boa constrictors and rats to skunks and rabbits. The show tells the story of America's forests, their wildlife and the steps being taken to counter the threats to both.

Flights of Wonder is a stage show starring live birds, and *Journey Into Jungle Book* is a musical show inspired by Rudyard Kipling's *The Jungle Book*. It stars actors and costumed animal characters who tell the story of the man-cub **Mowgli** who was raised by

Shopping

Disney commissioned more than 3,700 specially designed pieces of merchandise for sale in Disney's Animal Kingdom, including soapstone carvings from Kenya, Masai tribal face masks and painted gourds, and African jewelry.

The main shopping area is Mombassa Marketplace/Ziwani Traders, part of **Harambe Village** in Africa, the others are: The Outpost Shop, just outside the main entrance; Beastly Bazaar, Creature Comforts, Disney Outfitters and Island Mercantile in **Safari Village**; Chester and Hester's Dinosaur Treasures in **DinoLand USA**; and Out of the Wild at **Conservation Station**.

wolves in the jungle. You can see it in DinoLand USA.

March of the ARTimals is the zany twice-a-day parade which snakes its way around Disney's Animal Kingdom. Apart from a collection of fantasy animals, including 12 feet high preying mantises and giant spiders, there are street performers, jugglers, stilt walkers, acrobats and 'frog' musicians.

Getting hungry?

Rainforest Cafe — near the main entrance, is the park's only full-service restaurant and you can eat there without having to buy a ticket to enter the park. The restaurant's entrance is dominated by a huge waterfall and inside there are Audio-Animatronics® elephants, lions and monkeys to entertain diners. Classic American fare and great signature prime rib.

Flame Tree Barbecue — Safari Village, for burgers, chicken and ribs.

Pizzafari — Safari Village, for pizza and salads.

Restaurantosaurus — DinoLand USA, for burgers, salads and sandwiches.

Tusker House Restaurant — Africa, for burgers, salads, sandwiches and vegetarian dishes.

DISNEY-MGM STUDIOS

The Disney-MGM Studios Theme Park was opened in May, 1989 by Walt Disney's chairman Michael Eisner, with the words 'Welcome to the Hollywood that never was, and always will be'.

Today, you can experience the thrills of a working studio and all the attractions of a theme park. You get the opportunity to see behind the scenes, and can even take part in a live television show.

The park is set on a 110-acre (44-hectare) site and while there is a lot to see and do, the site is very compact and the best way to get around is on foot. There are always opportunities to sit down, either to watch a show, take a tour or get something to eat.

Getting there

By car exit I-4 at the sign marked Caribbean Beach resort, Walt Disney Village and the Disney-MGM Studios, or enter through the main Walt Disney World entrance off Highway 192 west. The parking lot can take 7,500 cars and there is a parking charge. Make sure you know which parking area you are in, and then catch one of the trams for the main gate. You can take a

Walt Disney World bus from The Magic Kingdom® Park or the resort hotels to the park.

Guests staying at the Dolphin, Swan, Beach Club or Yacht Club can take the launch to the park.

Arrival

As you enter through the main gate, you are in bustling, music filled Hollywood Boulevard. The palm-lined boulevard evokes the 1930s and 1940s and the shops on both sides, sell movieland memorabilia, autographed photos, old movie magazines and lots more. The information center is in the booth in the center of the boulevard straight ahead of you, and **Oscar's Super Service**, for strollers and wheelchairs is on your right, with the **Darkroom** camera center next door.

At **Cover Story** you can be photographed and appear on the front cover of your favorite magazine.

Hollywood Boulevard leads to the central plaza and this is the hub of the park with all the attractions spaced around it, although buildings, roads and turnings are planned in such a way that this is not always apparent. Almost half the park is off limits to visitors on

DISNEY – MGM STUDIOS

- The park is usually open between 9am and 7pm although it stays open later during the summer and on holidays and may close earlier in the winter.

- Visit **Crossroads of the World** in the entrance plaza for maps and the latest information about the day's special events and show times. The Guest Relations facility just inside the entrance can answer any questions you may have. It also deals with lost children and lost and found articles, and can provide maps in French, German and Spanish, as well as information for disabled visitors. Taped narrations are available for guests with sight-impairments, and written show descriptions are available for those with hearing difficulties.

- The **Production Information Window** near the entrance, can give you details about any productions being filmed that day, and whether they need audiences.

- The Studios Tip Board on the right at the corner of Hollywood Boulevard and the Central Plaza is constantly updated with the latest information about queues and waiting times at various attractions.

- Restaurant reservations must be made direct to the establishment you want to eat in.

foot, although most of this area can be visited on one of the excellent back-stage tours. The two tours are the **Disney-MGM Studios Backlot Tour** and **Backstage Pass**, and both are well worth doing. Both are described in detail later.

Entertainment

There are often strolling entertainers along Hollywood Boulevard, like the madcap group Citizens of Hollywood.

The Hollywood Hitmen play in Studio Courtyard off the boulevard, the Toon Town Trio croon in Mickey Avenue, while the Tubafours Quarter oom-pa in Hollywood Boulevard.

You can often meet celebrities and favorite Disney characters in the Soundstage Restaurant over breakfast, and the *Star Today* programme, which runs most of the year, brings stars of screen and television into the park each day, to take part in the parade, and if they are famous enough,

Essential Information

- There are baby changing and nursing facilities in the **Guest Services** building just inside the main entrance, and baby strollers are available for rent in limited quantities at **Oscar's Super Service** inside the entrance.

- There is an **automated bank teller** next to the Production Information Window at the main entrance, outside the turnstiles, and foreign currency can be exchanged at the **Guest Relations Window**.

- Cameras and videocamcorders can be rented from the **Darkroom** on Hollywood Boulevard. Film for 2 hour processing can be dropped in wherever you see the 'Photo Express' sign. Your prints can be collected from the Darkroom as you leave the park. The Darkroom will process film in 1 hour if you drop it in directly to them, and they even undertake minor camera repairs if you have a problem.

- While the park is very informal, shirts and shoes must be worn at all times. Lockers are available for rent next to Oscar's Classic Cars Souvenirs near the main entrance. Wheelchairs are available for rent at **Oscar's Super Service**, and to assist guests with disabilities, a special booklet is available from Guest Services.

get to leave their handprints on Hollywood Boulevard.

Two of the park's stage shows are *Beauty and the Beast* and *The Little Mermaid.*

Sorcery in the Sky Fireworks — Do not miss the spectacular firework display, a star late-night attraction held every night during the summer, but only on Fridays and Saturdays at other times. Check the entertainment schedules.

The award winning **Earffel Tower**, the huge elevated water tank with its Mickey Mouse ears, dominates the landscape, and is even more imposing when illuminated at night.

After lunch take in **Jim Henson's Muppet™ Vision 3D 4D, Star Tours** and **Monster Sound**, and then **Voyage of the Little Mermaid** and **The Magic of Disney**. Keep your eye on the time because you need to take in the last Indiana Jones show of the day and finish with a bang at **The Twilight Zone Tower™ of Terror.**

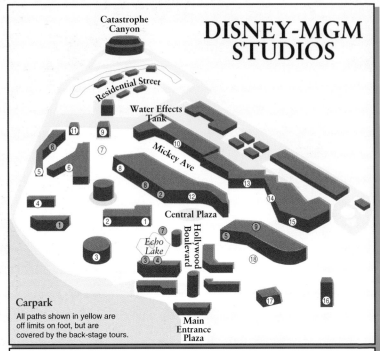

DISNEY-MGM STUDIOS

Catastrophe Canyon

Residential Street

Water Effects Tank

Mickey Ave

Central Plaza

Hollywood Boulevard

Echo Lake

Carpark

All paths shown in yellow are off limits on foot, but are covered by the back-stage tours.

Main Entrance Plaza

KEY TO MAIN ATTRACTIONS & PLACES TO EAT

1. SuperStar Television
2. ABC Sound Studio 1: Saturday Morning
3. Indiana Jones™ Stunt Spectacular
4. Star Tours
5. The Studio Showcase
6. Jim Henson's Muppet™ Vision 3D 4D
7. New York Street
8. Honey I Shrunk The Kids Movie Set Adventure
9. Goosebumps Fright Show
10. Backstage Pass
11. Disney's The Hunchback Of Notre Dame - A Musical Adventure
12. The Great Movie Ride
13. Voyage Of The Little Mermaid
14. Disney MGM-Studios Backlot Tour
15. The Magic Of Disney Animation
16. The Twilight Zone™ Tower Of Terror
17. "Beauty & The Beast" Live on Stage
18. Sunset Boulevard

Places to Eat

1. Backlot Express
2. ABC Commissary
3. 50's Prime Time Cafe
4. Hollywood & Vine
5. The Hollywood Brown Derby
6. Mama Melrose's Ristorante Italiano
7. Min & Bill's Dockside Diner
8. Sci-Fi Dine-In Theater Restaurant
9. Soundstage Restaurant

Opposite: *Twilight Zone™ Tower of Terror, Disney-MGM Studios*
(© Disney Enterprises, Inc)

Planning your visit

You need to spend at least a day exploring the theme park. Most people head straight for the **Indiana Jones Stunt Spectacular** and the **Twilight Zone™ Tower of Terror**, so get ahead of the crowds and go straight to the **Great Movie Ride** and then take in the two tours starting with the 30 minute **Backlot Tour** which runs continuously from 10am. You should then be back in good time to take in the **Backstage Pass** which will take you to lunchtime.

Park Attractions

You will come across the following attractions if you tour in a clockwise direction around the park.

ABC Sound Studio 1 Saturday Morning

This provides a lot of laughs as members of the audience are selected to create the sound effects for ABC's new Saturday Morning Show. You get a good idea of what to expect from the hilarious pre-show video. The film is screened first, and then played again without sound so that the selected sound effects crew can add thunder, creaking

doors and so on. The third running of the film shows the results, usually hysterical as the sound effects rarely match the action.

The show reveals how all sorts of special sound effects are created, and afterwards in the Soundworks you get the chance to try your hand using a range of weird machines. Play around with the voices of the stars at **Movie Mimics** and experience the virtual reality of 3D sound at **Soundsations**.

Indiana Jones™ Stunt Spectacular

As memorable for the ingenuity of this attraction, as for the stunts and excitement. Members of the audience are invited to take part as extras in the filming of various scenes in the huge 2,000 seat amphitheater which combines film set and theater. The director and stunt co-ordinator explain what goes on in front of and behind the cameras and then the action hots up as you see how various scenes were filmed. The desert finale, featuring an out of control aircraft, explosions, machine guns and lots of stunts is tremendous.

How one set can be transformed into another in just a few seconds is equally impressive.

Star Tours

Inspired by the *Star Wars* film this ride offers a trip aboard a

Starspeeder, for what is supposed to be a peaceful trip to the Moon of Endor. Everything goes wrong of course, and you find yourself hurtling through space. The space simulators, the same as those used for training jet fighter pilots, are synchronised with the film to maximise the assault on your senses. It is all good fun, but very young children, pregnant women and people with heart, back and neck problems are advised to give it a miss.

The American Film Institute Showcase

Actual costumes, props and set pieces used by the stars in recent movies.

Jim Henson's Muppet™ Vision 3D 4D

A charming 20 minute sight and sound spectacular featuring the Muppets and the troublesome Waldo — the Spirit of 3D. The show combines actual appearances by various Muppet characters, stunning on screen 3D effects, and a lot of other special effects which add to the enjoyment.

Beauty and the Beast Live on Stage

The characters of this popular Disney film appear in a live 25 minute musical show several times a day.

New York Street

Not an attraction but an example of how sets can be made to create almost any effect. If you stand at the end of the street and look up at the Empire State building and other skyscrapers, it is difficult to believe that it is all an illusion. The buildings are only façades, and the clever use of paint and perspective makes them look many times taller than they actually are. Great place for getting your photo taken.

Honey I Shrunk the Kids Movie Set Adventure

A playground for children where everything is enormous. The blades of grass are more than 20ft (6m) tall, you can slide down a piece of discarded film and try and dodge the water jets which squirt at random from a giant hosepipe.

Goosebumps™ Fright Show

New attraction to give you nightmares!

Visitors beware, you're in for a scare! The Goosebumps Fright Show will send you through real nightmares, straight from the pages of R L Stine's best-selling book series and hit TV show. You'll meet the grimmest of ghouls, including Slappy the ventriloquist's dummy, Curly the skeleton, Prince Khor-Ru the mummy, and many more of your spooky favorites.

Disney-MGM Studios Backlot Tour

A fascinating insight into the world of special effects. A funny pre-show video featuring Goldie Hawn and Rick Moranis keeps you entertained while you wait, but the lines move along quite quickly.

The tour begins at the outdoor water tank where two visitors are co-opted to act out scenes to show how realistic effects are created by combining models and close ups. In this case the close ups are of one visitor in the wheelhouse of a trawler, and the other as the skipper of a submarine in the conning tower. Models of the trawler, the submarine and the use of underwater explosions and other special effects create very realistic battle scenes which are then edited in with close up shots of the volunteers, who naturally get a soaking.

After a pre-show film about the history of the Walt Disney Studios, hop on a tram for a tour of the backlot buildings and the excitement of **Catastrophe Canyon**. People sitting on the left hand side of the trams may get wet so be warned!

The tram ride allows you to see inside many of the backlot buildings, some piled high with studio lighting, others crammed with costumes and working seamstresses, and all part of the real world of film and television. You drive around the motor pool where cars, boats and even a space ship are parked until they are next needed as a prop.

There is a storage area for a small forest of trees and shrubs in pots which are often used on sets to hide unsightly areas, and appreciate the skill of the topiarists who snipped the hedges into their various shapes.

You drive down Residential Street which features homes of various styles, which have been used in different productions, although they are only façades, and then enter the **Catastrophe Canyon**. Although the experience lasts only a few minutes, you have a first hand taste of just how special effects are created as you undergo first an earthquake, then a blazing inferno as an oil tanker explodes, and finally a flash flood. This is all very realistic, especially the blast of heat from the explosion. In a couple of minutes, however, everything is peaceful again, and you drive round the back of the canyon to see how it was all done.

It takes only 3.5 minutes to collect the 70,000 gallons of water used to produce the flood, just about enough time before the next tram load arrives. The tour finally takes in the impressive skyline of New York, another example of how scenery and forced perspective can be used to create amazing illusions of size and space.

Disney's: The Hunchback of Notre Dame — A Musical Adventure

A heart warming stage hit based on Disney's animated film which tells the story of bell ringer Quasimodo and the beautiful gypsy Essmeralda. A cast of Medieval puppets and 21 actors perform daily to the powerful soundtrack.

Disney's MGM Studios Backstage Pass

A Backstage Pass allows visitors to see real television production behind the scenes.

The Great Movie Ride

Housed in the Chinese Theater, this is a must. There are always lines but the pre-show as you shuffle forward is almost as entertaining as the ride itself. It takes about 25 minutes once you are through the doors of the theater to snake your way round the foyer to the ride. During this time you are entertained by film clips from many of the all time greats.

The ride itself, aboard open trams, transports you through the history of cinema with many of the screen's most famous names as your hosts. Each elaborate set, complete with Audio-Animatronics® figures, depicts a film genre — musicals, westerns, gangsters, through to science fiction, and, of course, cartoon animation. The finale of the show,

presented simultaneously on three screens, presents many of the cinema's most famous moments from Academy Award® winning films. The ride itself lasts for just over 20 minutes.

Voyage of the Little Mermaid

A 15 minute stage show which condenses the film into a series of charming musical highlights with the aid of animation, live performers, puppets, lasers and special effects.

The Magic of Disney Animation

Spend a very interesting 30 minutes or so discovering how cartoon characters come to life. After an 8 minute amusing film *Back to Never Land*, featuring Walter Cronkite and Robin Williams who introduce you to the world of animation, you then follow a route overlooking studios where Disney animators are working.

Overhead monitors explain each of the different processes as you proceed. If you think that you need about twenty-four separate drawings to produce just one second of animation, you can see what an enormous production task is involved in making a full length animated film. The tour ends in the Disney Classics Theater with a film showing how animation has improved over the years and finishing with clips from some of the all time great cartoons.

The Twilight Zone™ Tower of Terror

The park's latest attraction set in a vintage hotel where you are not advised to take the elevator! Explore haunted hallways before experiencing a thirteen storey free-fall plunge aboard the hotel's battered elevator. The hotel stands at the end of Sunset Boulevard.

Sunset Boulevard

Offers a range of shops, a ranch market restaurant, and the Tower of Terror.

Mulan: The Parade

Every day Shang, Cri-kee, the Matchmaker and Mushu join together in a triumphant Chinese celebration honoring Mulan, the brave and beautiful heroine of Disney's newest animated feature.

Getting hungry?

Backlot Express — for charboiled chicken and burgers, grilled hot dogs and salads. Counter service.

ABC Commissary — special sandwiches, burgers, salads and stir-fry. Counter service.

50's Prime Time Cafe and Tune-In Lounge — serves steaks, sandwiches, burgers and desserts. Table service. Reservations recommended.

Hollywood and Vine — serves rotisserie chicken, smoked baby back ribs, seafood, pasta, salads and is open from breakfast throughout the day. Buffet service.

The Hollywood Brown Derby — for fine dining in the grand Hollywood tradition. Steak, seafood, salads and memorable desserts. Table service. Reservations recommended.

Mama Melrose's Ristorante Italiano — offers gourmet brick oven pizza, pasta, chicken, steak and seafood. Table service. Reservations taken at the door.

Min and Bill's Dockside Diner — for sandwiches, snacks, fruit and soft-serve yoghurt.

Sci-Fi Dine-In Theater Restaurant — serves seafood, burgers, stacked sandwiches, pasta and salads as you watch vintage clips from sci-fi movies. Reservations recommended.

Soundstage Restaurant — for pasta and pizza, sandwiches, soup and salads. Counter service.

OTHER DISNEY ATTRACTIONS & RESORT HOTELS

Disney's Blizzard Beach Water Park

Blizzard Beach is the nation's first 'ski resort and water adventure park'. According to legend, it was created by a freak winter storm that dropped snow over the western side of the Walt Disney World Resort. Afterwards, as temperatures soared, water began to cascade down Mt. Gushmore and the park was born.

You can bobsled down the slopes of **Mt. Gushmore** or plunge at 60 mph straight down the **Summit Plummet**, the world's tallest, fastest free-fall speed slide.

Other rides include: **Teamboat Springs** — the world's longest family whitewater raft ride; each raft takes three to five passengers down a twisting, 1,200-foot series of rushing waterfalls — and **Toboggan Racer**, an eight-lane water slide.

Try the **Downhill Double Dipper**, the world's only side-by-side racing slides, and **Snow Stormers**, which has three switchback flumes descending from the top of the mountain.

Runoff Rapids is an innertube run with two open slides and one enclosed "blackhole."

You can take a chair lift to the summit of Mt. Gushmore while below, children can play in **Tike's Peak**, a mini-version of the mountain with snow-castle fountain play area.

For those who want more leisurely pursuits, there is **Melt-Away-Bay**, a one-acre bobbing Blizzard Beach **Ski Patrol Training Camp**, or you can just relax on the sandy beach and enjoy the sun.

At the east end of the beach is **The Village** with lockers, towel rental, first aid and souvenir shop. Eateries include the Lottawatta Lodge which serves burgers, hot dogs, pizza, deli sandwiches, salads, ice cream, and drinks; and the Avalunch and Warming Hut Snack bars.

Disney's Wide World of Sports

This showpiece sports complex is one of the most modern in the world and offers the chance to watch or participate in a wide range of sporting activities from baseball to Indi car racing.

Annual events include **Atlanta Braves** spring training, the PGA's **Disney Golf Classic**, the Indy Racing League's **Indy 200**, Nascar's **Chevy Truck Challenge**, Harlem Globetrotters **Basketball**, and the **Walt Disney World Marathon.** The complex is also home to the Amateur Athletic Union (AAU) and many of its annual championships.

The complex caters for 30 different sports and the 30,000-square-foot 5,000 seat **Fieldhouse** hosts basketball, gymnastics, wrestling, weight lifting and badminton. There is a vast track and field complex, **The Beach** for volleyball, a tennis complex, baseball, softball and sports fields for football and soccer. This is now the official warm weather training camp of the British Olympic Association. Several of their best known athletes can be seen training here.

Disney's All-Star Music Resort

This 1,900-room resort is dedicated to music of every kind. Even the décor has Broadway, Country, Jazz, Rock and Calypso themes from the three-storey high pair of cowboy boots to the guitar-shaped swimming pool and walk-through neon-lit jukebox. The resort offers a wide range of eating options from breakfast by the pool to the Intermission Food Court. Here meals are served all day and restaurants offer fine American dining.

There is even Pizza Delivery, with delivery to your room by pressing the special pizza button on the phone.

Disney's All-Star Sports Resort

For sports fans this 1,900-room resort has everything. The resort is based around five themed areas — football, baseball, basketball, tennis and surfing. There is access to five championship Disney golf courses, outdoor heated pools, arcade and playground.

The End Zone Food Court offers a choice of five cafes and restaurants offering American-style meals and snacks throughout the day. Specialties include pizza, pasta, hamburgers, sandwiches, salads, BBQ ribs, rotisserie chicken, freshly baked goods and family dinner platters. Continental breakfast is also available by the pool where sandwiches and snacks are served during the day.

The resort is next to Blizzard Beach.

Disney's All-Star Movies Resort

This new resort is built around five theme areas — 101 Dalmatians, Fantasia, The Love Bug, Toy Story and Mighty Ducks. With more than 1,900 rooms, the mid-range priced resort offers restaurant/bar; baby-sitting and child services, disabled-accessible rooms/facili-ties; laundry/valet services; non-smoking rooms/facilities, heated pool, recreation facilities and shops.

Downtown Disney Area

Downtown Disney is the com-plex's newest entertain-ment area and consists of three areas: **West Side** with dining, shops, 24-screen cinema and the Virgin record superstore; **Pleasure Island** with seven nightclubs and discos; and the **Marketplace** which is packed with exciting shops and restaurants.

Disney's BoardWalk

You can also stroll along **Disney's BoardWalk**, a seaside celebration with shopping, dining, dancing, a state-of-the-art sports bar, and live entertainment.

Downtown Disney West Side is like the bustling main street of a city offering food and fun for all ages. It is the latest addition to the Downtown Disney area of Disney Village and is popular throughout the day and evening.

Exciting eateries include the celebrity-studded **Planet Hollywood**, the incredible California cuisine at **Wolfgang Puck Cafe**, the spicy Latin music and tastes of Miami's

South Beach at **Bongos Cuban Cafe**, and live music and Cajun cuisine at the **House of Blues**. The **Wildhorse Saloon** is a country music restaurant fea-turing the best in contemporary country seven days a week with the resident Wildhorse Dancers show and a 1500-square-foot dance floor. Then enjoy a country music meal of barbecued ribs and chicken, steaks, chops, entree salads, and home-baked desserts.

Music lovers must visit the **Virgin Megastore** with its own outdoor stage for live concerts. There is also the **AMC Theatres Complex** with 24 screens, the largest theater complex in the Southeast, with more than 6,000 seats.

One of the latest attractions is **DisneyQuest**, the first-ever indoor interactive theme park.

You can shoot the rapids on a river raft in a virtual prehistoric world, experience a motion simulator and ride a roller coaster of your own design or fly a magic carpet through the bazaars of an ancient city.

Stores include Celebrity Eyeworks Studio, Copperfield Magic Underground, The Store, Guitar Gallery by George's Music, Hoypoloi selling art and sculptures, Magnetron with collector-quality magnets, Authentic All Star Sporting Goods, Sosa Family Cigars and nostalgia-laden Starabillias.

Downtown Disney Marketplace offers a wide range of shops and restaurants in a relaxing waterfront setting, complete with a marina. You can buy the latest fashions, unique Disney gifts and collectibles and dine at any of the several fine restaurants. The Marketplace also hosts a number of annual events such as the spectacular **Festival of the Masters** art show and seasonal holiday events.

Stores include the **World of Disney**, the newest and biggest Disney store on earth with 12 massive rooms each based on a different Disney classic. Have fun in the LEGO Imagination Center and Superstore. Check out the 30 foot tall LEGO sea serpent and then see what you can build. The **Art of Disney** is a gallery of Disney animation art and collectibles, **Team Mickey's Athletic Club** sells a range of sports clothing and equipment, and **Disney's Days of Christmas** offer year-round holiday enchantment.

Other shops include: Discover selling imaginative gifts, Eurospain with glass sculpting and engraving, the Gourmet Pantry, Harrington Bay Clothiers, Resortwear Unlimited, Summer Sands, Toys Fantastic,

2R's Reading & Riting and Studio M.

Check the event directory boards for special performances and events taking place at the waterfront **Dock Stage**.

Other attractions include boating and fishing on the 35-acre (14-hectare) **Lake Buena Vista**. Both activities are available through **Cap'n Jack's**.

Sand Street Station is a sand playground, train ride, and children's fun area, and see how many Disney characters you can spot in the cleverly sculpted topiaries.

Getting hungry?

For eating out, try —
The Rainforest Cafe which also sells rain-forest items from around the world;
Wolfgang Puck Express,
Ghirardelli Soda Fountain & Chocolate Shop,
McDonald's,
Fulton's Crab House,
Portobello Yacht Club,
Cap'n Jack's Oyster Bar
and **The Gourmet Pantry**.

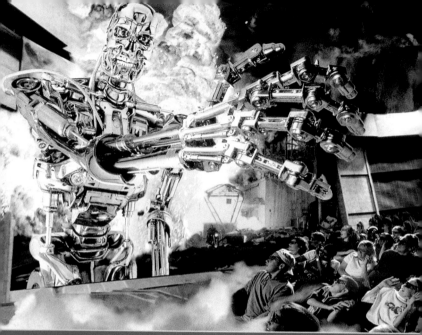

3 SEA WORLD, UNIVERSAL STUDIOS AND SPLENDID CHINA

SEA WORLD OF FLORIDA

Sea World of Florida is the world's most popular marine life park and shows perfectly how entertainment, education, research and conservation can go hand in hand. Getting close to nature is an important part of this education process, and being able to stroke a stingray or pat a manatee does leave a lasting and very favourable impression.

The park, which opened on 23 December 1973 and was taken over by Anheuser-Busch in 1989, features more than twenty major shows, attractions and educational and entertaining exhibits which have brought pleasure to tens of millions of visitors, but above all, they have increased enormously people's appreciation and understanding of marine life and their environments, and the need to protect and preserve them.

Above: *The new and exciting Terminator 2: 3-D experience at Universal Studios* (© Universal Studios Florida)

Sea World of Florida is an Anheuser-Busch Theme Park. Among the company's many other parks are Busch Gardens and Adventure Island in Tampa. You can buy combination admission tickets to Sea World and Busch Gardens at a discounted price.

A team is based at Sea World for the rescue and treatment of injured animal life, such as manatees injured by propellors from any of the million speed-boats in Florida.

Planning your day

When you park, make sure you know which parking zone you are in. Each zone is named after a Sea World celebrity. When

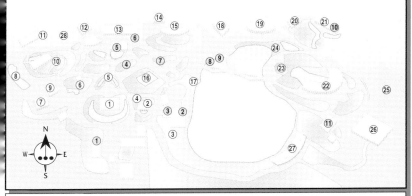

⇡KEY SEA WORLD® OF FLORIDA

① Tropical World & Flamingo Exhibit
② Dolphin Nursery
③ Pelican Exhibit
④ Tropical Rain Forest
⑤ Tide Pool
⑥ Turtle Point
⑦ Stingray Lagoon
⑧ Dolphin Cove
⑨ Key West at Sea World
⑩ Whale and Dolphin Stadium
⑪ Manatees: The Last Generation?
⑫ Special Events Pavilion
⑬ Penguin Encounter℠
⑭ Pacific Point Preserve℠
⑮ Sea Lion & Otter Stadium
⑯ Sea World® Theater
⑰ Sky Tower
⑱ Terrors of the Deep®
⑲ Nautilus Theater

⑳ Clydesdale Hamlet
㉑ Anheuser-Busch Hospitality Center
㉒ Shamu Stadium℠
㉓ Shamu Close Up!
㉔ Flamingo Lagoon
㉕ Shamu's Happy Harbor℠
㉖ Wild Arctic
㉗ Atlantis Water Ski Stadium
㉘ Journey To Atlantis Ride

Refreshments
① Treasure Isle Ice Cream
② Polynesian Luau
③ Bimini Bay Cafe
④ Buccaneer Smokehouse
⑤ Mama Stella's Italian Kitchen
⑥ Florida Citrus Grower's Plaza
⑦ Chicken 'n Biscuit
⑧ Waterfront Sandwich Grill
⑨ Smokehouse
⑩ The Deli
⑪ Mango Joe's Cafe

SEA WORLD
Essential Information

Sea World is located at the intersection of I-4 and the Bee Line Expressway, 10 minutes south of Downtown Orlando and 15 minutes from Orlando International Airport. It is very well sign-posted so there are no problems finding it.

Christmas, Easter and the week including 4 July are the busiest times of the year, and Fridays, Saturdays and Sundays tend to be the busiest days. Plan to spend at least 8 hours if you want to see all the shows and attractions. Normally a one day ticket is enough, but if you really want to spend longer at the park, buy a 2 day pass, which allows entry on the day of purchase and on any day within 7 days of this.

There is a car park fee and everyone aged 10 and over is classified as an adult for entry. Children under the age of 3 are admitted free.

The park is open year-round from 9am-7pm, although it stays open longer during the summer and on holidays, usually to 10pm. During the later opening summer months, it is worth delaying your visit until after lunch so that you can still pack in an 8 hour visit but during the cooler part of the day.

The park provides dolphin-shaped strollers, wheelchairs and lockers for rental. There is wheelchair seating at all the facilities and shows, and there are baby changing and nursing facilities throughout the park. Foreign currency can be exchanged at the Special Services window at the Main Gate, and there is an automated teller machine near the exit.

Cameras (35mm) can be loaned but most people opt for the disposable Kodak Funsaver cameras which are on sale. Film is also on sale. If you make purchases, you do not have to carry them around all day. Arrange to collect them as you leave from Parcel pick-up in **Shamu's Emporium** just before the exit. You must have your receipt and allow at least an hour between purchase and pick-up.

If your group becomes separated, go to the Information Center by the Main Gate. Staff are trained to look out for lost children and take them to the Information Center. If you lose your bearing in the park, just ask any member of staff who will be happy to assist.

you get your admission ticket, you also receive a location map showing where all the attractions and shows are, and times of performances. The maps are computer-generated and customised, telling you what time the park is open and any special events that might be taking place. It can even recommend the best order to see the shows. All the show times are also displayed just inside the entrance.

As soon as you arrive work out which shows you want to see and in what order. The shows are timed so that you can usually move leisurely from one to another, although during busy periods when the park is crowded, it is advisable to get an early seat as the stadiums fill up quickly. Remember, if you sit near the front at many of the shows you are likely to get wet.

The park is built around a large lake which is on your right as you enter. There are six shows during the day which have set times and you should reckon to see all of these, slotting in all the other attractions in between as appropriate.

As the middle of the day can be quite busy because of the way the show schedules are arranged, it is a good idea to snack your way around the park because there may not be time for lunch, and it is essential to take regular drinks as the sun can quickly dehydrate you.

Star Value

There are two excellent tours available. They leave every 30 minutes or so from the guided tour center next to the guest relations center near the main entrance. Sign up for one or both of the tours when you arrive, both are great value and cost only a few dollars each. There is a 90 minute guided tour which takes you behind the scenes of Sea World, and a 45 minute tour which concentrates on animal behaviour and training.

Shows and Stadiums

Hawaiian Rhythms is a swinging South Seas revue at the beach stage. The show lasts 25 minutes.

Sea Lion and Otter Stadium features Clyde and Seamore, the Park's sea lion comedy duo as well as otters and walruses in *Hotel Clyde And Seamore*. The show lasts 25 minutes. There is a 20 minute pre-show warm-up by mime artists.

Sea World Theatre highlights education and conservation projects with its presentation *Window To the Sea*. It also provides an interesting behind the scenes look at Sea World, going backstage to Shamu

93

Making the most of your day

Plan 1

1. If you are arriving early, head for the Whale and Dolphin Stadium for the first show of the day taking in the Harbor Seal Community and Stingray Lagoon on the way. You can always spend more time here later in the day as well.

2. Experience Journey to Atlantis and then visit Manatees: The Last Generation?, Penguin Encounter and Pacific Point Preserve, then cut back to the Sea World Theatre to catch the 20 minute show.

3. You should then have time to grab a drink and make your way to the Park's sea lions for the lunch time show.

4. Straight in to Terrors of the Deep and then the Shamu Stadium for the afternoon show.

5. Then head for the Bayside Water Ski Stadium to catch the afternoon show here.

6. Take in Wild Arctic and then retrace your steps to visit all those things you have not yet had time for on the right of the lake — Shamu's Happy Harbor, the Killer Whale Facility, the Clydesdale Hamlet and Anheuser-Busch Hospitality Center.

7. Finally, make your way leisurely back to the exit taking in on the way those attractions not visited on the left hand side of the lake — Tropical Reef, Dolphin Nursery, the Spoonbill and Pelican Exhibits and the Sand Sculpture.

There are sand sculptures, and artists creating them, opposite the Pelican Exhibit and between Wild Arctic and Shamu's Happy Harbor. The sculptures produced as you watch are quite fantastic.

The other attraction which you should take in if you have a head for heights and the weather permits, is the Sky Tower, approximately 400ft (122m) high, with its revolving platform. The tower dominates the skyline and makes a useful landmark if you want to find your bearings in the park, and the views from the top over the park and surrounding countryside are stunning. There is a small additional fee for this ride.

Plan 2

1. As everyone else might be following Plan I, start your day by visiting the Sea World Theatre, and then take in the Penguin Encounter and Terrors of the Deep.

2. You should have plenty of time then to get a good seat in the Shamu Stadium for the first show of the day.

3. Follow the crowds to the Bayside Water Ski Stadium for the midday show and then take in Wild Arctic.

4. You then work your way back round the back in an anti-clockwise direction, taking in Shamu's Happy Harbor, The Shamu Adventure, the Anheuser-Busch Hospitality Center and Clydesdale Hamlet.

5. Visit Pacific Point Preserve, Manatees: The Last Generation, Stingray Lagoon, Dolphin Nursery and Tropical Reef.

6. You can then head for the Whale and Dolphin Stadium to take in the late afternoon show and finally, catch the last performance at the Sea Lion and Otter Stadium and take The Journey to Atlantis.

It is worth pointing out that when the park is open in the evening the Shamu Stadium also stages Shamu Night Magic, a 20 minute long magic show performed under the stars.

The Sea World Theatre switches performances late in the afternoon to stage Water Fantasy, a 20 minute music, water and lights spectacular, and a very relaxing way of ending your day at Sea World.

Killer whales rise to the occasion (Sea World® of Florida)

Stadium, travelling on an ocean expedition, and boarding a deep sea research sub to study sharks. The presentation lasts 20 minutes.

The Shamu Adventure, in the Shamu Stadium, features Shamu and the world-famous killer whale family. The living documentary explores the unique relationship which exists between man and animal. The show lasts 25 minutes.

Whale and Dolphin Stadium features the *Whale and Dolphin Discovery* show which demonstrates the unique personalities of these animals which come from different oceans of the world. The show lasts 20 minutes.

Park Attractions

The attractions are dealt with as they are met in a clockwise tour of the park.

Tropical Reef and Flamingo Exhibit

After passing through the main gates, the broad avenue ahead takes you to the flamingo lagoon, behind which is the entrance to the **Tropical Reef**. The subdued lighting inside the air-conditioned exhibit allows you to better appreciate the glorious and colorful habitat that has been created. The center piece is a massive circular 160,000 gallon tank with observation windows, containing more than a thousand beautifully-colored tropical fish swimming around a man-made coral reef.

Key West at Sea World (includes Dolphin Cove)

A wonderful opportunity to get really close to these intelligent creatures. The open tanks allow the dolphins to splash and swim about and you can stroke them as they streak past hugging the side of the tanks. You can also buy fish to feed them as well. There are washing facilities at all the petting and feeding exhibits, plus some underwater viewing.

Tropical Rain Forest

A small but interesting exhibit showing the lush vegetation of a tropical rain forest, and providing an environment even hotter than the normal Florida weather.

Tide Pool

A fascinating hands-on exhibit which recreates a Caribbean tide pool and encourages closer examination of tropical fish and invertebrates such as sea urchins, starfish and anemones. There are normally Sea World experts on hand to answer questions and the exhibit is built so that even young children can put their hands in the warm water to interact with the fish and plant life.

Sea Turtle Exhibit

Another opportunity to feed the animals, although it is definitely not a good idea to try to pet them. It is fascinating just how noisy these animals can be when they know food is around, and how some of them show-off to attract your attention, if you happen to have a smelt in your hand.

Stingray Lagoon

One of the great thrills at Sea World, and the clearest demonstration of how attitudes can be changed. You have only to spend a few minutes watching these beautiful creatures swimming gracefully around their shallow tank, to appreciate how ill-deserved their reputation is. If you manage to stroke one of these creatures as it swims past, you can appreciate how gentle they can be.

Journey to Atlantis

Sea World's newest and most spectacular attraction is a water-coaster thrill ride unlike any other. As you search for the legendary lost city, you experience all the thrills of a roller coaster cum water ride plus the very latest in illusionary effects. Highlights of the ride are two of the steepest — almost freefall — wettest, fastest drops in the world.

Whale and Dolphin Stadium

The huge stadium is necessary because this is one of the most popular shows in the park. The show features six very acrobatic Atlantic bottlenose dolphins and two false killer whales. The spectacular out of the water leaps and pirouettes of the dolphins and whales are one of the strongest memories you will take home. Close-up shots of the whales and dolphins are broadcast on a giant screen in the stadium. One lucky child from the audience is selected every show to meet the dolphins and become an honorary trainer, while their family gets guest of honour seats in the pavilion to the right of the stage. If you want to 'volunteer' your child, get there early and speak to one of the stadium staff.

The show itself demonstrates the versatility and intelligence of these creatures and their spectacular acrobatic abilities, as well as the obvious bonds between trainers and animals.

If you do not want to get wet, keep out of the first four rows.

Manatees: The Last Generation

A new exhibit which affords a fascinating window of discovery to the mystery of these gentle creatures. The Florida manatee is threatened with extinction because of habitat destruction and encounters with power boats. Sea World believes the critical link to saving the manatee is public awareness and education, and this exhibition was specifically developed to help visitors appreciate the plight of these and other endangered species.

You enter the exhibit by walking through a lush, lagoon-like setting typical of its preferred habitat, which leads into a circular theater where a film gives an insight into the manatee's view of the world, and finally you get to meet the manatees themselves. There is a 126ft (38m) long underwater window into the 300,000 gallon tank, through which you can watch the creatures, which can weigh more than 2,000lb. The exhibit also includes a number of other animals and birds that would be typically found in the same habitat, including alligators.

In 1976 Sea World organised its Manatee Rescue and Rehabilitation Program in co-operation with the Department of the Interior, the National Marine Fisheries Service and

Observe at close quarters the manatees at Sea World
(Sea World® of Florida)

the Florida Department of Natural Resources. Since then the park, which is on 24-hour call year round, has responded to more than 1,000 calls, aiding ill, injured or orphaned manatees, whales, dolphins, otters, sea turtles and waterfowl. Some of the equipment used by the manatee rescue teams is displayed outside the exhibit.

Penguin Encounter

A delightful experience to leave the Florida sun outside and enter the ice-bound Antarctic. You step on to a moving walkway which transports you the length of the massive exhibit housed behind a thick glass wall. Inside, the many species of penguins slither around on the ice or show off their swimming prowess under water. There are even snow making machines built into the roof to add further touches of reality.

Feeding time is at 1pm and the exhibit naturally gets very busy at this time, but it is interesting with staff on hand to answer any questions you may have. The exhibit also features birds, such as puffins, razorbills and the like, which inhabit the Antarctic with the penguins.

Sea World Theatre

Window to the Sea highlights education and conservation projects being undertaken at Sea World and also gives a fascinating insight into the behind-the-scenes activities, including how the animals are trained. The presentation stresses that none of the animals are taught tricks, they are simply encouraged to do what they do naturally when in the wild.

Around 5pm, the presentation is replaced by *Water Fantasy*, a wonderful way to relax by just sitting back and watching the show. The show combines water jets, music and lights in a synchronised water ballet.

Sea Lion and Otter Stadium

A mime artist entertains before the show mimicking members of the audience, but it is good innocent fun and worth getting there early to see it. The show itself, *Hotel Clyde and Seamore*, is an action-packed comedy in which all the actors and animals, and some of the audience in the front rows, get wet. The show features Clyde and Seamore, the Park's sea lions, as well as a sea otter and walrus. It even features a conservation message. The plot centers on the 'hotel' bid to win an environmental housekeeping award, and a rival's attempt to thwart this. Although the shows change at regular intervals, the stars do not.

Pacific Point Reserve

A new 2.5-acre (1-hectare) exhibit, which used hundreds

of tons of crafted rock, moulded crag and mountains of cement and stone to recreate a rugged Pacific coastline. It is now the naturalistic home for species of pinnipeds, 'flippered' mammals, harbour and fur seals and the much larger Californian sea lions, who can dive from the cliffs into the water, or sunbathe on the rocky ledges. The habitat is filled with 450,000 gallons of chilled saltwater and has a wave maker capable of creating waves up to 2ft (half-m) high. Visitors are able to interact with these creatures above the water by leaning over the parapets of the round tank, and can watch their grace and agility through the underwater windows. Guests can purchase fish to feed the seals and sea lions.

Clydesdale Hamlet

Walk through the stables to see these magnificent beasts in their stalls. The horses, always immaculately groomed,

provide good photo opportunities.

Anheuser-Busch Hospitality Center

Just across the way from the Clydesdale Hamlet is the Hospitality Center, a feature of all Anheuser-Busch parks. Those aged 21 and over can sample the brewery's beers during the day, and you can snack on sandwiches and salads.

Shamu: Close Up!

Opened in the spring of 1994, this massive facility is another Sea World first. The one million gallon killer whale breeding and research facility offers a close-up underwater view of their breeding and nursery area.

Shamu Stadium

Sea World's most famous show now features Shamu, the park's most famous character, and Baby Shamu, who perform side by side in *The*

Terrors of the Deep

The world's 'largest and most terrifying collection of dangerous sea creatures ever assembled', including eels, barracuda, venomous and poisonous fish, and, of course, sharks. A moving walkway takes you through a thick glass tunnel with the sharks and fish swimming about over your head. You can observe the fish from other observation decks and there are a number of monitors running videos which give further information about the various species on display.

Shamu Adventure. Every graceful movement of these magnificent creatures is picked up by four live underwater cameras and displayed in a gigantic state-of-the-art video screen to bring visitors closer than ever before to these beautiful animals. The sight of these huge beasts hurtling up out of the water will stay with you forever.

There is a remarkable relationship between the whales and their trainers, and trainers can spend up to 18 hours a day developing the bonds with these magnificent killer whales, which can weigh up to 5,000lbs. The trainers not only have to be superbly fit and excellent swimmers, they must also be able to hold their breath for 2 minutes while swimming at a depth of 40ft (12m). You are likely to get very wet sitting in any of the first ten rows. At night, the show is replaced by *Shamu Night Magic*.

Shamu's Happy Harbor

A place for the children to let off steam in this 3-acre (1-hectare) well supervised playground, where they can crawl, slide, bounce and scramble to their heart's content.

Wild Arctic

The park's most ambitious project to date, combining thrilling flights over the frozen North, and real life encounters with the animals that live there. The adventure begins aboard a jet helicopter racing to take off in order to outrun an approaching storm. The 'stormy' trip ends at the research station — **Base Station Wild Arctic** — which leads to a frozen wonderland with seals, polar bears, walruses and Beluga whales, which can be viewed both above and below water.

Bayside Water Ski Stadium

Bayside Water Ski Stadium features the *Baywatch at Sea World Ski Show*, a stunning water ski display of acrobats, stunts and comedy. The show lasts 35 minutes

The *Gold Rush Ski Show* is the theme for Sea World's famous troupe of water skiers. The show features world-class water skiers who 'bring early American history to life' while performing daring tricks and high jinks on the water. It is great entertainment.

If you want to eat and watch the show at the same time, try and get a lakeside table at Mango Joe's Cafe. You can enjoy grilled fajitas, special sandwiches and salads, and have a ringside seat for the spectacular show.

At the end of the day, the Stadium is the venue for '*Mermaids, Myths and Monsters*', a water, lights, music, laser and firework spectacular.

Getting hungry?

Check at the food services information center near the main entrance as menus change seasonally and restaurant opening times can vary.

Treasure Isle Ice Cream — for refreshing ice desserts.

Polynesian Luau — you can try native delicacies and enjoy a complimentary drink as you enjoy the show featuring Polynesian dancers, musicians and entertainers. Seating is limited so early reservations are recommended.

Bimini Bay Cafe — next to the Dolphin Community Pool, offers full service dining and great views across the lake.

Buccaneer Smokehouse — serves barbecued, mesquite-style chicken, ribs and beef with all the trimmings.

Mama Stella's Italian Kitchen — handy for the Penguin Encounter and Whale and Dolphin Stadium. Serves homemade food such as spaghetti, pizza, garlic bread and garden salads.

Florida Citrus Growers' Plaza — across from Penguin Encounter, for freshly squeezed orange and grapefruit juice.

Chicken 'n Biscuit — near the Sky Tower, features Southern-fried chicken and fries, dinner salads and desserts.

Waterfront Sandwich Grill — near Sea Lion and Otter Stadium, for bulging ham and turkey sandwiches, burgers, salads and fresh baked goods.

Smokehouse — near Sea Lion and Otter Stadium, serves mesquite-grilled barbecued ribs, chicken and trimmings.

The Deli — serves carved turkey, beef and German sausages, fresh baked breads and homemade desserts.

Mango Joe's Cafe — for grilled fajitas, sandwiches and salads, and excellent views over the lake, especially if the water ski show is on.

Above left: *Sea World offers great entertainment with revues as well as the exhibits* (Sea World® of Florida)

Above right: *Enjoy the whale and dolphin presentations at Sea World* (Sea World® of Florida)

Below: *At Sea World there is a serious educational message alongside the fun* (Sea World® of Florida)

UNIVERSAL STUDIOS FLORIDA

Universal Studios Florida opened the park in 1990. It covers 444 acres (178 hectares), cost $650 million, and is now the third most popular theme park in the USA after Walt Disney World® Resort and Disneyland. Like the competition, it is continuously updating and introducing new attractions to keep the crowds pouring in. There are more than forty rides, shows and movie set streets to enjoy, and as many restaurants and boutiques. Do not think you only need to visit one or other of the studio theme parks. Both offer great and very different days out.

Getting there

Clearly signposted just north of Exit 30B off I-4, close to the junction of I-4 and the Florida Turnpike, or from Turkey Lake Road (turn off I-4 onto Sand Lake Road at junction 29 and follow the signs). Gas (petrol) is available at the Turkey Lake Road entrance. There is a car parking fee.

Cameras and videocamcorders can be rented at the **Lights, Camera Action Shop** near the main entrance. The **Dark Room** on Hollywood Boulevard can carry out minor camera repairs, and offers one hour film processing.

The First Union National Bank near the main entrance exchanges foreign currency, cashes traveler's cheques and makes cash advances against credit cards.

Lockers are available for rent near Guest Services if you have items you do not want to carry around, and Guest Services also handle lost children and lost and found.

Getting around

The theme park covers a large sprawling area, with the attractions spaced around the Lagoon. It is essential to have a route worked out that covers everything in the shortest possible distance, especially if you have young children. Try to take in attractions as you meet them on your planned route, rather than rushing all

HOT TIP

Take advantage of the **Baby Swap** if you have very young children. One adult can enjoy a ride while the other minds the baby, and they can then swap places without having to wait all over again.

The park is open every day of the year at 9am. Closing times vary so check. It normally closes at 7pm but stays open to 10pm and later during the summer and on special holidays.

Mondays to Wednesdays followed by the weekend are the busiest days of the week, with Thursdays and Fridays the least busy.

You need a very full day to see and do everything available. Universal experts reckon you need 12 to 14 hours. If this sounds too daunting, you can either buy a two day pass and do the visit at a more leisurely pace, but at greater expense, or make a list of things you want to see in the time available, accepting that there will not be time for others.

If you decide a second day is necessary once inside the park, buy the second one-day ticket before leaving. This way you will only be charged as if you have bought a two day pass, cheaper than buying two separate one-day tickets. Or, you can sign up for one of the two VIP Tours, one lasts 4 hours and the other 8, which allow you to whiz round as you can jump all the lines. Naturally you pay for the privilege. On a number of occasions during the year, one day ticket holders are offered the chance of a second day free provided the tickets are exchanged while they are still at the theme park. Check with the information desk.

As soon as you arrive visit Guest Services in the Front Lot just inside the entrance for maps and latest information on show times and shooting schedules. There are Studio Information Boards outside Mel's Drive-In and the Studio Stars Restaurant which are constantly updated with waiting times at the main attractions, revisions to show times and so on.

The Production Schedule near the entrance also gives details of filming or taping taking place that day. If you want studio audience tickets ask at the Nickelodeon Studios and Tour.

over the place, which will waste time and tire you and your family out.

A suggested lightning tour on arrival is to head straight from the **E.T. Adventure** and then **Kongfrontation**, as both these get very busy later on, and then to work your way round the park in a clockwise direction taking in the rest of the main attractions. Skip the street sets until last and take these in if you have time, before buying your souvenirs and heading home.

For a more thorough one day tour, start at **Back to the Future...The Ride**, and then work anti-clockwise round the Lagoon taking in the Wild, Wild, Wild West Stunt Show, Jaws, Earthquake — The Big One, Beetlejuice's Graveyard Revue and Kong-frontation before lunch. Grab a quick snack and then head for Twister followed by the two tours — Nickelodeon Studios and Tour and the Production Tram Tour.

Then visit the Gory, Gruesome and Grotesque Horror Make-Up Show, followed by Alfred Hitchcock: The Art of Making Movies, and then across 8th Avenue for the Hercules and Xena: Wizard of the Screen. Finally stroll down Sunset Boulevard before making a right turn for the E.T. Adventure. The new 440-acre (162-hectare) Back Lot has

sets which whisk you round the world from New York Sideways, Fisherman's Wharf in San Francisco, to the Garden of Allah!

The **Funtastic World of Hanna-Barbera**, should not be missed even when time is tight, and the Blues Brothers, a band of musicians who cruise in their Bluesmobile and give regular performances outside 70 Delancey in New York, are great.

The studios also have the largest assembly of working film and TV animal actors in the world, including Benji the dog, cats, primates, penguins, vultures and parrots. They appear in the Animal Actors show.

Main attractions

The Front Lot

An area of shops, boutiques and eateries, and the Plaza of the Stars.

Production Tram Tour

Production Central covers large areas of the park and includes working stage areas, as well as popular attractions like **Hercules & Xena**. The guided tram tour takes you around the park, past **The Boneyard** where props are stored in case they are needed again, and there is a non-stop commentary pointing out things

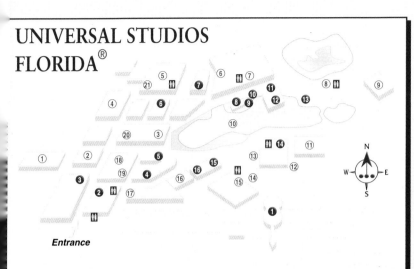

UNIVERSAL STUDIOS FLORIDA®

Entrance

Key to Map

Places of Interest

① Nickelodeon Studios®
② The Funtastic World of Hanna-Barbera™
③ Hercules and Xena: Wizards of the Screen℠
④ Twister
⑤ Kongfrontation
⑥ Beetlejuice's™ Graveyard Revue
⑦ Earthquake® - The Big One
⑧ Jaws®
⑨ Wild, Wild, Wild West Stunt Show℠
⑩ Dynamite Nights Stuntacular®
⑪ Back to the Future®… The Ride℠
⑫ A Day in the Park with Barney™
⑬ Animal Actors Stage®
⑭ Fievel's® Playland
⑮ The E.T. Adventure®
⑯ The Gory Gruesome & Grotesque Horror Make-Up Show
⑰ Terminator 2:3-D™
⑱ Alfred Hitchcock The Art of Making Movie
⑲ Lucy: A tribute
⑳ Studio 54
㉑ Universal Studios Islands of Adventure Preview Center

Places to Eat

❶ Hard Rock Cafe®
❷ Beverly Hills Boulangerie
❸ Studio Stars Restaurant
❹ Schwab's℠ Pharmacy
❺ Mel's Drive-in
❻ Finnegan's
❼ Louie's Italian Restaurant
❽ Pier 27
❾ Chez Alcatraz
❿ Richter's
⓫ San Francisco Pastry Co
⓬ Lombard's Landing
⓭ Boardwalk Snacks
⓮ International Food Bazaar
⓯ Animal Crackers
⓰ Café La Bamba

of interest on the way, and letting you into a few backstage production secrets. It lasts about 20 minutes.

Nickelodeon Studios and Tour

The Production Tram Tour returns you to the end of Nickelodeon Way where you cross over the road to take the **Nickelodeon Studios and Tour** which explains how a television show is put together for the world's only television network especially for children. The shows are actually made here and you can normally expect to see something being taped, as well as seeing where the show's young stars get their hair and make up done. At the end of the tour, enjoy the Game Lab with all its hands-on attractions.

The Funtastic World of Hanna-Barbera

Yogi Bear in the pre-ride video, introduces you to the attraction which combines flight simulator and video-interactive display. As soon as you are seated, you suddenly find that you are now part of the cartoon you were watching. After the ride spend some time playing with the various inter-active computers. You can dub your own voice over one of the Flintstones, or re-paint some of your favorite cartoon characters. The ride lasts about 6 minutes. Very young children, pregnant women and people who suffer from motion sickness, heart, back or neck problems are not advised to ride.

Lucy: A Tribute

On the corner of Plaza of the Stars and Rodeo Drive, a collection of costumes worn by and memorabilia used by Lucille Ball. As you walk through the exhibit, monitors overhead play clips from the *I Love Lucy Show*. Allow about 20 minutes.

Hitchcock's 3-D Theatre

A great show and fitting tribute to the master of horror. The 3-D effects are stunning as you are dive bombed by seagulls in *The Birds*, and visitors are recruited to re-enact the famous *Psycho* shower scene, so that you can see just how it was done. The show lasts 40 minutes.

Hercules and Xena: Wizards of the Screen

Based on the globally popular television shows and featuring dazzling special effects. The attraction takes audiences behind the scenes enabling guests to battle shoulder to shoulder with the blockbuster TV stars in a specially produced interactive episode featuring exotic location footage filmed in New Zealand, home of both TV stars.

New York Metro

The New York Metro set offers lots of good photo opportunities as every street corner has a surprise view in store. **The Blues Brothers** perform a live stage show on Delancey Street and there are Ghostbusters and Kongfrontation, two great attractions.

Twister

Based on the 1996 film which broke box office records, this is the latest attraction at the park and pits humans against Mother Nature at her most furious. Experience the awesome live spectacle and destructive nature of an actual tornado — just 20ft (6m) away. Twenty-four hundred people an hour can experience the intense winds and pounding rain of the five-storey-tall cyclone created by circulating more than 2 million cubic feet of air a minute.

Kongfrontation

The entrance to the ride is modelled on a New York subway station although you board an aerial tram and not a train to flee the city under attack from the 35ft (11m)-tall King Kong. As the tram turns the corner, however, Kong blocks the path and attacks your tram. This is all good fun and the monster is driven away by gun-toting helicopters as you make good your escape.

Because of the jerky nature of the ride, it is advised that pregnant women and people with heart, back or neck problems avoid it.

Beetlejuice's Graveyard Revue

An award-winning live stomping, rock and roll musical based on the hugely popular 1991 movie. The show has proved so popular that a 1,300 seat covered area has been added to the open-air amphitheater. Great music and a lot of laughs with a cast that includes Wolfman, Dracula, Phantom and his bride and Frankenstein. The special effects, lighting and pulsating amplified sound make for a very memorable 20 minutes.

Earthquake — The Big One

Situated in the **San Francisco/ Amity** area of the theme park. As you wait for the main attraction, visitors are invited to take part in re-takes of scenes from the movie *Earthquake*, which are displayed on the overhead monitors. You then board your subway car for one of the great rides at Universal. You are subjected to a massive earthquake and then have to cope with fire, floods and blackouts. Everyone survives, some people get wet and some continue to shake long after the earthquake tremors have died down. The show lasts about 12

Above: *Beetlejuice's Graveyard Revue*
(© Universal Studios Florida)

Right: *Enjoy the Nickelodeon Game Lab with its hands-on attractions* (© Universal Studios Florida)

Below: *One of the great rides at Universal Studios, Earthquake – The Big One, a 5-minute thrill spectacular* (© Universal Studios Florida)

Opposite page: *Jaws tests your mettle in a thrill-a-second boatride* (© Universal Studios Florida)

minutes and the ride lasts 5 minutes. Very young children, pregnant women, and people with heart, back or neck problems or who suffer from motion sickness are advised not to board.

Jaws

Off Amity Avenue is **Jaws**, a thrill-a-second boatride trying to escape the massive killer shark. Each time you think you have escaped the monster, it comes back with a vengeance. Real thrill seekers are recommended to do the ride after dark so that you cannot see Jaws coming. The ride, which is hugely popular, lasts 6 or 7 minutes but feels longer, and like Earthquake — The Big One, has the same restrictions.

Wild, Wild, Wild West Stunt Show

The 2,000 seat amphitheater echoes to the sounds of shootouts and explosions in this action-packed show, laced with lots of comedy and death defying stunts. By the end of the 16 minute show, the entire stage area has been wrecked one way or another by the stunt men and women, who are then happy to chat to you and pose for pictures.

A Day in the Park With Barney

Brings to life Barney's make-believe pre-school play-world in a state-of-the-art, imaginatively interactive musical show and hands-on educational playground.

Back to the Future... The Ride

Crossing the Lagoon bridge, you arrive in **Expo Center**. Bear to the right for perhaps the most exciting ride of its kind anywhere — **Back to the Future... The Ride**. You enter your time-travelling vehicle and are then hurtled off into a journey through space. The effects of the flight simulator are magnified many times by the massive seven-storey-high screen enveloping you, so you really do get the impression that you are being thrown all over the place. Very exciting and worth the wait, even though the lines can be massive. The ride lasts about 5 minutes.

Fievel's Playland

Children love this larger than life playground with state of the art games, climbs and rope bridges, a 200ft (61m) water slide and much more.

E.T. Adventure

Children love the pre-attraction waiting area, an eerie forest scene with E.T. trying to avoid the search party looking for him. Then you climb on your bicycles for a delightful journey through the trees and magical gardens before soaring up into the sky heading for the moon. A 5-minute gentle ride although very young children must ride alongside an older person. As you might expect, this show had to be sponsored by a phone company!

The Boneyard

The Boneyard is an open-air inter-active area containing many of the largest and most memorable and famous props used in the Studio's films.

The Gory, Gruesome & Grotesque Horror Make-Up Show

Learn how to really scare your friends at Halloween with this 25-minute-long show which lets you into the secrets of horror make-up. Very young

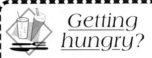

Getting hungry?

Hard Rock Cafe — guitar shaped and great fun. Burgers and deafening rock music. You can eat in the café without going into the theme park. Table service.

International Food Bazaar — offers a wide range of ethnic foods from American to Italian and Greek to Chinese.

Lombard's Landing — offers a setting resembling a nineteenth-century San Francisco warehouse.

Mel's Drive-In — for burgers and fries in a 50s diner with appropriate music.

Studio Stars Restaurant — offers good value all you can eat buffet.

Finnegan's — an Irish pub offering traditional food and drink to the accompaniment of the Finnegan Boys, an Irish folk music group.

Richter's — fun dining in an 'earthquake-hit' restaurant. The cracks in the walls are not real!

children may be frightened by some of the effects, but older kids love them.

Terminator 2: 3-D

Features Arnold Schwarzenegger and the original 72-member cast in a $60 million 'virtual adventure' experience. Frame for frame the 12-minute long film is the most expensive live action film ever produced. Three 23ft (7m) high by 50ft (15m) wide screens help create **Terminator 2: 3-D**'s massive, sensory experience.

The Hi-Tones

A 50s style acapella group who perform around Hollywood Boulevard.

Lagoon

At the center of the park, the Lagoon is the setting for the **Dynamite Nights Stunt Spectacular**, presented at 7pm nightly. Around a story of cops and drug smugglers, a remarkable stunt show with a difference has been created, as it is performed on speed boats at night. The show lasts 20-minutes but the best viewing spots fill up early. The attraction features the studio's recent films and you can currently see props used in both the '*Flintstones*' and '*Jurassic Park*'.

Universal Studios Escape

This new 800-acre (324 hectare) resort, is situated next to the existing attraction between I-4 and Turkey Lake Road. There will be three main areas:

Universal Studios Islands of Adventure

Where the worlds of myths, legends and superheroes come alive. The theme park features five unique islands — **Seuss Landing, The Lost Continent, Jurassic Park, Toon Lagoon** and **Marvel Super Hero Island.**

Universal Studios CityWalk

This impressive complex is an endless celebration of sight, sound and taste, offering a "best of the best" gathering of nightclubs, themed restaurants, shops and cinemas.

Universal Studios Escape Resorts

Three world class hotels are also included in the plans for the park. The Portofino Bay Hotel opened in 1999 and is based upon the Italian seaside village of Portofino. The Royal Bali Hotel opens the following year along with a Tom Fazio designed 18-hole championship golf course. Other facilities include a 300-unit golf lodge and villa complex; a championship tennis center, state of the art convention and meeting centers and expanded film and television production facilities.

SPLENDID CHINA

Splendid China is situated 3 miles (5km) west of I-4 (exit 25B), 1 mile (2km) west of the Walt Disney World® Resort entrance on US192 and 5 miles (8km) east of US27. It opened on 19 December 1993, taking two years to build.

It is without doubt the most tranquil of all the Greater Orlando area theme parks with piped Chinese music accompanying you around the park. Splendid China is a near-duplication of the original which is situated at Shenzhen in China, close to Hong Kong. The latter park opened in 1989 and is now one of the most popular attractions in the Far East.

The attraction cost $100 million, and reproduces either in full size or miniature, more than sixty of China's best known scenic, historic and cultural sites. Conceived as

Left: *The Dazu Grotto, one of over fifty superb exhibits*

Below: *The Great Wall of China, recreated at Splendid China with millions of tiny bricks*

Splendid China Florida

Key to Map

Exhibits

1. Mogao Grottoes
2. Grotto #257
3. Yungang Grottoes
4. Longmen Grottoes
5. Leshan Grand Buddha Statue
6. Buddhist Stone Sculpture in Dazu
7. Midair Temple
8. Cliffside Tombs
9. Stone Forest
10. Shanhaiguan Pass of The Great Wall
11. Nine Dragon Wall
12. Mongolian Yurt
13. Mausoleum of Genghis Khan
14. The Great Wall
15. 1000 Eyes and 1000 Hands - Guanyin Buddha Statue
16. Xiang Fei's Tomb
17. Id Kah Mosque
18. Panda Playground
19. Bai Dwelling Houses
20. Three Ancient Pagodas
21. Dai Village
22. Jingzhen Octagonal Pavilion
23. Potala Palace
24. Lijiang River Scenery
25. Foshan Ancestral Temple
26. Zhenghai Tower
27. Dwelling Houses of the Hakkas
28. Water Village
29. Tengwang Pavilion
30. West Lake Scenery
31. Town God Temple
32. Chinese Gardens
33. Temple of Confucius
34. Summer Palace
35. Zhaozhou Bridge
36. Marco Polo Bridge
37. Imperial Palace/Forbidden City
38. Jin Gang Bao Zuo Pagoda
39. White Pagoda
40. Yingxian Wooden Pagoda
41. Terra Cotta Warriors
42. Big Wild Goose Pagoda
43. Jiayuguan Pass
44. Ancient Star Observatory
45. Temple of Zhuge Liang
46. Buyi Village
47. Miao Village
48. Dong Village
49. Yueyang Pavilion
50. Yellow Crane Tower
51. Feihong Pagoda
52. Shaolin Temple
53. Pagoda Forest
54. Jin Ancestral Temple
55. Temple of Heaven
56. (Dr.) Sun Yat Sen's Mausoleum
57. Harmony Hall Theater

Dining Guide

58. The Great Wall Terrace
59. Wind and Rain Court
60. Pagoda Garden
61. The Seven Flavors
62. Suzhou Pearl

Route to include all must see exhibits

Entrance

115

a 10,000 mile (16,100km) journey through 5,000 years of Chinese history and culture, it claims to offer visitors the most extensive and authentic close-up look of China possible without actually visiting the country.

Star attractions include the half-mile (1km) exact reproduction of **The Great Wall**. To recreate the 4,200 mile (6,762km) wall, each of the 3ft (1m) building blocks were transformed into bricks 1 and 2 inches long. Each one of these 6.5 million mini-bricks was then placed by hand to faithfully reproduce the original.

There are the breathtaking miniatures of the **Forbidden City**, **Temple of Heaven**, the imposing **Potala Palace**, the brooding **Leshan Buddha** — 30ft (9m) high, compared with 236ft (72m) in real life, the awesome natural wonder of the **Lunan Stone Forest** and more than sixty other impressive sites and settings.

Splendid China occupies a total of 76 acres (30 hectares). It introduces the visitor to China, its various culinary styles, and its merchandise from works of art and fashions to bonsai trees.

Visitors enter the park through **Suzhou Gardens**. The first part of this is a replica of a commercial street in the 'water-city' of Suzhou in eastern China, often referred to as the Venice of the East. The scene is set some 700 years ago. In fact, the buildings incorporate techniques in use at that time. There are a variety of shops, a cinema giving an introduction to China and two restaurants.

Leaving the shops behind, a path leads around by various replicas of grottoes and statues of the Buddha. These include the **Mogao Grottoes**, built to a tenth of the actual size, which are in the north of China. This complex consists of 492 caves constructed 1,600 years ago on the Silk Road. They became covered by desert sand and were not re-discovered until 1900. There is also a model of the **Leshan Buddah**. At 236ft (72m) high, it is the largest

Getting hungry?

The **Seven Flavours** is a cafeteria-style place offering both Chinese and American food. The **Suzhou Pearl** is perhaps the best restaurant of all here, offering authentic gourmet Chinese cuisine in an elegant setting. There are a limited number of western dishes available and the restaurant is definitely recommended.

Buddah statue in the world. This model is an eighth of the full size. It is a sobering thought that over 100 people can sit on each foot of the original!

The grottoes are built around the **Lunan Stone Forest** feature. These pinnacles of carved limestone cover 65,765 acres (26,306 hectares) near Kunming in southern China, yet another of a whole string of incredible statistics.

However it is the **Exhibit Park** which is perhaps the most memorable part of this theme park. It is simply breathtaking what has been achieved. It is incredible in some respects when one sees the carved detail on some of the buildings. They display craftsmanship rarely seen in the west these days.

Each exhibit has a board giving detail of the original feature including its age. They incorporate a scale used to date the feature which shows parallel happenings elsewhere in the world to the time the original exhibit was constructed. For example, the **Nine Dragon Wall in Peking** was built just after 1420, when the Medici came to power in Florence.

Major exhibits

The Great Wall

One of the wonders of the world, China's 4,200 mile (6,762km) Great Wall is the only man-made site visible to astronauts in space. Even scaled down to a half-mile (1km) in length, the Florida version of The Great Wall is enormous and destined to become one of the most photographed scenes in America.

The Forbidden City and Imperial Palace

The largest and grandest **Imperial Palace** ever built is the 9,999 room centerpiece of Peking's famed and infamous Forbidden City. It was built in 1420 and was the setting for the Academy Award-winning motion picture *The Last Emperor*. The city and palace was the home and seat of power for several emperors including their families, military and political staffs and administrative personnel. The site is so vast that some emperors lived their entire lives within its walls. In Splendid China, The Imperial Palace has been reproduced stone by stone, tile by tile and brush stroke by tiny brush stroke.

The Potala Palace

This striking and imposing reproduction of the renowned palace in Tibet, is one of the visual highlights of Splendid China. As it does in its original setting, the palace sits high on the side of a mountain, projecting its majesty and grandeur like a beacon. For most of us, our impressions of the palace are restricted to the familiar view of the most imposing side. Here one can go around and see what the rear view looks like. The grassed area has hundreds of little models of people, cattle, carts etc. There are thousands of these around the park, with incredible numbers of them at some exhibits such as the Imperial Palace, all painted in different costumes. They make some of the exhibits absolutely stunning.

The Ancient Star Observatory

In the year AD279, 1,200 years before Galileo, the famous astronomer Guo Shoujing erected twenty-seven observatories throughout China, the centerpiece of which was Zhou Gong Temple, since renamed the **Ancient Star Observatory**. The main part of the structure is an inverted funnel-shaped brick platform and sky measuring scale. The Florida replica is built to scale.

Terra Cotta Warriors and Horses

In 1974, one of the world's major archaeological discoveries was made with the uncovering of over 6,000 life-sized and individually carved statues of soldiers and horses. An overwhelming example of ancient excesses and sweeping Imperial power, the statuary army was a guard of honour for the spirit of Quin Shihuang, protecting both his memory and his mausoleum. It also remains as an unsurpassed ancient military museum. Even in this reduced scale, the exhibit is incredible in its detail.

The Mausoleum of Genghis Khan

Located in inner Mongolia, this is the burial palace of the famous or infamous conqueror, whose Empire stretched from mid-Asia to Europe. The war lord died in 1227 but his coffin was moved time and again until finally transported to this magnificent site in 1954.

At set times you can take a rest at the **Temple of Light Theater** and see the young dancers in their beautiful costumes. It is close to the **Panda Playground** where extracting your children from their enjoyment can be a distinct problem. There are three restaurants in the Exhibit Park where you can also rest up for a while.

At 6.30pm the evening parade moves through the Suzhou Gardens towards the main entrance where dancers and acrobats delight the crowd. Once again, the lovely costumes steal the show.

A huge Asian Business Centre is being built next to Splendid China, with convention facilities, offices and exhibition space.

4 OTHER ATTRACTIONS

ORLANDO

Orlando and the surrounding area has much more to offer than just the enormous theme parks. There are some of the world's most attractive miniature golf courses or there are go-karts and bungee-jumping for those who want a bigger thrill; there are the shopping malls, packed with all kinds of goods, and often at a fraction of the prices compared to other countries, and literally thousands of places to eat, catering for every taste and budget; for those who want to party into the small hours, there are clubs, bars and discos. After a few days of negotiating the endless parking bays and seething crowds of the major attractions, many visitors will find it a refreshing change to seek more peaceful venues and enjoy some areas of natural beauty before pitching back into the fray.

Above: *Surfing at Kissimmee; Water Mania offers 38 acres (14 hectares) of slides, flumes and pools*

Things to see and do

Brazil Carnival Dinner Show, 7432 Republic Drive: A dinner show featuring the sights and sounds of Brazil performed by native artists while you enjoy a four course dinner. Dinner shows: 6.30 and 9pm ☎ (407) 352-8666.

Caruso's Palace Italian Ristorante, 8986 International Drive, Orlando: A $5 million dollar Italian Renaissance restaurant with strolling musicians ☎ (407) 363-7110.

Celebration City, south of the 192/I-4 junction is going to be a city of 75,000 people with its own schools, hospitals and facilities when completed. The first multi-storey offices school, hospital and homes have been built and the project will take at least twenty-five years to complete.

Central Florida Zoological Park, on US 17-92 east from exit 52 off I-4: covers 110 acres (44 hectares) and has been much transformed in recent years as it continues to expand. There are all the usual animals but the zoo specializes in rare cats, especially the smaller ones. The elephants, otters and snakes are popular, as is the **Animal Adventure**, the petting area for children. Open: 9am-5pm daily ☎ (407) 323-4450 (allow 2-3 hours).

Church Street Station, 129 West Church Street, Orlando: A massive self-contained shopping, eating and entertainment complex to keep you amused for hours. Home of the world-famous **Rosie O'Grady Saloon** and **Good Time Jazz Band**, the **Cheyenne Saloon** and **Opera House, Orchid Garden Ballroom** offering live music from the 50s to the 90s, and lots, lots more. Open: 11am-2am daily ☎ (407) 422-2434.

Fun 'N Wheels, at 6739 Sand Lake Road, Orlando: Four go-kart tracks, miniature golf, bumper boats, waterslide, ferris wheel, kiddie and arcade area, snack bar. Open: hours vary according to season ☎ (407) 351-5651.

Fun World, Highway 17-92 between Orlando and Sandford: 2 mini golf courses, 9 batting cages, bumper boats and cars, 3 go-kart tracks, carousel, 300 arcade games and more. Open: 10am-midnight Friday to Sunday ☎ (407) 645-1792.

Gator Jungle, on E. Highway 50 in Christmas, east of Orlando: A 'jungle' cruise through gator swamps, wildlife shows. Open: 9am-6pm daily ☎ (407) 568-2885.

King Henry's Feast, 8984 International Drive, Orlando: Enjoy a four-course banquet in a sixteenth-century fortified English mansion with continuous entertainment and lots of audience participation. Open: every night ☎ (407) 351-5151.

calendar
Orlando

- Florida Citrus Bowl Football Classic, Orlando Stadium
- Camelia Society of Central Florida Show, Winter Park Mall
- Scottish Highland Games, Central Florida Fairgrounds

- Walt Disney World® Village Wine Festival
- National Championship Rodeo Finals, Orlando Arena
- Annual Central Florida Fair, Central Florida Fairgrounds

- St Patrick's Day Street Party, Church Street Station
- Nestlé Invitational PGA Tour Event, Bay Hill Club
- Winter Park Sidewalk Arts Festival

- Orlando Shakespeare Festival, Lake Eola Amphitheater
- Easter Sunrise Services, Sea World's Atlantis Theater
- Easter Parade, Main Street, Magic Kingdom
- Orlando International Fringe Festival, throughout Downtown Orlando

- Up, Up and Away Air Show, Orlando International Airport

- 4th of July Parade, Orlando and Walt Disney World® Resort

- Oktoberfest, Church Street Station

- Universal Art Show, Central Florida parks
- Walt Disney World® PGA Golf Tournament
- Autumn Art Festival, Winter Park
- Pioneer Days Folk Festival, Folk Art Center, Pine Castle

- Festival of the Masters, Art Exhibition, Downtown Disney Village Marketplace
- Light Up Orlando, Downtown Orlando

- Pet Fair and Winterfest, Loch Haven Park
- Nativity Pageant, Downtown Disney Village Marketplace

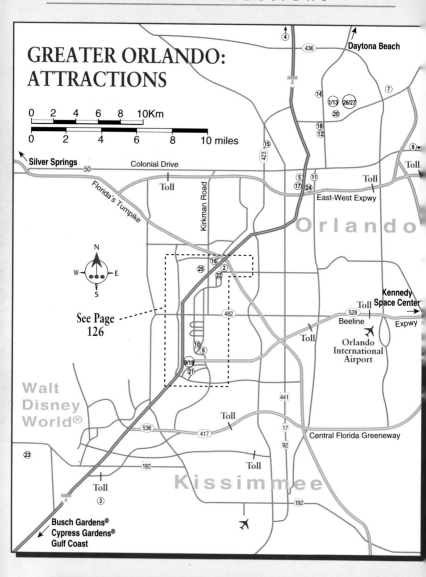

GREATER ORLANDO: ATTRACTIONS

Silver Springs

Daytona Beach

Kennedy Space Center

Walt Disney World®

Kissimmee

Busch Gardens®
Cypress Gardens®
Gulf Coast

See Page 126

Colonial Drive

Florida's Turnpike

Kirkman Road

East-West Expwy

Beeline

Orlando International Airport

Central Florida Greeneway

Orlando

Toll

Opposite page: Church Street Station (in downtown Orlando) is a huge shopping, eating and entertainment complex

KEY TO MAIN ATTRACTIONS

① Audubon Center for Birds of Prey
② Belz Factory Outlet
③ Celebration City
④ Central Florida Zoological Park
⑤ Church Street Station
⑥ Circus Maximus
⑦ Fun World
⑧ Gator Jungle/Christmas
⑨ Hilarities Comedy Theater
⑩ Historical Research and Development
⑪ Lake Eola Park
⑫ Leu Botanical Gardens
 Loch Haven Park
⑬ Maitland
⑭ Maitland Art Center
⑮ Mark Two Dinner Theater
⑯ Mystery Fun House
⑰ Orlando Arena

⑱ Orange County Historical Museum
 John Young Planetarium
 Orlando Science Center
 Civic Theater of Central Florida
 Orlando Museum of Art
⑲ Orlando International Toy Train Museum
⑳ Rollins College
 Cornell Fine Arts Museum
 Morse Museum of American Art
㉑ Sea World® of Florida
㉒ Sleuths Mystery Dinner Theater
 Brazil Carnival Dinner Show
 Wet 'N Wild
㉓ Splendid China
㉔ Terror on Church Street
㉕ Universal Studios Florida
㉖ Winter Park/Mead Park and Gardens
㉗ Winter Park Farmer's Market

Belz Factory Outlet Mall
5401 W. Oakridge Road,
Orlando
Shopping at factory direct
prices at more than 150
stores. Open: 10am-9pm
Monday to Saturday,
10am-6pm Sunday.

Church Street Exchange
129 W. Church Street,
Orlando
Dozens of shops and
restaurants on several storeys.
Open: 11am-2am daily.

Church Street Market
55 W. Church Street, Orlando
Speciality shops and
restaurants. Open: 10am-9pm
Monday to Saturday,
12noon-6pm Sunday.

Colonial Plaza Mall
2560 E. Colonial Drive,
Orlando
Major stores and seventy-five
other fine shops. Open: 10am-
9pm Monday to Saturday,
12noon-5.30pm Sunday.

**Crossroads of
Lake Buena Vista**
I-4 and exit 27 for
Lake Buena Vista
Twenty-five shops,

restaurants, bank, post office
and 24 hour supermarket.
Open: 10am-10pm daily.

The Florida Mall
8001 S. Orange Blossom Trail,
Orlando
Massive shopping mall with
major stores and more than
200 speciality shops and
restaurants. Open: 10am-9pm
Monday to Saturday, 11am-
6pm Sunday.

The Great American Bazaar
7551 Canada Ave, Orlando
A shopping and entertainment
experience. More than 700
stalls in the open-air market
place, plus restaurants, live
entertainment.
Open: 10am-10pm.

**The Market Place at
Dr Phillips**
7600 Dr Phillips Blvd, Orlando
Gift and shops in a European
setting with seven ethnic
restaurants. Open: all hours.

**Mercado Mediterranean
Village**
8445 International Drive,
Orlando
Shop, dine and be entertained
in a Mediterranean village
setting. More than sixty shops.

Open: 10am-10pm daily
(restaurants stay open later).

Orange Blossom Market

5151 S. Orange Blossom Trail, Orlando
Citrus fruit, juice and souvenirs.
Open: 8am-6pm daily.

Orlando Fashion Square

3201 E. Colonial Drive, Orlando
Big name fashion stores and more than 130 shops plus food court. Open: 10am-9pm Monday to Saturday, 12noon-5.30pm Sunday.

Park Avenue

Park Avenue, Winter Park
Exclusive shopping and stores and restaurants. Open: daily.

Quality Outlet Center

5527 International Drive, Orlando
Factory outlet shopping in twenty-five stores. Open: 9.30am-9pm Monday to Saturday, 11am-6pm Sunday.

Sunbelt International Shoppers

9649 Tradeport Drive, Orlando
Duty free shopping at Orlando International Airport.
Open: 8am-11pm daily.

Luau, South Seas Music and dance over dinner, 6.30pm daily. Sea World ☎ 1-800-227-8048.

Lake Eola Park, a family park established more than 100 years ago. There are swan-shaped pedal boats and the park is very popular with walkers and families. The **Walt Disney Amphitheater** on the lake, is home of the annual spring **Shakespeare Festival**, and regular weekend community concerts. Open: daily 7am-midnight.

Maitland, another city suburb north of Orlando, and home of the **Florida Audubon Society Madlyn Baldwin Center for Birds of Prey**, on Lake Sybelia Drive, off Audubon Way. The center treats hundreds of injured birds of prey every year. Many are able to return to the wild after treatment, and those that can not may be observed in the center's aviaries. Open: 10am-4pm Tuesday to Saturday ☎ (407) 645-3826 (allow 1-2 hours).

The Maitland Art Center, on Packwood Avenue near Lake Sybelia: Housed in buildings designed by Andre Smith. Work on the buildings started in 1937 and reflects the Mayan and Aztec influences on the artist. The museum displays the artist's work and also stages exhibitions. The chapel in the grounds is very popular for

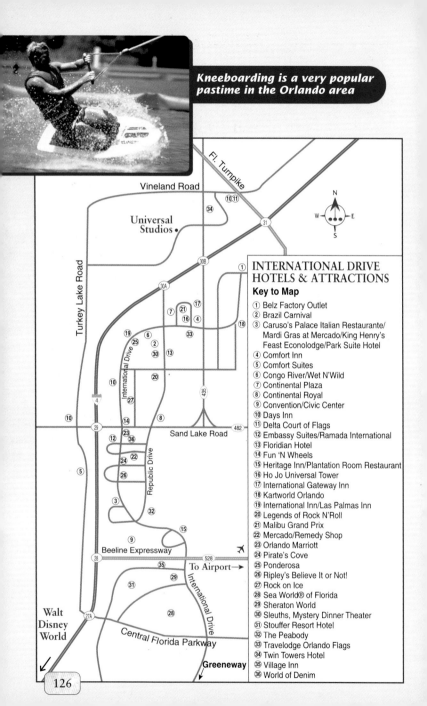

Kneeboarding is a very popular pastime in the Orlando area

Fl. Turnpike

Vineland Road

Universal Studios •

Turkey Lake Road

International Drive

Republic Drive

Sand Lake Road

Beeline Expressway

To Airport →

International Drive

Walt Disney World

Central Florida Parkway

Greeneway

INTERNATIONAL DRIVE HOTELS & ATTRACTIONS
Key to Map

① Belz Factory Outlet
② Brazil Carnival
③ Caruso's Palace Italian Restaurante/ Mardi Gras at Mercado/King Henry's Feast Econolodge/Park Suite Hotel
④ Comfort Inn
⑤ Comfort Suites
⑥ Congo River/Wet N'Wild
⑦ Continental Plaza
⑧ Continental Royal
⑨ Convention/Civic Center
⑩ Days Inn
⑪ Delta Court of Flags
⑫ Embassy Suites/Ramada International
⑬ Floridian Hotel
⑭ Fun 'N Wheels
⑮ Heritage Inn/Plantation Room Restaurant
⑯ Ho Jo Universal Tower
⑰ International Gateway Inn
⑱ Kartworld Orlando
⑲ International Inn/Las Palmas Inn
⑳ Legends of Rock N'Roll
㉑ Malibu Grand Prix
㉒ Mercado/Remedy Shop
㉓ Orlando Marriott
㉔ Pirate's Cove
㉕ Ponderosa
㉖ Ripley's Believe It or Not!
㉗ Rock on Ice
㉘ Sea World® of Florida
㉙ Sheraton World
㉚ Sleuths, Mystery Dinner Theater
㉛ Stouffer Resort Hotel
㉜ The Peabody
㉝ Travelodge Orlando Flags
㉞ Twin Towers Hotel
㉟ Village Inn
㊱ World of Denim

weddings. Open: 10am-4pm Monday to Friday, 12noon-4.30pm Saturday and Sunday ☎ (407) 539-2181.

Malibu Grand Prix, 5901 American Way, Orlando: Experience Indy and Formula One racing in authentic scaled down cars, plus miniature golf, bumper cars, batting cages and arcade. Open: 10am-midnight daily ☎ (407) 351-4132.

Mardi Gras at Mercado, 8445 International Drive, Orlando: A four-course dinner and 2 hour musical extravaganza of the carnivals of the world with international acts. Open every night ☎ (407) 351-5151.

Mark Two Dinner Theater, 3376 Edgewater Drive, Orlando: A fully-staged Broadway show after a buffet dinner. Shows nightly Wednesday to Sunday, matinees Wednesday, Thursday and Saturday ☎ (407) 843-6275.

Murder Watch Mystery Theatre, Grosvenor Resort Hotel, Lake Buena Vista: Musical mystery buffet show with audience participation. Saturdays 6-9pm ☎ (407) 828-4444.

Mystery Fun House, 5676 Major Boulevard, Orlando: Fun for all the family, Wizard's 15 surprise chambers, explore an Egyptian tomb, play Starbase Omega, the Ultimate Laser Game, miniature golf, arcade and more. Open: 10am-10pm

year round, later opening during high season ☎ (407) 351-3356 (allow 3-4 hours).

Orlando International Toy Train Museum, 5253 International Drive, Orlando: Massive model train layout, with many related exhibits. Open: 10am-10pm during the summer, 10am-7pm rest of year ☎ (407) 363-9002.

Pirate's Cove Adventure Golf, 8601 International Drive, Orlando: Two 18-hole adventure golf courses in spectacular landscaping. Open: 9am-11.30pm daily ☎ (407) 352-7378 (allow 1-1.5 hours).

Plantation Dinner Restaurant, 9861 International Drive, Orlando: Dine in Victorian Florida elegance and be entertained by the Plantation Dinner Theater. Shows nightly 7pm ☎ (407) 352-0008.

Ripley's Believe It Or Not!: A museum on International Drive like no other, full of weird and wonderful exhibits collected by Robert Ripley. Themed galleries feature antiques, miniatures, oddities and even disasters. Even the building is unusual because it was deliberately built to look as if it is falling down. Open: 10am-11pm daily ☎ (407) 363-4418 (allow 2-3 hours).

Rock On Ice, 7500 Canada Ave, Orlando: Family entertainment center with ice skating arena. Skate to lights and music with live DJs, snack bar and arcade. Open: 9am-11pm daily ☎ (407) 352-9878 or 1-800-424-0680.

Sleuths Mystery Dinner Theater, 7508 Republic Drive, Orlando: Solve the murder as you enjoy your dinner. Four different mystery shows each week. Shows 6pm and 9pm ☎ (407) 363-1985.

Terror on Church Street, 135 S. Orange Ave, Orlando: A House of Horrors with theater and fantastic lighting and sound effects. Open: 7pm-midnight Tuesday to Thursday and Sunday, 7pm-1am Friday and Saturday (allow 1.5-2 hours).

Wet 'N Wild, 6200 International Drive, Orlando: More than 25 acres (10 hectares) of water park with spectacular slides like the 500ft (152m) twisting **Black Hole**, and the **Bubba Tub**, a triple dip slide in a tube big enough for the whole family. The Children's Park has mini-versions of all the rides. Open: 10am-6pm spring, 9am-9pm summer, 10am-5pm autumn ☎ (407) 351-1800/1-800-992.

Winter Park

Winter Park, once the winter playground for people from up north, is now an elegant suburb of Greater Orlando, although a city in its own right, with lots of good shops and a number of interesting things to see. The community nestles around three lakes connected by canals built more than 100 years ago. There are lots of fine old homes and Park Avenue offers trendy boutiques and eateries. After shopping, you can cool off under the shade of the old trees in Central Park, or take the hour-long **Scenic Boat Tour**, which cruises 12 miles (19km) through the lakes and around the Rollins College campus. The cruises leave from the dock at the end of East Morse Boulevard every hour. Winter Park is home to the following:

Rollins College, in Park Avenue, reveals many fine old Spanish-style buildings. The Knowles Memorial Chapel is home of the Bach Festival Society, and the **Cornell Fine Arts Museum**, has an impressive collection of American and European art, the largest in Central Florida. **The Charles Hosmer Morse Museum of American Art**, on Park Avenue, has a number of permanent exhibitions including stained glass windows, Louis Tiffany glass, pottery, jewelry and American art spanning the last 200 years.

The Winter Park Farmer's Market, is held every Saturday on the parking lot just over the railway tracks from Park Avenue.

Mead Park and Gardens, 55 acres (22 hectares) on Denning Avenue, is an area of minimally-managed traditional wetlands. A favorite with walkers and joggers, it is a good place to spot wildlife from the trails that follow the creek.

Leu Botanical Gardens (56 acres, 22 hectares) is a gardener's dream. Established by industrialist Henry Leu more than 100 years ago, there are massive oaks, a huge floral clock, a stunning camelia collection in bloom from autumn to spring, and the **Mary Jane's Rose Garden**, in honour of his wife, is the largest rose conservatory in the South-east. The museum, in what was the family home, shows how wealthy Floridians lived at the turn of the century. Open: gardens 9am-5pm daily, museum 10am-3.30pm Tuesday to Saturday, 1-3.30pm Sunday and Monday ☎ (407) 246-2620.

Loch Haven Park

Loch Haven Park, entrances on Rollins and Princeton Streets, and home to the following:

Orlando Science Center, The Orlando Science Center is a new hands-on fun education center aimed especially at children. It features **Kids Town**, a child-sized town for children aged eight and under where they can have fun and make discoveries. The center also includes the *CineDome 3-D Light Shows*, Nature Works of Florida habitats,

Cosmic Tourists, Body Zone, the Observatory and much more. 777 East Princetown Street. Open: 9am-5pm Monday to Thursday, 9am-9pm Friday and Saturday, 12 noon-5pm Sunday ☎ (407) 896-7151.

Orange County Historical Museum, answers almost all your questions about the area, its history, development, and wildlife. Do not miss the fire station behind the museum housing fire fighting exhibits. Open: 9am-5pm Monday to Saturday, 12noon-5pm Sunday ☎ (407) 897-6350.

Orlando Museum of Art, houses a collection of nineteenth- and twentieth-century American art which changes regularly, plus a permanent exhibition of pre-Columbian art. There are lots of hands-on activities for children. Open: 9am-5pm Tuesday to Saturday, 12noon-5pm Sunday. Tours 2pm Wednesday and Sunday September to May ☎ (407) 896-4231.

Civic Theater of Central Florida, stages mainstream productions year-round. The smaller stage offers fringe theater, and there is also the **Theater for Young People**.

Loch Haven Park, during March, is the venue for the **Kite Festival**, and the Florida Symphony Orchestra stages a number of outdoor performances here during the year.

Kissimmee and St Cloud

Things to see and do

Airboat/canoe rentals: 4266 W. Vine Street, Kissimmee: Pilot an airboat or paddle a canoe through backwaters and cypress swamps and see the real Florida. Open: 9am-5pm. You can rent by the hour or day ☎ 417-847-3672.

Alligatorland Safari Zoo: 4580 W. Irlo Bronson Memorial Highway (192), Kissimmee: Animals from around the world plus lots of alligators. Open: 8.30am-dusk (allow 1.5 hours) ☎ (407) 396-1012.

Arabian Nights Dinner Attraction: 6225 W. Irlo Bronson Memorial Highway,

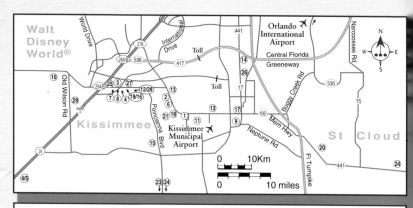

KEY TO KISSMMEE-ST CLOUD ATTRACTIONS

① Airboat/Canoe Rentals
② Alligatorland Safari Zoo
③ Arabian Nights Dinner Attraction
④ Baseball City Stadium
⑤ Boardwalk and Baseball
⑥ Capone's Dinner & Show
⑦ Crystal City Music Palace
⑧ Elvis Presley Museum
⑨ Fighter Pilots USA
⑩ Florida's Splendid China
⑪ Flying Tigers Warbird Air Museum
⑫ Fort Liberty/Brave Warrior Wax Museum
⑬ Fun'N Wheels
⑭ Gatorland
⑮ Green Meadows Farm

① Haunted House of Old Town
② Kissimmee Antique & Classic Cars
③ Medieval Life/Times Dinner & Tournament
④ Old Town Shopping and Dining
⑤ Osceola County Center for the Arts
⑥ Osceola County Historical Society
⑦ Osceola Schools Environmental Study Center
⑧ Poinciana Horse World
⑨ Reptile World Serpentarium
⑩ Ski US
⑪ Tupperware Awareness Center
⑫ Water Mania
⑬ Wild Bill's Wild West Dinner Show
⑭ World of Orchids

Above: *Lake Eola Park and the Orlando skyline*

Below: *Leave this to the experts at Gatorland!*

calendar
Kissimmee & St Cloud

FEBRUARY
- Livestock Show and Osceola County Fair
- Silver Spurs Rodeo

MARCH
- Kissimmee Bluegrass Festival
- St Cloud Spring Fling
- Osceola County Wagon Train & Trail Ride

APRIL
- Spring Boating Jamboree
- Kissimmee Jazzfest

JUNE
- Summer Boat-A-Cade

MAY
- Spring Flower Festival, Cypress Gardens

JULY
- Kissimmee Old Fashioned 4th of July Celebration
- St Cloud 4th of July Lakefest

SEPTEMBER
- Osceola Arts Festival

OCTOBER
- The Fall Boating Jamboree
- Florida State Air Fair
- Annual Mustang Roundup, Cypress Gardens

NOVEMBER
- Tournament of Champions basketball competition

DECEMBER
- Great Florida Shoot-Out basketball tournament
- Christmas Boat Parade

Kissimmee: More than 80 Arabian horses in a spectacular 2-hour 25-act four-course dinner show ☎ 1-800-553-6116.

Brave Warrior Wax Museum: 5260 W Irlo Bronson Memorial Highway, Kissimmee: Displays on the exploration of the West and tableaux featuring six Indian nations. Open: 11am-7pm (allow 1-2 hours) ☎ (407) 351-5151.

Capone's Dinner and Show: 4740 W. Irlo Bronson Memorial Highway, Kissimmee: Features a 2-hour Broadway-style revue, complete with song, dance and comedy as you dine in an underworld 'prohibition speakeasy' ☎ (407) 397-2378.

Crystal City Music Palace: 5770 W. Irlo Bronson Memorial Highway, Kissimmee: Top contemporary Christian music artists perform live as you eat. No alcohol is served ☎ (407) 396-2112.

Cypress Island: Wildlife and camera safaris, boat trips daily from 9am from Cypress Island County Store. 1541 Scotty's Road, Kissimmee ☎ (407) 935-9202.

Fighter Pilots USA: 3033 W. Patrick St. Kissimmee: Fly your own plane coached by an F-16 fighter pilot. Yes, it is a real plane, not a simulator! Open: 8am-6pm Wednesday to Sunday (allow 3-4 hours) ☎ 1-800-56-TOPGUN.

Fantasy of Flight: off I-4 Polk City: A new aviation themed attraction easily found because of the 162ft (49m) high red and white check water tower. There are vintage aircraft, aviation exhibits and flight simulators. Open daily 9am-5pm (8pm during peak periods) ☎ 941-984-9417.

Flying Tigers Warbird Air Museum: 231 Hoagland Blvd, Kissimmee: World War II Aircraft Restoration Facility specialising in bombers, thus its nickname 'Bombertown USA'. The museum houses vintage planes in the hangar with more outside. Open: 9am-5.30pm (allow 1.5-2 hours) ☎ (407) 933-1942.

Fun 'N Wheels: 3711 West Vine Street, Kissimmee: Four go-kart tracks, bumper boats, waterslides and other attractions. Open: hours vary according to season ☎ (407) 870-2222.

Gatorland: South Orange Blossom Trail: More than 5,000 alligators and crocodiles, three shows, including Gator Jumparoo, Gator wrestling and Snakes of Florida, plus tours. Open: 8am-8pm spring and summer, 8am-6pm autumn and winter (allow 3-4 hours) ☎ 1-800-393-JAWS.

Green Meadows Farm: Poinciana Blvd, Kissimmee: A guided 'hands-on' farm animals tour with tractor drawn hayrides and pony rides. Open: 9am-5pm (allow 2-3 hours) ☎ (407) 846-0770.

Haunted House of Old Town: Old Town, Kissimmee: Frightening fun rather than grissly gore with secret passages, ghosts and lots of other fun. Open: 10am-11pm daily ☎ (407) 847-7552.

Kissimmee Antique & Classic Cars: 609 W Vine Street, Kissimmee: Air-conditioned automobile collection. Open 9am-5pm, Sunday 12 noon-5pm (allow 1 hour) ☎ (407) 931-0051.

Kissimmee Rodeo: calf roping, bull riding and all other rodeo attractions. Friday

8pm. Kissimmee Sports Arena, follow signs off Hoagland Bld ☎ (407) 933-0020.

Larzland: 5720 W. Bronson Highway: An old indoor arcade with larger than life games. Next to Old Town ☎ (407) 396-0777.

Medieval Life: 4510 W Irlo Bronson Memorial Highway, Kissimmee: Step back 1,000 years into a medieval village with authentically clad artisans at work. Open: 1-9pm. (allow 1-2 hours) ☎ 1-800-229-8300.

Medieval Times Dinner and Tournament: 4510 W. Irlo Bronson Memorial Highway, Kissimmee: Knights on horseback compete in jousts plus lots of other entertainment over 2 hours as you eat medieval-style in an eleventh-century castle ☎ 1-800-229-8300.

Old Town Shopping and Dining: Turn-of-the-century shops, restaurants and giant ferris wheel ☎ 1-800-843-4202.

Osceola County Center for the Arts: 2411 W Irlo Bronson Memorial Highway, Kissimmee: Monthly exhibitions in the art gallery and live theater from the Osceola Players. Open: ring for details as times vary. Free admission to museum and gallery ☎ (407) 846-6257.

Osceola County Historical Society Spence-Lanier Pioneer Center: 750 N Bass Road, Kissimmee: Rural Florida life in 1900 in four beautifully-landscaped acres plus almost 8 acres (3 hectares) of nature reserve of woodland, remnant prairie and swamp. Open: 10am-4pm, Sunday 1-4pm. Admission free, donations welcomed (allow 1-2 hours) ☎ (407) 396-8644.

Below: *The themed dinner attraction at Medieval Times*

Above: Take to the air in an authentic World War II aircraft at the Kissimmee-based Flying Tigers Warbird Air Museum

Below: The Arabian Nights Dinner attractions at Kissimmee has a two-hour horse extravaganza

Osceola Schools Environmental Study Center: 4300 Poinciana Blvd, Kissimmee: A 200-acre (80-hectare) wildlife reserve with deer, otters, bobcats, alligators, bald eagles and other species of animals. A visitor's center houses educational displays and nature video presentations. Open: 10am-5pm Saturday, 12noon-5pm Sunday (allow 1-2 hours). Admission free ☎ (407) 870-0551.

Poinciana Horse World: 3705 Poinciana Blvd, Kissimmee: Horseback riding through 750 acres (300 hectares) and petting zoo. Open: 9am-6pm (allow 3-4 hours if you want to ride) ☎ (407) 847-4343.

Reptile World Serpentarium: 5705 E Irlo Bronson Memorial Highway, St. Cloud: The only venom show of its kind in America. The venom from poisonous snakes is collected for scientific research. Open: 2-5.30pm Tuesday to Sunday ☎ (407) 892-6905.

Ski US: W Irlo Bronson Memorial Highway, Kissimmee: A 145-acre (58-hectare) lake with swimming pool, sandy beach, volleyball and jet ski rental. Open: 9am-6pm (stay as long as you wish) ☎ (407) 396-1998.

Tupperware Awareness Center: 3175 N Orange Blossom Trail, Kissimmee: The Tupperware World headquarters in beautifully-landscaped gardens and lakes. Self-guided tours featuring manufacturing process and a museum of historic food containers dating back to 400BC. Open: 9am-4pm (allow 30 minutes-1 hour) ☎ (407) 847-3111.

Water Mania: 6073 W Irlo Bronson Memorial Highway, Kissimmee: 38-acre (15-hectare) water theme park with slides and flumes, giant raft ride, wave pool and two children's pools. The water is heated. Open: 10am-5pm (allow at least 4 hours) ☎ 1-800-527-3092.

Wild Bill's Wild West Dinner Show. At Fort Liberty, 5260 W Irlo Bronson Memorial Highway, Kissimmee: Two hour cowboy and Indian spectacular as you dine ☎ 1-800-776-3501.

World of Orchids: 2501 N. Old Lake Wilson Rd, Kissimmee: Thousands of orchids in an indoor tropical garden with guided tours and laboratory demonstrations. The plants can be shipped worldwide. Open: 10am-6pm daily ☎ (407) 396-1887.

shopping
Kissimmee & St Cloud

Kissimmee Manufacturers' Mall
2517 Old Vineland Road Kissimmee
Factory owned and operated retail outlets featuring top names.
Open: 10am-10pm, Sunday 11am-5pm.

Old Town
5770 W Irlo Bronson Memorial Highway, Kissimmee
Return to turn-of-the-century shopping. Around 70 stores.
Open: 10am-11pm.

Original Downtown Kissimmee and Lakefront Park
23 Broadway, Kissimmee
Attractive and interesting shopping area in historic buildings.
Open: 9am-9pm, Sunday 9am-5pm.

Osceola Flea and Farmers Market
2801 E Irlo Bronson Memorial Highway, Kissimmee
Around 900 indoor booths selling new and used merchandise.
Open: 8am-5pm.

Osceola Square Mall
3831 W Vine Street, Kissimmee
More than 30 stores, food court and two cinemas.
Open: 10am-9pm, Sunday 9am-6pm.

Parkway Pavilion
2901 Parkway Blvd, Kissimmee
Wide range of shops, closest shopping plaza to Disney.
Open: 9am-11pm.

The Neighbourhood Shops
2 blocks south of Hwy 192 on 17-92, Kissimmee
Restored turn-of-the-century homes, gift shops, galleries
and eateries.
Open: 10am-5pm, Saturday 10am-3pm.

5 IDEAS FOR DAYS OUT

Bok Tower Gardens

After a day at a theme park, a visit to Bok Tower Gardens makes a refreshing change. The atmosphere is peaceful and serene, and even the wildlife seems to know that it is protected. There are lots of squirrels and racoons, but while friendly, they are not tame and may scratch.

Bok Tower Gardens are 3 miles (5km) north of Lake Wales. It is an hour's drive south from Orlando. Take I-4 to US27 then cut across to Alternate US27 and follow the signs.

Bok Tower is one of Florida's most famous landmarks, located on the peninsula's highest point — 298ft (91m) above sea level. The historic 200ft (61m) bell tower, made of pink and grey Georgia marble and Florida limestone, is set in the center of 128 acres (51 hectares) of magnificent gardens, and houses one of the

Above: Cypress Gardens contains more than 8,000 different plants and flowers from 75 countries

world's greatest carillons — 57 bronze bells ranging in weight from 17lb to nearly 12 tons. Note the elaborate carvings on the walls of the tower and on the massive brass door.

The gardens contain thousands of azaleas, camelias, magnolias and other flowering plants which provide a year round display of color. There are 126 species of wild birds and all sorts of other wildlife to be seen from a hide where you can relax and watch turtles, other creatures and, maybe an alligator just a few feet away.

The gardens, formerly Mountain Lake Sanctuary, were presented to the nation in 1929 by publisher and author Edward Bok. The gardens were created in 1923 when Bok asked landscape architect Frederick Olmsted Junior to create a beautiful sanctuary out of the sandy scrub and pine covered hill known as Iron Mountain. The carillon was added in 1929 as a reminder to Bok of his native Netherlands, and the tower and sanctuary were dedicated by President Calvin Coolidge.

Old Cracker House, the visitor's center, presents an audiovisual tour of the garden, and has exhibits about the founder. There are daily carillon concerts with special events at Christmas and Easter and moonlight recitals.

Strollers and wheelchairs are available free of charge. There are free guided walking tours between mid-January and April Monday to Saturday at 12noon and 2pm, 2pm only on Sundays. There is a café and gift shop offering plants. Open: daily 8am-6pm. The bells chime every half hour and there is a recital of bell music every afternoon at 3pm ☎ 941-676-9412.

On your way home detour to Lake Wales and follow the signs for **Spooks Hill**, off US17 at the junction of North Avenue and 5th Street. The idea is to drive a little way up the hill, stop at the mark on the road, put the car in neutral and take your foot off the brake after making sure that there is nothing behind you. The car will start to roll slowly backwards down the hill, but if you look out of the rear window you will be certain that you are going uphill. No one knows how this illusion is created but there are lots of local yarns to explain why the hill got its name.

Cypress Gardens

Cypress Gardens combines a botanic garden, theme park and world famous water-ski spectacular. It opened on 1 January 1936 as Florida's first theme park, and is now the State's oldest continuously running attraction. It offers a delightful,

139

peaceful day out in a beautiful setting, but with other things to see and do to keep the family amused. Apart from the superb gardens, the park is equally famous for its water ski show and Southern Belles. The water ski shows started during World War II as a free attraction for servicemen stationed nearby, and many of the stunts now used in water-ski shows around the world were developed here. The ski show celebrated its fiftieth anniversary in 1994.

Take I-4 west to US27 south exit, through Winter Haven and then turn right at Waverly on Highway 540 west for about 5 miles (8km). The park is well signposted. There are two main parking areas, and parking is free. The park is open daily from 9.30am and closes at 5.30pm, although it stays open later during the summer. The information office is just inside the main entrance.

Baby strollers, wheelchairs and 35mm cameras can be rented from the **Bazaar Gift Shop.** Lockers are available for rent just inside the main entrance

If you want a behind-the-scenes tour of the nurseries, or a guided tour of the botanic gardens, call in advance to make arrangements.

Cypress Gardens covers 223 acres (89 hectares) and contains more than 8,000 plants and flowers from 75

Southern Belles

The Southern Belles, or Flowers of the South, are a unique feature of the park. It is said that after one particularly devastating winter storm which caused considerable damage in the garden, the owners had the women staff dress in the crinolines and hooped skirts worn before the Civil War. The aim was to distract the visitors away from the most badly damaged areas of the park. The idea was so successful, it is still a very popular feature of the park, and you never know when you are going to spot one of the Southern Belles, at strategically photogenic spots around the park.

countries worldwide. It is a delight throughout the year but especially so during the spring months.

The park is split into three areas with the botanic gardens on your right as you enter the main entrance, Lake Eloise, where the water ski show is performed, straight ahead, and the attractions on your left.

Take the guided **Botanical Gardens Cruise** around the park to see just how diverse the plant life is, then explore on foot, visiting the Florida Pool,

Oriental and French Gardens, the giant banyan tree and Overlook Vista. All the plants are labelled.

Attractions

You must see the 30 minute **Water Ski** show, full of stunts and amazing acrobatic feats, which climaxes with Cypress Garden's famous human pyramid on water skis.

The **Crossroads Arena** stages a spectacular 25 minute airborne show, featuring trapeze and trampoline artists and high-wire jugglers, while the **Cypress Theater** offers a very endearing bird show.

There is an antique radio museum, the American Water-skiing Museum, and a fascinating exhibit about the Popes, who created the park.

Cypress Junction boasts the biggest model railway, and certainly the best laid out, in the USA.

If you have a head for heights, you must experience **Kodak's Island in the Sky.** The structure takes you from ground level to 150ft (46m) above the park, and then the platform revolves to give you spectacular views over the surrounding countryside.

The **Wings of Wonder Butterfly Conservatory** set in four new gardens, is the latest exhibit, offering the opportunity to see hundreds of butterflies flying around in near-natural habitats. For further information ☎ 813-324-2111 or in Florida ☎ 1-800-282-2123.

Silver Springs

Silver Springs is the world's largest natural spring formation, created when Florida heaved itself up from the ocean half a million years ago. There are fourteen springs with names like Blue Lagoon, Bridal Chamber, Mammoth Spring and Florida Snowstorm. Every day 550 million gallons (2,500 million litres) of crystal clear pure water are pumped by Mother Nature through the springs. The water is so pure that with sunlight shining on it, you can see to incredible depths — well over 80ft (24m) down.

The water is also so clean that it is home to a huge variety of fish, and some of the largest striped bass found anywhere. There are also alligators, turtles, shellfish and more than 100 varieties of water plants.

The famous glass bottomed boats, which allow you to explore the underwater world of the springs, were invented here almost 100 years ago. You can take a 2.5 mile (4km) water safari through the park which contains more than 300 species of animals from many continents. The setting is so stunning that it has been used as the location for more than 200 film and TV shows, including many

Above: One of the colorful exhibits at Cypress Gardens

Below top: Boating on one of the many crystal-clear lakes in Seminole County

Below bottom: Wekiwa Springs State Park has lots of nature trails to explore around the cool, refreshing waters of Wekiwa Springs

Below: Sanford's Historic Waterfront district

of the Tarzan films. At **Animal Encounter**, children can pet the animals, and even get a giraffe to eat out of their hands. There are also reptile shows, and a vintage car collection.

Located just off I-75, 1 mile (2km) east of Silver Springs and 72 miles (116km) from Orlando (1.5 hours) the park is open year round from 9am-5pm, with extended opening during the summer. There is free parking and all the safari boats have covers just in case there is a shower.

Next to the park is **Wild Waters** a water theme park with giant wave pool and seven fast flumes.

Open: late March to mid-September ☎ 800-234-7458.

If you have time it is worth visiting **The Appleton Museum of Art**, 4333 E. Silver Springs Blvd, Ocala: a museum which spans 5,000 years of history featuring exhibits from around the world ☎ (904) 236-5050, and Don Garlits **Museum of Drag Racing**, 13,700 S.W 16th Ave, Ocala: dedicated to drag racing. Open: 9am-5.30pm daily ☎ (904) 245-8661.

Seminole County

North of Orlando lies Seminole County, an area full of clean

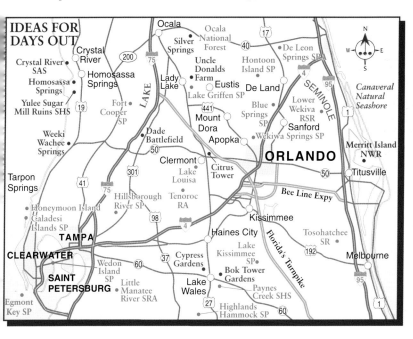

lakes, clear running rivers and lush tropical vegetation. It covers 344sq miles (892sq km) making it one of Florida's smallest counties, but it offers a wealth of opportunities if you are interested in sports and outdoor recreations. There are nine 18-hole golf courses and a number of public tennis courts.

Seminole County gets its name from the Indians who used to inhabit the area. The first white settlers did not arrive in force until after 1812 when the USA acquired Florida from Spain. The region developed quite fast, however, because of the St Johns River which was capable of carrying steamboats and paddleboats, Seminole County became a booming trade center and port.

By 1870, the area went through another significant transformation when General Henry Shelton Sanford, former lawyer and diplomat, bought a large plot of land because of its location and fertile soil. As a result, **Sanford** was born as well as Belair, a large orange grove and important experimental garden. A decade later, the region's expansion was boosted again with the building of the South Florida Railroad. It was completed in 1884 and linked Sanford with Longwood, Maitland and Orlando. A year later it had been extended to Jacksonville.

Rivers and lakes

Seminole County is bordered by the Wekiva River to the west, the St Johns River to the east and Lake Monroe to the north. In fact, the southern border is the only access without having to cross a bridge. The area is typified by pine woods and oak hammocks in the higher and drier areas, with lush cypress swamps and marshlands bordering the many lakes and rivers traversing the county. The St Johns is the longest navigable freshwater waterway in Florida, and the St Johns Basin and surrounding wetlands provide a natural habitat for a wide variety of plants and animal life, including the Florida alligator and endangered manatee.

Steamboats continued to operate, however, and were widely used by the federal government to bring in new settlers and ship the Seminole Indians out. Side-wheel steamboats were used because they were better able to manoeuvre the bends on the St Johns River. The river was used until the 1930s to carry both trade and tourists, but the newer, faster railroads then took over.

The large expanse of water makes the area ideal for fishing. There are more than 2,000 freshwater lakes providing world-class fishing for bass, bream, catfish and crappie year-round. There are a number of fishing camps along the St Johns and Wekiva, as well as on Lake Monroe, and expert guides are readily available. Fishing boats are available for rent or charter from the many marinas. Lake Jessup boasts the largest number of alligators per acre of lake anywhere in the USA.

If you fancy some gentle exercise, hire a canoe and go paddling off down the Wekiva River ☎ (407) 628-1482, or get an aerial view of the St Johns River aboard a seaplane ☎ (407) 331-5155.

The 6,398-acre (2,559-hectare) **Wekiwa Springs State Park**, on the Wekiva River, is central Florida's favorite watering hole, offering miles of clear spring-fed river meandering through an ancient and delicate semi-tropical forest. The water is always inviting, with a constant year-round temperature of 72°F (22°C). Picnic areas, 13 miles (21km) of trails for hiking and an 8-mile (13-km) horseback trail, as well as canoe rentals are available.

In addition, eighteen county-operated parks are located throughout Seminole County providing a wide range of recreational opportunities from fishing and camping to tennis and racquetball. Most are situated in untouched forests, along the shores of the area's many lakes, or under the shades of ancient oaks and pines.

The county's main areas of population are: Altamonte Springs, Casselberry, Lake Mary, Longwood, Oviedo, Sanford and Winter Springs. They are mostly residential cities with small business communities, but there are restaurants and many have older districts of historical interest.

Longwood is named after an 1876 Boston suburb, and like most of the cities in the area, is mainly a residential community. It does have, however, a very attractive restored historic district with gift and antique shops and restaurants. There is a brochure for a self-guided walking tour of the historic district. The impressive Longwood Hotel has served the Central Florida community for more than 100 years.

Sanford

Sanford has an interesting historic district and is also the southern terminal for the **Amtrak Auto Train**, which travels daily between Lorton,

145

Virginia, near the Washington D.C. area and Central Florida saving motorists the lengthy drive down from the north.

Main attractions

Big Tree Park, General Hutchinson Parkway, Sanford: Home of 'The Senator', the oldest and largest cypress tree in the world. This 3,500-year-old tree towers to 138ft (42m) and has a diameter of more than 17ft (5m), rivalling any Californian redwood in size and age.

Central Florida Zoological Park, Highway 17-92, Sanford: Home to more than 300 native and exotic animals, including birds, monkeys, reptiles and sea lions. Recent additions to the zoo include the endangered clouded leopard and the American bald eagle, and there is a new cheetah exhibit. Children can enjoy the petting zoo, as well as pony and elephant rides. Open: 9am-5pm daily ☎ (407) 323-4450.

Henry Shelton Sanford Memorial Museum, in 'historic Sanford': Houses books, pictures and furniture once owned by Sanford's founder. Open: daily ☎ 407 322 2212.

Sanford's Historic Waterfront District: Part of Florida's Main Street preservation project, Sanford's waterfront district has excellent examples of classic Victorian and 'Cracker-style' architecture typical of nineteenth-century Florida. Brochures for self-guided walking tours are available (allow 1 hour).

Seminole Historical Museum, Bush Boulevard: Contains exhibits of early Florida agriculture, transportation, steamboats and railroads, as well as a reproduction of the interior of a typical nineteenth-century Floridian family home. Open: daily ☎ 407 321 2489.

shopping
Seminole County

Altamonte Mall: On SR436 half a mile (1km) east of I-4 One of Florida's largest malls with four department stores and more than 175 shops plus restaurants.

Flea World: On Highway 17-92 between Longwood and Sanford.
America's largest flea market with 1,500 booths on the 104-acre (42-hectare) site, selling everything from antiques and arts and crafts to clothing and electronics. Fun World, to keep the children occupied, is next door. Open: every Friday and Saturday 10am-5pm.

Student Museum and Center for Social Studies, Sanford, on Highway 46 just west of 17/9: The fourth oldest school in Florida. Students can experience pioneer life by exploring a log cabin, trying on authentic costumes and performing the tasks of merchants and farmers. The museum is open to the public weekdays from 8am-3.30pm.

For further information:

Seminole County Convention and Visitors Bureau, PO Box 160816, Altamonte Springs, FL 32716-0816
☎ 1-800-800-7832
or (407) 834-3304.

Above: *Uncle Donald's Farm at Lady Lake*

Left: *The Florida Citrus Tower in Lake County*

Lake County

Lake County lies to the west and north-west of Orlando, and is named after the hundreds of shimmering lakes which occupy more than 200sq miles (518sq km) of the county's total 1,200sq miles (3,110sq km). It is part of the Central Highlands with most of the land between 50ft and 190ft (15m and 58m) above sea level, making it one of the few places in Florida to boast rolling hills, albeit not very high ones.

Like Seminole County, it is an area made for outdoor activities and sports. There is gliding, parachuting, tennis, golf, cycling and hiking, and, of course, an enormous range of water-based activities.

Fishing, especially for bass, attracts amateurs and professionals alike, and there are a number of big-dollar competitions. Other fish which are plentiful and popular are blue bream, shellcrackers, stripers, speckled perch and catfish. There is no shortage of bait and tackle shops, and most lakes have boat ramps to provide easy access.

Boats of all sizes can be found on the lakes and the Chain of Lakes allows craft to make their way to the Atlantic Ocean. The Dora Canal, which connects Lakes Dora and Eustis, was once described as 'the most beautiful half-mile of water in the world.' A number of boat owners offer cruises along the Dora Canal.

The area's most famous landmark is the **Florida Citrus Tower**, 15 miles (24km) north-west of Orlando on US Highway 27 in Clermont. The views from the top of the tower are stunning and show just how much water there is in Lake County. The communities of Lake County have a special charm all of their own. **Mount Dora** is typical of most with its lovingly preserved turn-of-the-century homes, covered sidewalks and fascinating

Florida Citrus Tower

Florida Citrus Tower, Clermont. Built in 1956 on one of the highest hills in the State, the tower rises 226ft (69m) and the top is the highest point in Florida. Two of the tower's observation decks are reached by elevator from the first flooor lobby. Before the big freezes of 1983 and 1985 which decimated the citrus groves, the views from the top of the tower used to embrace more than 17 million citrus trees. At the top of the tower, built to withstand winds of 190 miles (306km) an hour, are carillon bells which chime at regular intervals. There is a restaurant and gift shop, as well as a glass artists' workshop and the Carolyn Candies manufacturing plant. There is a shop, of course, so that you can buy the finished sweets ☎ (904) 394-8585.

stores. **The Lakeside Inn** in Mount Dora was built in 1883 and is now listed in the National Register of Historic Places. Eustis, Tavares, Leesburg and Clermont all have their historic buildings and delightful antique and crafts shops.

The **Renningers Antique Market** in Mount Dora which opens on Saturdays and Sundays can have up to 500 dealers showing their antiques and collectibles.

Clermont has been hugely successful in attracting world-class athletes and is now known as the triathlon capital of the world. This gruelling race involves a 2.4-mile (3.8-km) swim, followed by a 112 mile (180km) cycle ride and then a full marathon over 26.2 miles (42.1km).

Places to Visit

House of Presidents Wax Museum, on US27 in Clermont ☎ (904) 394-2836.

Lake County Fairgrounds, at Eustis: Used for rodeos and a number of other activities.

Lake Griffin State Recreation Area, three miles (5km) north of Leesburg on 441/27: A 427-acre (171-hectare) park with camping, nature study, swimming, canoe rental and picnic pavilion. Famous for its bass fishing.

Lake Louisa State Park, on Lake Nellie Road, 2.5 miles (4km) off SR561: A 1,790-acre (716-hectare) State Park with bath house and picnic tables.

Lakeridge Winery and Vineyards: The winery and vineyards in Clermont give you the chance of visiting one of Florida's two vineyards and sampling the produce (with grape juice for the children). Florida is the home of American wine because the first wine was produced by French Huguenots using local Muscadine grapes around 1562. The vineyards will eventually cover 110 acres (44 hectares) when the current 3-year planting programme is completed. Open: 10am-6pm Monday to Saturday, 12noon-6pm Sunday ☎ (904) 394-8627.

Ocala National Forest, three miles (5km) north of Altoona on SR19: A 450,000-acre (180,000-hectare) national forest with nature, cycling and riding trails and campsites.

Uncle Donald's Farm, in Griffin Avenue, Lady Lake: An educational petting and real working farm. There are hayrides, birds of prey exhibit and a wildlife rehabilitation refuge. Open: 10am-5pm Tuesday to Saturday, 12 noon-4pm Sunday (January to April) ☎ (904) 753-2882.

calendar
Lake County

JANUARY

- **Leesburg:** fishing tournament on Chain-of-Lakes
- **Eustis:** Lake County Farmer's market, every Thursday throughout the year at the Lake County Fairgrounds

FEBRUARY

- **Mount Dora:** Art Festival which attracts thousands of visitors
- **Eustis:** Washington's Birthday Celebrations & Miss Eustis Pageant
- **Clermont:** Lakeridge Winery Winefest

MARCH

- **Leesburg:** Fun and Arts Festival
- **Mount Dora:** Antique Boat Festival
- **Altoona:** Lake County Boys Ranch Professional Rodeo, Boys Ranch Arena
- **Clermont:** Spring Sprint Triathlon

APRIL

- **Eustis:** Lake County Fair
- **Sorrento:** Derby Day Harness Racing, Simpson Training Center

- **Mount Dora:** Antique Auto Show and Tour, Mount Dora Sailing Regatta
- **Fruitland Park:** Fruitland Park Day, parade, bazaar, arts and crafts
- **Clermont:** Great Clermont Triathlon

MAY

- **Mount Dora:** Arts in the Park
- **Clermont:** Scholastic Rowing Regatta
- **Groveland:** Liz Allen Open Water Ski Tournament, Lake David

JUNE

- **Lady Lake:** Ice Cream Social, entertainment, antique car show

JULY

- **Groveland:** The Superstars Water Ski Tournament, Lake David (4th of July weekend).
- 4th of July Celebration and Miss Groveland Pageant.
- Groveland Fire Department Car Show
- **Clermont:** Melon Man Triathlon

- **Tavares:** 4th of July Celebration and fireworks display
- **Leesburg:** 4th of July Parade

AUGUST

- **Groveland:** Summer Sizzler Triathlon

SEPTEMBER

- **Clermont:** Labor Day Festival on the lake, arts and crafts, races

OCTOBER

- **Clermont:** Florida Challenge Triathlon, Great Floridian Triathlon
- Octoberfest arts and crafts festival
- **Lakeridge** Winery October Wine Festival
- **Sorrento:** Octoberfest
- **Mount Dora:** Invitational Golf Tournament
- Bicycle Festival
- Annual Mount Dora Craft Fair

NOVEMBER

- **Clermont:** Triathlon Championships
- **Eustis:** Annual Eustis International Folk Festival
- **Tavares:** Annual Christmas-by-the-Lake Arts and Crafts Festival

DECEMBER

- **Umatilla:** Christmas Parade, arts and crafts show
- **Mount Dora:** Tree Lighting, Christmas Parade
- **Leesburg:** Tree Lighting ceremony and Christmas Parade
- **Tavares:** Tree Lighting
- **Groveland:** Christmas Parade
- **Clermont:** Light-Up Clermont and lighted boat parade, arts and crafts show
- **Astor:** Christmas Boat Parade

The John P Donnelly House at Mount Dora, built in 1893

STATE NATIONAL PARKS, HISTORIC SITES & RECREATION AREAS

Blue Spring State Park

Located to the west of Orange City on French Avenue.

The botanist John Bartram was asked to carry out an exploration of the St Johns River in 1755, 3 years after England acquired Florida from Spain, to see if it had any resources which might be useful to the Crown. His account, written up on 4 January 1766, described his visit to Blue Spring. It has always been an important area for flora and fauna, and is an important winter home for the manatees who gather in the spring's constant 72°F (22°C) waters. Also on offer is camping, fishing, swimming, snorkelling, canoeing and boating in the adjoining Blue Spring Run and St Johns River. Cabins are also available for rent but must be booked in advance.

De Leon Springs State Recreation Area

Located in De Leon Springs on the corner of Ponce De Leon and Burt Parks Road.

A wonderful place to picnic and swim in the crystal clear waters of the springs which deliver 19 million gallons (86 ml) of water a day. There are canoes to rent and you can make breakfast pancakes at the Old Spanish Sugar Mill Restaurant.

Highlands Hammock State Park

Located on SR6, 3.4 miles (6km) west of Sebring.

This 3,800-acre (1,520-hectare) park opened in 1931 and is evidence of Florida's long standing commitment to preserve public lands for all to enjoy. Local citizens concerned that the woodland area was to be cleared for farming, campaigned to preserve it, and then handed it over to the Florida Park Service which was created in 1935. It is an area rich in wildlife, and an excellent place to spot white-tailed deer and alligators. The interpretative center explains the park's history and wildlife and is worth a visit before walking the many trails. There are camping and horse-riding facilities.

Hontoon Island State Park

Six miles (10km) west of De Land.

A 1,650-acre (660-hectare) park whose first settlers were Timucuan Indians. Their mounds can still be seen close to the park's nature trail. Before being bought by the State in 1967, the island had a boat yard, cattle ranch and pioneer homestead. Today it is only accessible by private boat or the free passenger ferry which operates daily from 9am till one hour before sunset. There are facilities for camping, fishing, canoeing, boating and picnicking, and there are cabins for rent. There is also an 80ft (24m) observation tower.

Lake Kissimmee State Park

Off SR60, 15 miles (24km) east of Lake Wales.

In the heart of pioneer cattle country, the 5,030-acre (2,012-hectare) park consists of a huge wilderness area and a living history exhibition of an 1876 'cow camp'. The park, offering great fishing, surrounds Lake Kissimmee, Florida's third largest, and Lakes Tiger and Rosalie. There are canoes for hire, boat ramps, wilderness campsites and facilities for group camping. The wildlife is abundant and there is an observation tower which can be scaled to give spectacular views over the woodlands and water. From the tower or the 13 miles (21km) of nature trails, you can spot white-tailed deer, bald eagles, sandhill cranes, turkey vultures and the occasional bobcat. The park has nine distinct plant communities and more than fifty endangered or special-concern animals.

Lower Wekiva River State Reserve

Nine miles (14km) west of Sanford on SR46.

This 4,636 acre (1,854 hectare) reserve is ideal for watching Central Florida's wildlife. The reserve is bordered by St Johns and Blackwater Creeks and the Wekiva River. The plant life is particularly rich, but its main attraction is the unique system of blackwater streams and wetlands, which provide ideal habitats for black bears, otters, alligators, wood storks and sandhill cranes. There are facilities for canoeing, hiking, camping and wilderness camping although numbers are restricted to protect the environment.

Paynes Creek State Historic Site

Half a mile (1km) east of Bowling Green on SR664A.

The site of a trading post set up to attract the Indians because the white settlers wanted to keep them away from their own settlements around what is now Tampa. When the Seminoles attacked the trading post and killed two of the clerks, a chain of forts was planned along the northern boundary of the Indian Reservation to protect the white settlers. The first fort was built 1.5 miles (2km) from the trading post. There are exhibits telling the story of the Seminole Indians and the trading post. Facilities for picnics, hiking and fishing.

Rock Springs Run State Reserve

In Sorrento off SR46 via SR433.

The reserve spreads out for 12 miles (19km) along the frontage of Rock Springs Run and the Wekiva River and offers hiking, wilderness and group camping, horse riding trails and canoeing. Permits are required for wilderness camping and numbers are controlled.

Tenoroc Recreation Area

North-east of Lakeland on SR659.

An excellent bass fishing area in what was once the site of a large open cast phosphate mine. The area has been reclaimed and now offers wilderness camping, hiking, fishing, horse riding trails and boating. There is a boat ramp and picnic areas. You should check with the

park rangers about what water craft are allowed.

Tosohatchee State Reserve

Off SR50 on Taylor Creek Road in Christmas.

Mainly a wildlife and nature study area covering 28,000 acres (11,200 hectares) and with 19 miles (31km) of frontage on the St John's River. There are also facilities for wilderness camping, hiking, horse riding, cycling and fishing. The reserve is a vast area of swamps, marshes, pine flatlands and wooded hammocks, the result of centuries of alternating fire, caused by lightning, and flood.

Wekiwa Springs State Park

On Wekiwa Springs Road off SR434 or 436 near Apopka. A 6,900-acre (2,760-hectare) park with a wide variety of flora and fauna. The springs are the headwater for the Wekiva River which flows for 15 miles (24km) into the St John's. It is the southern range for the black bear. Activities include wilderness camping, 13 miles (21km) of hiking trails, group camping, an 8 mile (13km) horseback riding trail, canoeing, swimming and nature study. Canoes are available for rent.

Highlands Hammock State Park

6 CENTRAL GULF COAST

TAMPA

The warm waters, golden sands and year round sunshine of the Central Gulf Coast make the Tampa area an ideal holiday location. It is an area steeped in rich history and tales of pirates and buried treasure abound. It is an area that caters to all tastes. The beaches, sea and attractions make it ideal for families, the wealth of open-air activities have earned it the title '*World Capital of Sport*' and at night there is wining, dining and dancing and a host of other entertainments to attract you, whatever your interests.

History

In the early sixteenth century, the first European explorers visited the Gulf Coast. It is likely that Ponce de Leon sailed into Tampa Bay during his exploration along the west

Above: The Flying Montu ride at Busch Gardens®

coast of Florida in 1521, and in the spring of 1539 Hernando de Soto, Governor of Cuba, sailed into Tampa Bay in search of gold. An Indian fishing settlement was called *Tanpa*, meaning 'Sticks of Fire' and this somehow got changed over the years into Tampa.

In 1772 a Dutch cartographer Bernard Romans named the area around Tampa Bay as Hillsborough, in honour of Lord Hillsborough, Secretary of State for the Colonies. Many of the early settlements were attacked by Indians, and it was not until the Seminole Wars of the nineteenth century that an army base was established at Fort Brooke in 1824. Many soldiers who were posted there returned after the wars to settle in the area. By 1846 Tampa had acquired town status, and the pace of settlement speeded up.

During the Civil War, the Confederates surrendered the fort after being bombarded by Union gunboats.

The railroad arrived in 1883, the brainchild of Henry Plant. The Southern Florida Railroad, connecting Tampa with markets throughout the USA, attracted new business and industry as well as rich entrepreneurs. A causeway was built over the Gulf and piers for ocean going vessels. Plant also started a steamship line sailing between Tampa, Key West and Havana. The port expanded and the railroad helped the area develop as a tourist resort. In 1885 Vincente Martinez Ybor moved to the area from Key West, and the following year established the first cigar factory. Cigars are still made in **Ybor City** (pronounced Ee-bor), now Tampa's Cuban Quarter.

Did you know that Tampa...

- hosts the Florida State Fair every February;
- is invaded by pirates every February during the month-long Gasparilla Festival;
- has the seventh largest port in the USA and is the largest in Florida;
- has the longest continuous sidewalk and the smallest park in the USA;
- has the world's only fully-rigged pirate ship. The *José Gasparilla* sets sail every year during the Gasparilla Festival to invade the city; and...
- produces 90 per cent of tropical fish found in aquariums in the USA

An old Tampa joke is to say that 'my mother was a stripper and my father a boxer'. Both refer to different jobs on the cigar-rolling assembly line. At one time almost 12,000 people worked in the 200 cigar factories.

In 1891 Plant opened the 511-room **Tampa Bay Hotel**, based on a Moorish Temple, and in 1898 Colonel Theodore 'Teddy' Roosevelt and his Rough Riders trained in the extensive grounds before sailing for Cuba during the Spanish-American War. The hotel, the first in Tampa to have electric power, is now used as offices by the University of Tampa, and also houses a small museum. It is now a National Historic Landmark.

Present day

Tampa's waterfront includes a picturesque harbor and elegant walkways, shops and restaurants, as well as the port, the seventh largest in the USA. New terminals are being built to handle the growing number of ships sailing into the port. During 1994, Carnival Cruise Lines and American Family Cruises joined Holland America, Regency Cruises and Odess America who operate from Tampa. You can dine by the water's edge or take a dinner cruise aboard a paddlewheeler or luxury yacht.

The **Garrison Seaport Center** incorporates the **Florida Aquarium**, the $70 million Whydah Pirate Collection, a new cruise ship terminal, a 16,000 seat amphitheater, cinema complex, shops and restaurants.

Downtown Tampa has long been noted for its patronage of the arts, and a brochure of public art on display is available from the Art in Public Places office, or from local museums and galleries. Many of these works of art are in the lobbies of company offices, but members of the public are allowed access during normal business hours.

Among the many fine works on display are Geoffrey Naylor's 90ft (27m) tall aluminium wall relief sculpture in the lobby of the First Florida Bank, on the corner of Tampa and Madison streets; William Severson's solar powered hanging sculpture on the corner of Franklin and Zack Streets; and Charles Fager's ceramic work hanging in the lobby of Tampa City Center.

Tampa's Museum of Science and Industry was trebled in size in 1995 and includes a 350-seat Omnimax Theater where films are projected on an 85ft (26m) high domed screen — another first for Florida. The **Tampa Museum of Art** has also been remodelled and expanded — it has both permanent and changing exhibitions.

KEY TO MAIN ATTRACTIONS

1. Boatyard Village
2. Boyd Hill Nature Park
3. Florida Military Aviation Museum
4. Great Explorations
5. Largo Heritage Park & Museum
6. Marine Aquarium & Science Center
7. Moccasin Lake Nature Park
8. Museum Of Fine Arts
9. Ruth Eckerd Hall
10. Fort De Soto Park
11. St Petersburg Historical & Flight One Museum
12. St Petersburg Pier
13. Salvador Dali Museum
14. Sawgrass Lake Park
15. Science Center
16. Sea Screamer
17. Suncoast Botanical Gardens
18. Suncoast Seabird Sanctuary
19. Sunken Gardens
20. Busch Gardens
21. Tampa Jai - Alai Fronton
22. Tampa's Rocky Point RA
23. Whydah Pirate Complex
24. Tampa Bay Downs
25. Sacred Heart
26. Tampa Stadium
27. Tampa Bay Convention Center
28. José Gasparilla
29. Tampa Greyhound Track
30. Fairground Factory Outlet Mall
31. East Lake Square Mall
32. Eyes Mind Museum
33. Adventure Island
34. Museum of Science & Industry
35. Henry Plant Museum
36. University of South Florida
37. West Shore Plaza
38. Schlitz
39. Bobby's Seminole Indian Village
40. Ben T Davis Municipal Beach
41. Garrison Seaport Center
42. Kopsick Palm Arboretum
43. Gamble Plantation Historic Site SP

Hillsborough County

Tampa has a population of around 280,000 and surrounding it is Hillsborough County, with a total population of 834,000. It offers a wide range of activities and entertainments and attracts about 4.5 million visitors a year. While the area is a rich farming region, especially strawberries and citrus, there are also around thirty-six golf courses, including ones designed by Arnold Palmer and Robert Trent Jones. The **Saddlebrook Golf and Tennis Resort**, 12 miles (19km) north of Tampa, is set in 480 acres (194 hectares) and is now the world headquarters for the Arnold Palmer Golf Academy, which offers courses of varying durations for all ages and

abilities. There are rivers to canoe along, hiking and horse riding trails and an abundance of wildlife to spot. There are more than 1,000 public and private tennis courts, waterfront boulevards for running and cycling, and Hillsborough's 100 parks offer freshwater fishing, swimming, canoeing, horseback riding and hiking.

While Tampa itself does not have any beaches, it does have a number of resort complexes, as well as major attractions. The nearby Gulf and lakes offer swimming, jet skiing, windsurfing and parasailing. You can rent motorboats, paddleboats and pontoons, and further out, you can try your hand at scuba diving or deep sea fishing among the reefs and wrecks.

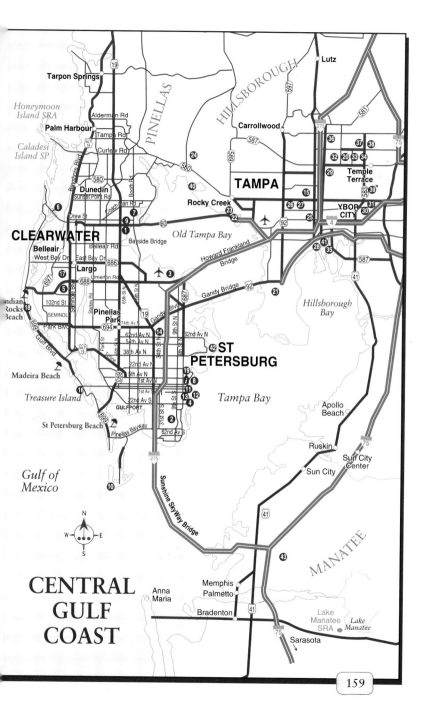

CENTRAL GULF COAST

159

Getting Around

Tampa is on Florida's Gulf Coast in Hillsborough County which covers 1,000sq miles (2,592sq km) of land and includes two interstate highways and an express toll road.

Almost every attraction and hotel is within 5 miles (8km) of either I-275 which runs north to south, or I-4, which runs east to west. Tampa's Crosstown Expressway runs from Gandy Boulevard east to the Brandon area.

The speed limit in residential areas and business districts is 30mph (48kph). There is plentiful parking throughout the area and metered parking is enforced between 8am and 5pm Monday to Friday.

Tampa International Airport is one of the best in the USA and the largest on the Gulf Coast. The facilities are excellent and it is consistently voted one of the best international airports worldwide. Whether arriving on domestic or international flights, there is very clear sign-posting with moving walkways and shuttles to most areas, including the massive new parking complex. All the major car rental companies are at the airport and there are courtesy coaches to most of the hotels, as well as taxi and limousine services.

The HART Line (Hillsborough Area Regional Transit) provides most of the public transport in the area. There are forty-two bus routes throughout the Tampa area and the main terminus is in Marion Street in Downtown Tampa. The PeopleMover monorail provides transportation downtown and to and from Harbor Island.

Greyhound buses operate out of Tampa and are located at 610 Polk Street, while Amtrak stops at the station at the junction of Nebraska Avenue and Twiggs Street.

Busch Gardens

Undoubtedly the Gulf Coast's main attraction and not to be missed. A 300-acre (120-hectare) combination of theme parks, rides, non-stop entertainment, zoo and the world's largest brewery, Busch Gardens has a lot to offer and is constantly adding new attractions to appeal to the thrill-seekers in particular.

Busch Gardens is based on turn-of-the-century Africa, the Dark Continent, and there are ten themed areas. The zoo is the fourth largest in the USA, and one of the best ways of seeing the hundreds of animals is to take the Skyride cable car which allows you to look down on the wildlife roaming free on the Serengeti Plain. You can also take the Trans-Veldt railway which circles the park. Moats and natural barriers, rather

— BUSCH GARDENS —
Essential Information

- Arrive well before opening time or wait until later to avoid waiting.

- If planning to visit other Busch attractions (Sea World of Florida or Adventure Island) take advantage of combination tickets.

- On arrival pick up a schedule giving show times and a map of the park.

- Apart from the regular shows there are often special performances and details of these are listed on the Daily Entertainment Schedule in Morocco.

- If you need assistance or information, ask at the Guest Relations window.

- If you have a baby, there is a baby changing and nursing area in Dwarf Village.

- Cameras are available on loan from the One Hour Photo shop near the Main Entrance. Film is sold at gift shops throughout the park.

- Foreign currency and travelers cheques can be exchanged at the Guest Relations Office.

- Plan your day and work round the park in a logical order (anti-clockwise), fitting in attractions between shows.

- Some rides are restricted to children above or below a certain height. There may also be size and physical condition restrictions.

- Wear loose casual clothing and comfortable shoes while visiting the park, and remember items may fall out of your pockets while on some rides.

- Protect cameras while on wet rides such as the Congo River Rapids.

- You do not have to carry purchases around with you all day. Pick them up from the Sahara Traders Gift shop after leaving the park and remember to keep your receipt.

- If, you have trouble with your car when leaving, lift the hood and the roving Parking Patrol will come to your aid.

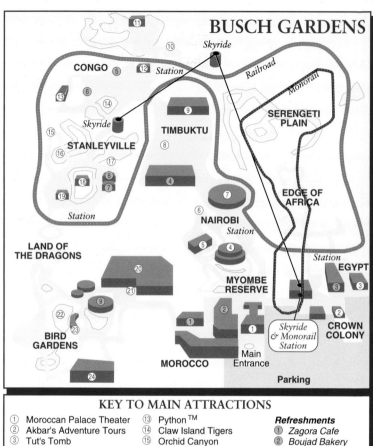

BUSCH GARDENS

KEY TO MAIN ATTRACTIONS

1. Moroccan Palace Theater
2. Akbar's Adventure Tours
3. Tut's Tomb
4. Curiosity Caverns
5. Animal Nursery
6. Petting Zoo
7. Asian Elephants
8. Scorpion
9. Dolphin Theater
10. Kumba
11. Congo River Rapids
12. Umbanga-Banga Bumper Cars
13. Python ™
14. Claw Island Tigers
15. Orchid Canyon
16. Tanganyika Tidal Wave
17. Stanley Falls
18. Stanleyville Theater
19. Zambesi Pavilion
20. Anheuser-Busch Brewery
21. Eagle Canyon
22. Flamingo Island
23. Bird Show Theater
24. Koala Display

Refreshments
1. *Zagora Cafe*
2. *Boujad Bakery*
3. *Crown Colony House Restaurant*
4. *Festhaus*
5. *Vivi Restaurant*
6. *Python Ice Cream*
7. *Stanleyville Smokehouse*
8. *Bazaar Cafe*
9. *Hospitality House*

than bars, are used to keep the animals in.

Members of the Conservation Information staff can be found throughout the park offering brief presentations and willing to answer any questions you may have.

The following is a description of the themed areas, touring

Above: Join the Egypt sand dig at Busch Gardens
Left: Getting close to the gorillas at Myombe Reserve

spectacular, *Around The World On Ice*, the park's most popular show. Other attractions include the **Tangiers Theater**, and a wide range of shops and gift stores. If you want to eat, try the Zagora Cafe or the Boujad Bakery, where delicious pastries are cooked daily. The Ice Cream Parlor specializes in strawberry-topped waffle cones crammed with the ice cream flavour of your choice.

Busch Gardens in an anti-clockwise direction, as this is the most convenient way.

Morocco

This is the first of the themed areas immediately inside the main entrance. There are belly dancers and snake charmers who perform daily in the **Sultan's Tent**. There is the **Mystic Sheiks Marching Band** and the **Moroccan Palace Theater** which features an ice

Egypt

Travel through time and discover the mystery and intrigue of Egypt then soar at 60mph (96kmph) and more on **Montu**, the largest inverted roller coaster in the world.

Visit a meticulous re-creation of Tutenkamun's tomb, and take part in your own archaeological dig. Take in *Akbar's*

Adventure Tours, a fast-paced motion picture adventure with audio-animation, the latest in flight simulation technology special effects and sound which combine to provide a fun but hair-raising trip.

Myombe Reserve

One of the newest themed areas featuring gorillas and chimpanzees in a spectacular tropical environment, which allows you to watch the animals from literally a couple of feet away. There are also audio-visual presentations and park staff on hand to tell you more about these creatures.

Crown Colony

This is on the right hand side of the park between Morocco and Myombe Reserve and many people must rush past it in their haste to get to the rides. You should head there if you want to take the Skyride, Monorail or Questor, or see the magnificent Anheuser-Busch Clydesdale Shire horses.

At the **Anheuser-Busch Hospitality Center** you can enjoy a beer (if old enough) and enjoy a pizza or deli sandwich. If you prefer a more substantial meal, dine in the **Crown Colony House Restaurant** with splendid views over the **Serengeti Plain**.

Nairobi

Features Asian elephants, a petting zoo and an animal nursery.

The nursery is in Nairobi's **Field Station** and you can discreetly watch very young animals who are ill or have been rejected by their mothers and have to be reared by human surrogate mums. Visit **Curiosity Caverns** where you can watch strange creatures flying, eating and exploring in naturalistic surroundings. The Kenya Kanteen offers snacks, drinks and other light refreshments. The **Trans-Veldt Railroad** runs from the Nairobi station touring the Serengeti Plain and stopping at the Congo and Stanleyville Stations. **The Backbones of Life** exhibit explains how creatures evolved on earth.

Edge of Africa

Edge of Africa is the park's latest themed area. It is a safari adventure offering closer than ever before encounters with some of the world's most fascinating animals. The 15-acre (7-hectare) attraction is a recreation of the African Serengeti and is packed with hippoes, giraffes, lions, baboons, meerkats, crocodiles, hyenas and many other species.

Visit the **welcome center** first to find out what animals have been sighted and where. Your journey aboard safari vehicles takes you through the remains of an old fishing village where you can observe hippoes from both above and below the water, a deserted Masai village and a research center. Roaming safari guides and naturalists offer informal talks about the animals and their habitat, adventure guidebooks are also available so that you can identify what you see. Mealtimes in Edge of Africa are staggered so that the animals don't get into daily routines but you can get a grandstand view by first checking the mealtime roster in the welcome center.

For those who don't want to explore the area on the safari trucks, the Monorail offers a bird's eye view.

The Serengeti Plain

Wildlife, including exotic birds, baboons, buffalo, impala, camels, zebras, giraffes, gazelles, camels, hippos and rhinos can move around freely as they would on the African plains in the 160 acre (64 hectares) paddock.

Timbuktu

Just beyond the elephant enclosure **Timbuktu** has rides for all ages, including the near heart-stopping **Scorpion**, another of the roller-coaster rides for which Busch Gardens has become famous. This one has a 360 degree loop. This themed area also includes the **Dolphin Theater**, which stages the *Dolphins of the Deep* several times daily, and Das Festhaus, offering German style food and entertainment in a family Oktoberfest atmosphere. There are many children's rides, as well as shops, crafts, bazaars and arcade and fair games.

The Congo

Home to several of the park's most popular attractions. Rare white Bengal tigers prowl on the aptly-named Claw Island, and for the thrill seekers, there are the **Kumba** and **Python** roller coasters. The Python is a double corkscrew ride and is not for the faint hearted. There are also the white-water rapids on the Congo River to navigate and, as you are likely to get wet, make sure cameras are protected. If you have valuables which you want to protect, lockers are provided for those people waiting to take rides on Kumba or the Congo River Rapids. Other attractions include Ubanga-Banga Bumper Cars, Monstrous Mamba and many children's rides and games. Apart from the gift shops there is the Vivi Storehouse Restaurant, and Python Ice Cream.

Stanleyville

Named after the famous 'Dr Livingstone, I presume' explorer, this is the next themed area. If you really like getting wet, head for the **Tanganyika Tidal Wave.** After a deceptively peaceful journey through Orchid Canyon, the boat starts to climb and then hurtles down the drop for the water splash. Or, climb aboard a 'dug out canoe' for a journey over the Stanley Falls.

Also find time to take in the variety show at the **Stanleyville Theater** and the improvised comedy routines at the **Zambesi Theater**. The Stanleyville Smokehouse offers chicken, beef and ribs slow smoked for hours, while the Bazaar Cafe sells Bar-B-Q beef sandwiches. Other exhibits include **Orchid Canyon**, featuring plants and exotic animals from the tropics. Animals on display elsewhere include orangutangs and snakes.

The Bird Gardens

This is the final themed area, full of shaded walks and hidden away places to delight children. There is Flamingo Island, Eagle Canyon, the Koala Display and a host of exotic birds.

Above: *Akbar holds a hornbill and ball python as he prepares to lead "Akbar's Adventure Tours" at Egypt, Busch Gardens*

Time for a beer

One must not forget that Busch Gardens is the home of the world's largest brewery. At the Hospitality House if you are aged 21 or over, you can try two complimentary samples of beer while listening to the shows which alternate between the rocking 60's and country music. You may be asked for identification to prove your age.

The brewery visit is also worth making time for. You learn how the beer is made and take in a trip to one of the world's most modern bottling plants.

An African lion cub at home in the Nairobi area of Busch Gardens

The Bird Show Theater has hourly shows featuring birds of the world, and the **Hospitality House Stage** offers musical variety including jazz and ragtime.

There are lots of games and rides for children, shops and gift stores, while the Hospitality House and Gingerbread House offer refreshments.

The latest attraction is *'Hollywood Live On Ice'*, a 35 minute tribute on ice to some of Hollywood's most memorable moments from the silent movies to today.

Lorikeet Landing

Themed with waterfalls, floral landscapes and ponds is the park's latest aviary habitat.

Other Tampa Attractions

The map for this section can be found on page 159.

Bobby's Seminole Indian Village is a tax haven. As it is Indian land, it has its own laws and taxes which is why you can often see people waiting to buy duty-free cigarettes. Because of the tax laws, gambling is also allowed for big money, especially Seminole Bingo, when very large cash prizes can be paid out ☎ (813) 620-3077.

To learn more about the Seminole Indians and their culture, visit the **Seminole Culture Center** on North Orient Road. There is a Seminole Indian village of thatched (chickee) houses and a museum tracing their history in Florida. There is also the chance to buy goods at the trading post, and there are regular shows featuring snakes and alligator wrestling.

Next door to Busch Gardens, and owned by the same company is **Adventure Island**, a 19-acre (8-hectare) water adventure park with beach area, slides, chutes and wave machines that produce very realistic and endless surf. **Aruba Tuba** allows you to hurtle through open and closed tube sections seated on inner tubes, and travelling at 20ft (6m) a second. Open: 10am-5pm daily spring to fall. Late opening during summer ☎ (813) 987-5600.

The *José Gasparilla*, docked on Bayshore Boulevard, is claimed to be the world's only full-rigged pirate ship.

Children's Museum of Tampa, 7550 N. Boulevard with indoor and outdoor educational and entertaining activities ☎ (813) 935-8441.

Eye's Mind Museum, on East Busch Boulevard, was opened by the Raja Yoga Education and Research Foundation and has a number of displays which aim to illustrate the meaning of many of the Foundation's beliefs, such as reincarnation, Karma and God.

The **Florida Aquarium**, at Garrison Seaport Center, on

the Downtown Waterfront, opened in 1995 costing $84 million. It is one of the largest and most modern aquariums in the USA. Visitors to the 152,000sq ft (14,128sq m) attraction follow the path of a drop of water from the freshwater springs and limestone caves of the aquifer, through rivers and wetlands, to the beaches and open seas.

The three-level, glass-domed structure features four exhibit areas: springs and wetlands; bay and barrier beach; a coral reef and the Gulf Stream and open ocean. It also has a collection of more than 450 animals and exhibits focussing on Florida conservation issues. ☎ (813) 273-4000.

Canoe Escape, 9335 East Fowler Avenue, Thonotosassa, Tampa Fl 33592, allows you to paddle your own canoe through Hillsborough County's 16,000 acre-(6,400-hectare) **Wilderness Park**. You can rent canoes for a couple of hours or all day and spot alligators, otter, deer, turtles and scores of birds. Open: 8am-5pm Monday to Friday, 8am-6pm Saturday and Sunday ☎ (813) 986-2067.

Downtown Trolley Services run a trolley service between Downtown and Ybor City, port, aquarium and Convention Center.

Harbor Island is a totally renovated area and now contains hotels, luxury apartments and the **Harbor Island Market**, a very upmarket shopping mall. The **PeopleMover** monorail transports you to and from the island and to Downtown Tampa.

The **Henry Plant Museum**, 401 West Kennedy Boulevard, is on the university campus, and has an exhibition depicting the life of Plant and how he shaped Tampa at the end of the nineteenth century. Open: 10am-4pm Tuesday to Saturday, 12noon-4pm Sunday ☎ (813) 254-1891.

Lowry Park Zoo, 7530 North Boulevard, offers the opportunity to see many of Florida's native species in their natural habitat, including the endangered manatee. There is even a manatee hospital to treat the injured mammals, particularly vulnerable to injuries from the outboard motors of boats.

You can also see in the 12-acre (5-hectare) **Florida Wildlife Center**, armadillo, white tailed deer, black bear, river otter, alligators and Florida panthers and many species of birds. Even bison and wolves, which once roamed northern Florida, are exhibited. The rest of the zoo is well laid out with lots of trees for shade and picnic areas. There is also a children's area where smaller animals can be petted. The zoo is in Lowry Park which has picnic facilities and nature trails. Open: 9.30am-5pm daily

The Museum of Science and Industry

The Museum of Science and Industry, at 4801 East Fowler Avenue opposite the University of Southern Florida, is Florida's largest museum and specializes in hands-on exhibits. It has a planetarium, a butterfly encounter exhibit, and many other hands-on natural phenomena, including one that allows you to feel a shark's tooth. Every hour you can experience what it feels like to be caught in a hurricane. An exciting $35 million expansion more than tripled the museum's size in 1995, making it the largest science center in the South-east. The additions include **Omnimax Theater**, permanent exhibitions, more nature trails and the first public library in a US museum. The various nature trails cleverly take you through different Florida habitats. Open: 9am-5pm Sunday to Thursday, 9am-9pm Friday and Saturday ☎ (813) 985-5535 or (813) 987-6300.

during winter, 9.30am-6pm rest of year ☎ (813) 935-8552.

Museum of African-American Art, 1308 Marion Street, opened in 1991 and is devoted to visual art by and about people of African descent. It also houses the **Barnett-Aden Collection** of more than 140 works of African-American art, one of the most historically significant and outstanding collections in the USA. Open: 10am-4.30pm Tuesday to Saturday,1-4.30pm Sunday. Closed Monday ☎ (813) 272-2466.

The Sacred Heart on Florida Avenue is worth visiting because of its beautiful Romanesque architecture and rose window.

Schlitz on 30th Street is another brewery which offers a very interesting 30 minute tour on weekdays between 10am and 3pm and, of course, there is a chance to try the product free if you are old enough.

The **Tampa Bay Hotel** (part of the university campus) with its thirteen silver-topped Moorish minarets (one for each month of the Muslim year), cost a staggering $3 million to build in 1891. The hotel was built by Henry Plant who also built the railway, which is why guests arrived in private railcars along a spur from the main track. There are free tours of the hotel at 1.30pm each Tuesday and Thursday.

The **Tampa Museum of Art**, 601 Doyle Carlton Drive, has a wide range of exhibits, both changing and permanent, from contemporary American and European paintings to ancient works of art from Egypt, Greece and Rome. There are also hands-on exhibits for children in the Lower Gallery. Open: 10am-5pm Tuesday to Saturday, 1-5pm Sunday. Closed Monday ☎ (813) 223-8130.

The **Tampa Bay Performing Arts Center**, 1010 N. MacInnes Place, has a busy season of concerts, shows and productions in one of its many venues, which include the Festival Hall, Playhouse, Jaeb Theater and Tampa Theater, on North Franklin Street, originally built as a cinema in 1926 and affectionately known as The Pride of the South. The original theater organ has been restored to its full glory. The new Off Center Theater presents shows by local theater groups, musicians, poets, dancers and improvisational groups ☎ (813) 221-10455 for further details.

University of South Florida Contemporary Art Museum, in East Fowler Avenue, was opened in 1989 and has a collection of contemporary and international exhibits. Open: 10am-5pm Monday to Friday, 1-4pm Tuesday to Saturday ☎ (813) 974-2849.

The **Whydah Pirate Complex** focuses on the history of the *Whydah* pirate ship, the only pirate shipwreck ever discovered. The 175,000sq ft (16,000sq m) pirate museum includes a full-scale replica of the 110ft (35m) *Whydah*. Actors recreate life aboard and a movie recounts the salvaging of the vessel. There is also a

Below: The Florida Aquarium at the Garrison Seaport in the center of Tampa

THE FLORIDA AQUARIUM

Above: The former Tampa Bay Hotel at the University of Tampa

Ybor City

Ybor City the Cuban quarter of Tampa famous for cigar making, now bustles with craftsmen who work from houses and small factories that have changed little over the decades. There are still cobblestone streets, intricate wrought iron balconies and Spanish tiles in abundance. The Cubans brought their cigar making skills with them, and soon Ybor City became home to many other immigrant groups including Germans, Jews and Italians.

The history of the city, now part of Tampa, is told in the

Below: Tampa Rico Cigar Company welcomes visitors to see cigars being made

motion-based simulation ride enabling visitors to experience being shipwrecked.

Ben T Davis Municipal Beach is Tampa's only saltwater beach running along the 9 mile (14km) Courtney Campbell Causeway which links Tampa with Clearwater. Very popular with the locals and can get very crowded.

Simmons Regional Park is almost 450 acres (180 hectares) of bayfront and channel land with a fine sandy but narrow beach. Good for swimming, birdwatching and canoeing. Camping is permitted on the marked waterfront sites and there is good fishing.

Ybor City State Museum, and it makes a useful first port of call as you can pick up a map and self-guided walking tour of the area. The museum on the corner of 9th Avenue and 19th Street is dedicated to the city's founder, Don Vicente Martinez Ybor. His settlement attracted thousands of immigrants and their special skills so that Ybor City quickly established itself as the cigar capital of the world. The first cigar factory opened in 1886 and until the 1930s, Ybor City was a flourishing community.

The rich history of the city is preserved at the museum, once a bakery (open 9am-12noon and 1-5pm, Tuesday to Saturday). You can also visit La Casita, a restored cigar worker's home (open 10am-12noon and 1-3pm Tuesday to Saturday).

The first cigar factory was in Ybor Square, 8th Avenue and 13th Street, now a shopping mall specialising in antiques and memorabilia. Many of the restaurants reflect the ethnic traditions of the early settlers. The Don Quixote restaurant specializes in authentic Cuban cuisine, and try the fresh baked Cuban bread at La Segunda Central Bakery on 15th Avenue, which will give you a conducted tour of the premises if you ask in good time. There are organised tours around the mechanised cigar factory of Villazon & Co on Armenia Avenue, although the traditional methods of hand rolling are still demonstrated.

Day Tours

The **Visitors Information Center** at 111 Madison Street, Suite 1010, or PO Box 519, Tampa, Florida 33601-0519, recommends the following excursions for those visitors wishing to get to know Tampa and the surrounding area:

Tour 1 • The Heart And Soul Of Tampa

Day I

Tampa's heart is **Ybor City**, its colorful Latin Quarter, where you can still smell the flavour of this turn-of-the-century boomtown. Taste the freshly baked Cuban bread, see cigars being rolled by hand, and take in one of the free guided walking tours through this historic neighbourhood. Lunch at one of the many restaurants and then browse through the shops and galleries, before returning to your hotel for dinner and a pleasant evening.

Day 2

Visit the Henry Plant Museum in the minaret-capped **Tampa Bay Hotel** to learn more about the man who did most to create this thriving city. Then cross the Hillsborough River to visit the **Tampa Museum of Art**. Enjoy lunch at one of the many open-air restaurants or cafes in **Old Hyde Park Village** and then spend an afternoon window-shopping or buying from the many shops and boutiques.

A pleasant way to watch the sun go down is to make your way to the waterfront at **Harbor Island**, where you can enjoy drinks on the terrace and watch the boats on the bay. If you really want to splash out, dress up for a night at **Bern's**,

renowned for its menu and wine list, reputed to be the biggest in the world. Or, visit the theater or one of the many productions staged by the **Performing Arts Center**. There is guaranteed to be something to suit all tastes.

Day 3

Spend the day at **Busch Gardens**, remembering to plan carefully so that you can fit in all the sights and rides between the various shows and presentations.

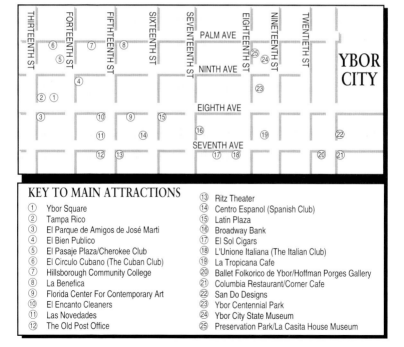

KEY TO MAIN ATTRACTIONS

① Ybor Square
② Tampa Rico
③ El Parque de Amigos de José Marti
④ El Bien Publico
⑤ El Pasaje Plaza/Cherokee Club
⑥ El Circulo Cubano (The Cuban Club)
⑦ Hillsborough Community College
⑧ La Benefica
⑨ Florida Center For Contemporary Art
⑩ El Encanto Cleaners
⑪ Las Novedades
⑫ The Old Post Office
⑬ Ritz Theater
⑭ Centro Espanol (Spanish Club)
⑮ Latin Plaza
⑯ Broadway Bank
⑰ El Sol Cigars
⑱ L'Unione Italiana (The Italian Club)
⑲ La Tropicana Cafe
⑳ Ballet Folkorico de Ybor/Hoffman Porges Gallery
㉑ Columbia Restaurant/Corner Cafe
㉒ San Do Designs
㉓ Ybor Centennial Park
㉔ Ybor City State Museum
㉕ Preservation Park/La Casita House Museum

Walking Tour

1 Start in **Ybor Square**, built by Vincente Ybor in 1886 and the city's first cigar factory. You can also visit Tampa Rico where cigars are still rolled by hand.

2 Across the road from the square is **El Parque de Amigos de José Marti**, once the site of the home of a Cuban-American patriot who sheltered José Marti. On 14th Street, there are the Marti Steps, now an entrance into Ybor Square.

3 Walk up 44th Street to **El Bien Publico**, built in 1895 as the Ybor Land and Improvement Company. At the turn-of-the-century it became a clinic and remained as one until 1980. The name means 'The Good of the People'.

4 Across the road is **El Pasaje Plaza** and the Cherokee Club, which was founded as an elite gentlemen's club in 1888. Eight years later they built the El Pasaje Hotel and the club moved in. Today the building houses Cafe Creole which offers traditional Creole cuisine and an authentic New Orleans brunch every Sunday between 12noon and 4pm.

5 Near the corner of 44th and Palm Avenue is **El Circulo Cubana** (The Cuban Club). It was one of six Ybor City mutual aid societies, and this glorious building, built in 1918, is one of the area's architectural treasures, particularly the grand entrance.

6 Walk along Palm Avenue, past Hillsborough Community College, to 15th Street and **La Benefica**, originally the United Secret headquarters which administered a number of men's clubs, and then later a clinic looking after the health and welfare of Spanish immigrants.

7 There are a number of interesting shops and craft centers along 15th Street, including a glass studio and the Florida Center for Contemporary Art, opposite El Encanto Cleaners, an Ybor City family business that has survived for three generations. Las Novedades, built in 1917 and once an award-winning restaurant, now houses the Tracks nightclub.

8 The **Old Post Office** is across the road on 7th Avenue. It was designed by Francis Kinnard, who was responsible for many of the early buildings, and next door is the Ritz Theatre, built in 1917 and now a nightclub.

9 Cross over into 16th Street past the **Spanish Club** (Centro Espanol) founded in 1892 to help needy immigrants. It was the first of the ethnic clubs and is now a National Historic Landmark.

A little further up the street and on the other side, is the **Latin Plaza**, with its statue dedicated to motherhood in the courtyard. Every Mothering Sunday, the base of the statue is festooned with flowers.

⑩ Further along 7th Avenue is the **Broadway Bank**, originally the Bank of Ybor City. Built in 1910, it now houses Art Moderne, and across the road is **El Sol Cigars** and **L'Unione Italiana** (The Italian Club). Built in 1914, the club is still active today.

⑪ Continuing along Seventh Avenue you reach **La Tropicana Cafe**, a restaurant and publishing office of *La Gaceta*, the only tri-lingual newspaper in the USA. A little further up on the other side of the road is the Hoffman Porges Gallery, and Head's Flag, a flag rental and sales store, and then the **Ballet Folklorico de Ybor**, specialising in Flamenco and other traditional dance from Spain, Cuba, Italy, Mexico and the Caribbean. On the corner of 7th Avenue and 21st Street is the **Columbia Restaurant and Corner Cafe**, Florida's oldest restaurant, founded in 1905 and occupying the whole block. The Corner Cafe was the original restaurant where cigar workers gathered to drink Cuban coffee and hear the latest news from home. Opposite is San Do Designs, a Spanish tile factory.

⑫ It is also worth visiting the **Ybor Centennial Park** on 8th and 9th Avenues and 18th and 19th Streets, before crossing over the road to visit the **Ybor City State Museum** and **La Casita House Museum** in Preservation Park.

shopping
Tampa

Big Top Flea Market
9250 E Fowler Avenue
Open: 8am-5pm daily.
600 booths of bargain
shopping from Western
boots to fresh produce.

Eastlake Square Mall
5701 E Hillsborough
Avenue
Wide variety of reasonably-
priced shops, stores and
restaurants.
Open: 10am-9pm Monday
to Saturday, 12noon-
5.30pm Sunday.

Fairground Factory
Outlet Mall
6302 Dr Martin Luther
King Jr Blvd
An upmarket shopping
mall.
Open: 10am-9pm Monday
to Saturday, 12noon-6pm
Sunday.

Florida Flea and
Farmer's Market
9309 N Florida Avenue
More than 800 stalls selling
a huge variety of goods at

bargain prices, as well as
collectibles and antiques.
Open: 9am-5pm Friday,
Saturday and Sunday.

Gulf Coast Factory Shops
5461 Factory Shops Blvd,
Ellenton
Famous name manu-
facturer's outlets offering
big savings.
Open: 10am-9pm, Monday
to Saturday, 12noon-6pm
Sunday.

Old Hyde Park Village
On Swann and Dakota near
Bayshore
Shops and restaurants in an
outdoor setting.
Open: 10am-6pm Monday
to Wednesday, 10am-9pm
Thursday and Friday. 10am-
6pm Saturday, 12noon-5pm
Sunday.

The Shops on
Harbor Island
601 South Harbour
Island Blvd
Shops, galleries,
restaurants, food court

and year-round events.
Open: 10am-9pm Monday
to Saturday, 12noon-5pm
Sunday.

Tampa Bay Center
3302 Dr Martin Luther
King Jr Blvd
A huge shopping complex
featuring more than 160
stores.
Open: 10am-9pm Monday
to Saturday, 12noon-6pm
Sunday.

University Mall
2200 E Fowler Ave
Fashion the emphasis in
130 plus shops.
Open: 10am-9pm Monday
to Saturday, 12noon-6pm
Sunday.

West Shore Plaza
253 Westshore Blvd
Tampa Bay's premiere mall
with almost 100 fine stores.
Open: 10am-9pm Monday
to Saturday, 12noon-
5.30pm Sunday.

Ybor Square
1901 N 13th Street
Shops, ethnic restaurants
and the nostalgia market.
Open: 10am-9pm daily.

Tour 2 • The Tampa Adventure

Day 1

Visit the **Museum of Science and Industry** with more than 200 hands-on exhibits to fascinate child and adult alike. Visit the planetarium and the new butterfly experience and then spend some time at the **Lowry Park Zoo**, one of the best city zoos in North America. Make time for the Florida exhibit featuring local wildlife in their natural habitat. You can even stroke a manatee. Take a swim and then enjoy leisurely dinner from the scores of restaurants to choose from before taking in the nightlife.

Day 2

Visit **Busch Gardens** and spend the day doing the rides and seeing the animals. Spend a little time relaxing back at your hotel before heading for **Ybor City** and a night of dancing, dining and music.

Day 3

Start the day by visiting Ybor City. Visit the **Yboy City State Museum** and take in the shops and galleries, before enjoying lunch at one of the many ethnic restaurants.

Work off your lunch by spending the afternoon leisurely paddling down the **Hillsborough River** where you can spot alligators and turtles.

Tour 3 • For Water Lovers

Day 1

Take in **Ybor City**, close to Tampa docks, and then visit the shops before lunch at one of the many ethnic restaurants. In the afternoon, visit the **Henry Plant Museum** and then make your way down to the waterfront at **Harbor Island** for a quiet drink on one of the terraces as the sun sets over the bay. Then to continue the nautical theme, enjoy an evening dinner cruise after having freshened up at your hotel.

Day 2

Take a charter from Tampa's **Rocky Point** recreation area or one of the other embarkation points. After lunch at sea or in one of the waterfront restaurants, try water skiing or jet skiing, or just laze by the water before enjoying dinner and the rest of the evening.

Day 3

Enjoy a day out at **Adventure Island** for exciting rides, surf and sun.

Tour 4 • Getting Around

Day 1

Visit Busch Gardens and then enjoy dinner at one of the waterfront restaurants.

Day 2

Drive to **St Petersburg** (about 30 minutes) and take in the **Salvador Dali Museum** which

Above: *Old Hyde Park Village on Swann and Dakota near Bayshore*

Opposite page: *Explore the 16,000 acre (6,400 hectare) Wilderness Park in Hillsborough County*

houses the world's most comprehensive collection of the artist's work. Enjoy the famous St Petersburg hands-on museum, then drive on to **Tarpon Springs** with its sponge fishing boats and delightful waterfront restaurants for dinner.

Day 3

Enjoy top class golf, laze at the beach or shop for all those gifts you have to take back. After lunch drive down to **Sarasota** (40 minutes) and visit the **Ringling Circus Museum** before returning for dinner at one of Tampa's many and varied ethnic restaurants.

Further Information

Tampa Visitor Information Center: Corner of Ashley and

Above: *The Bay Market at Tampa Bay Center*

Madison Streets (Exit 25 off I275). There are also Visitor Centers located inside Ybor Square, Harbor Island and the Tampa Convention Center ☎ (813) 223-1111.

Florida Bicycle Association: for information on where to cycle, clubs, organised rides ☎ 1-800-FOR BIKE.

St Petersburg and Clearwater

St Petersburg and Clearwater occupy the Pinellas peninsula in Pinellas County. The name Pinellas means 'Point of Pines' and was given by Spanish explorers in the early 1500s.

St Petersburg and Clearwater make ideal bases for holidays, especially for those looking for a relaxed vacation near the water. The Gulf is warm and safe to swim in, and the sandy beaches are ideal for lazing on and sunbathing. But the area offers a lot more than sea, sun and sand. There are sophisticated shops, cultural events and activities, a galaxy of sporting opportunities, attractions and entertainments, and excellent dining.

The two cities and surrounding communities and suburbs, make the area the most densely populated in all Florida. There are lots of trips that can be made if you want to explore further afield. The attractions of **Walt Disney World® Resort** and **Greater Orlando** are less than one and a half hours away, or you can explore south to **Sarasota**, or north to **Tarpon Springs** and beyond.

The **Pinellas Suncoast** includes eight communities and is famous for its 28 miles (45km) of snow white sandy beaches, and warm blue waters. Virtually every kind of water activity can be catered for, from deep sea fishing, sailing, wind surfing, parasailing, to jetskiing and diving. There are thirty-two golf courses, and a huge range of land-based sports and leisure activities, as well as shopping and dining opportunities galore.

The Suncoast stretches from Tarpon Springs in the north to Tierra Verde in the south, and includes Dunedin, Clearwater Beach, Indian Rocks Beach, Madeira Beach, Treasure Island and St Petersburg.

Getting Around

The St Petersburg–Clearwater International Airport is serviced by a growing number of international charters. The airport is linked to the interstate highway system and accessible from I-75, I-275 and I-4.

Some beaches areas are serviced by trolley cars. Public transportation throughout Pinellas County is provided by the Pinellas Suncoast Transit Authority (PSTA) ☎ (813) 530-9911.

Sun Capital of America

St Petersburg boasts the title 'Sun Capital of America', largely because of a record 768 consecutive days of sunshine. Between 1910 and 1986 the St Petersburg *Evening Independent* was given away free on days when the sun did not shine. In 76 years, the paper was given away free only 295 times, less than four times a year. It is very much a resort city with its palm-lined trees, bustling waterfront, shops and restaurants, and three museums — Museum of Fine Arts, Salvador Dali Museum and the Great Explorations children's museum.

St Petersburg was founded in 1876 by John C Williams of Detroit and Peter A Demens. They built a railroad which was finished in 1888 and the railhead was named after Demens' birthplace in Russia. The area was explored by the Spanish more than 300 years earlier and Fort De Soto, built in 1513, can still be visited.

Because of its Gulf-side location, St Petersburg has long been popular with holiday makers and in the 1940s the city actively encouraged vacationers to spend their retirement years there. As a result, St Petersburg is now largely a resort city connected by a series of bridges with Tampa and by causeways to the **Holiday Isles** to the west.

There is some industry and for many decades St Petersburg has been a seat of learning. The **Stetson University College of Law** was founded in 1901, 2 years before St Petersburg was granted city status. The **Museum of Fine Arts** was opened in 1961.

Clearwater, nestling along Clearwater Bay, was granted city status in 1912, and is connected to Tampa by the Courtney Campbell Causeway. Odet Phillippe, a surgeon in Napoleon's navy settled in the area in the mid-1830s and planted citrus groves. Following the establishment of Fort Harrison in 1841, other settlers arrived led by James Stevens.

The first town was known as Clear Water Harbor although it did not grow significantly until after the arrival of the **Orange Belt Railroad** in 1888, and it was not until after World War II that there was urban and industrial expansion. Clearwater, as the city became known, is connected to Clearwater Beach by the **Garden Memorial Causeway,** which offers excellent swimming and sandy beaches for sun bathing.

Above: The beach at Clearwater

There is a bustling sport fishing fleet based at the **Clearwater Marina** which is also the home of **Sea-Orama,** a museum and aquarium opened in 1954 and concentrating on the wildlife of the Gulf. There are all sorts of sea trips on offer from deep sea fishing, dolphin spotting and dinner specials to watching the sun set at sea. Concerts and Broadway shows are staged at the **Ruth Eckerd Hall,** and you spend an interesting and educational afternoon at the **Clearwater Marine Science Center.**

Tarpon Springs and the Pinellas Suncoast

Tarpon Springs is known as *'the world sponge capital'* and Florida's *'Little Greece'.* The Greek influence is very strong as Greek fishermen and sponge divers helped settle the area in 1876. By the 1890s there was a thriving port and there is still a Mediterranean atmosphere as you wander round the sponge dock.

Apart from sightseeing around the town, you can take a 3 hour cruise down the Anclote River, or visit Spongeorama and learn about the area's history. It is worth visiting the St Nicholas Greek Orthodox Church, and of course, you should take advantage of the excellent sponges on offer and sea cruises. Every year on Epiphany (6 January) the Greek Orthodox Church stages a procession through the streets, and then young men dive to retrieve a gold cross thrown into the water. The one who finds it is said to be blessed with good luck for the coming year.

Dunedin lies north of Clearwater and was founded by Scottish settlers in 1870. There are two state parks which are ideal for peaceful days out by the beach. You can take a ferry from Honeymoon Island to Caladesi Island and see what life was like when the coastline was being explored by the Spanish in the 1500s. There are unspoiled beaches, nature trails and a wealth of wildlife. The area's heritage is vividly borne out every year by the Highland Games.

Indian Rocks Beach actually consists of seven different communities which make up a very peaceful resort area, ideal for family holidays. You can visit the **Suncoast Seabird Sanctuary** on the Gulf and see their work in treating injured seabirds, or enjoy the Heritage Park and Museum in Largo and see how early pioneers to the area lived. You can also visit the 60-acre (24-hectare) Suncoast Botanical Gardens, or take a paddle-wheel dinner cruise on the Intracoastal waterway.

Madeira Beach is the fishing capital of this stretch of coast, and the scenic harbor is full of

Below: *The harbor at Tarpon Springs*

calendar
Central Gulf Coast

JANUARY

- **Hall of Fame Bowl**, New Year's Day football game.
- Epiphany procession and celebrations, **Tarpon Springs.**

FEBRUARY

- **Gasparilla Pirate Fest Weekend**: Hundreds of boats fill Hillsborough Bay to accompany the world's only fully rigged pirate ship as it sets sail for Tampa Convention Center. The pirates then parade along Bayshore Boulevard and the streets of Downtown Tampa.
- **Florida State Fair**: One of the largest in the country with nationally known entertainers and best food, arts, crafts and livestock on the 325 acre (130ha) site.
- **GTE Suncoast Classic**: The senior PGA Tour's top money-winners competing for a $500,000 purse.

- **Fiesta Day and Illuminated Night Parade** through Ybor City.
- **Doug Williams Heritage Weekend Golf Tournament**
- **Gasparilla Distance Classic**.

MARCH

- **Florida Strawberry Festival** at Plant City.
- **Gasparilla Sidewalk Arts Festival**.
- **President's Cup Regatta**.
- **Winter Equestrian Festival** at the Bob Thomas Equestrian Center at Florida Expo Park.
- Late March/early April **Festival of the States**, St Petersburg.

APRIL

- **Do Soto Celebrations**, Bradenton.
- **Dunedin Highland Games.**
- Late April/early May **Fun 'n Sun Festival**, Clearwater.

SEPTEMBER

- Late September/early October **Beachfest**, St Petersburg.

OCTOBER

- **Taste of Florida**.
- **Ruskin Seafood Festival**.
- **Mailou Art Festival**.
- **Southeast Street Rod Nationals**, the largest street rod show in the south-east.
- **Guavaween**, Latin-style Halloween celebrations.
- Late October John's Pass **Seafood Festival**, Madeira Beach.

NOVEMBER

- St Petersburg **Grand Prix Power Boat Race**.
- **Florida Classic**, the State's oldest continuing football match

DECEMBER

- **Brandon Marathon** and **Brandon Balloon Festival**.
- **First Night**. Celebration of the arts in Downtown Tampa.

commercial and charter fishing boats. There is an old fashioned boardwalk with charming shops and more than 2.5 miles (4km) of sandy beaches.

Treasure Island is an unspoiled beach area nearly 4 miles (6km) long for those who want to get away from it all. The beach is very wide which allows everyone to spread out, but there are lots of water sports and activities for those who want them, as well as fishing charters available and sightseeing cruises.

St Petersburg Beach offers almost 7 miles (11km) of splendid beaches. You can visit historic Fort De Soto, built in 1513, enjoy deep sea fishing, dine and dance aboard the dinner boats, or just enjoy the sun, sea and sand.

Attractions

Boatyard Village, on Fairchild Drive, Clearwater, is a recreated 1890s fishing village nestling in its own cove in Tampa Bay. There are also restaurants, shops, galleries and a theater.

Boyd Hill Nature Park, 1101 Country Club Way South, St Petersburg, is a 216-acre (86-hectare) park with nature trails for walking and cycle paths. It is interesting because the park covers a number of different habitats from lakeside and marsh to dry scrubland. There is a list of natural history-related activities throughout the year,

and a night walk is organised on the second Monday of every month. Open: daily 9am-5pm ☎ (813) 893-7326.

Caladesi Island, Dunedin, is accessible only by boat but worth making the effort for. It is one of the State's few remaining undisturbed barrier islands and ideal for swimming, shell collecting, picnics, skin and scuba diving, and nature study. There is a 3 mile (5km) nature trail.

Derby Lane, St Petersburg, features greyhound racing from January to June ☎ (813) 576-1361.

Florida Military Aviation Museum, next to the St Petersburg-Clearwater International Airport, features restored aircraft and aviation artifacts dating from World War II. Open: 10am-4pm Tuesday, Thursday and Saturday, 1-5pm Sunday ☎ (813) 584-6208.

Fort De Soto Park, south of St Petersburg Beach, features a fort built during the Spanish American war. The park covers 900 unspoiled acres (360 hectares), 7 miles (11km) of beach and camping and picnic areas.

Great Explorations, 1120 4th Street South, St Petersburg, is a must, especially if you have children. It is located just inland from the Salvador Dali Museum. It is a hands-on museum where visitors can touch, move and interact with scores of exhibits that are designed to educate and entertain. Open: 10am-5pm Monday to Saturday, 12noon-5pm Sunday ☎ (813) 821-8992.

Honeymoon Island, Dunedin, accessed by the Dunedin Causeway, is another get-away-from-it-all location and ideal for those who like shell collecting. Open: daily 8am-sunset ☎ (813) 469-5942.

Inness Paintings, 57 Read Street, Tarpon Springs, features the largest collection of works by George Inness Junior the American landscape painter, whose most notable works were done in the area. They are displayed in the Universalist Church on Read Street. Open: 2-5pm

Tuesday to Sunday, October to May ☎ (813) 938-5378.

Konger Coral Sea Aquarium, Dodecanese Boulevard, Tarpon Springs, features a 100,000 gallon main tank with a wide range of fish indigenous to the Gulf of Mexico and Caribbean. Open: 10am-6pm daily ☎ (813) 938-5378.

Kopsick Palm Arboretum, on North Shore Drive, St Petersburg, has a wide variety of native palms with swimming and picnic areas nearby. Open: daily.

Opposite page: Sponge boats are a regular sight in the harbours of the Central Gulf Coast

Right: The Salvador Dali Museum at St Petersburg

Below: Fort De Soto Park, south of St Petersburg Beach

Largo Heritage Park and Museum 125th Street, Largo is a fascinating collection of restored homes and buildings on a 21-acre (8-hectare) wooded site. The museum concentrates on the early pioneers. Spinning, weaving and other craft exhibitions are held, and on the fourth Sunday in October, the park is host to the Country Jubilee ☎ (813) 582-2123.

Marine Science Center, Windward Passage, Clearwater, is a research and rehabilitation facility, although there are very interesting live and model displays of local marine life. The tanks of baby sea turtles, and Sam, the bottlenose dolphin, are the most popular exhibits. There are daily tours. Open: 9am-5pm Monday to Friday, 9am-4pm Saturday, 11am-4pm Sunday ☎ (813) 447-0980.

Moccasin Lake Nature Park, on Park Trail Lane, Clearwater, is an environmental and energy education center set in a 50-acre (20-hectare) park featuring lake, upland forest, wetlands and most of the plant and animal species native to the area. There is a 1 mile (2km) nature trail which winds through the park taking in the Interpretative Center. The sun and wind provide the park's power supply. Open: 9am-5pm Tuesday to Friday, 10am-6pm Saturday and Sunday. Closed Monday ☎ (813) 462-6024.

Museum of Fine Arts, 255 Beach Drive NE, St Petersburg, houses a fine collection of American and European works dating from the eighteenth to twentieth century, as well as ancient, Oriental, and Renaissance art and furniture. There is also an exhibit of early photographs and the famed collection of Steuben Crystal. There are guided tours of the museum which nestles in its own peaceful gardens. Open: 10am-5pm Tuesday to Sunday ☎ (813) 816-2667.

Philippe Park, Safety Harbor, Bayshore Drive is named after Count Odet Philippe, a surgeon under Napoleon, who settled the site in the 1830s and introduced the first grapefruit trees into the New World. Before his arrival, it was an Indian settlement and a base for Spanish exploration.

Port Royal Sunken Treasure Museum on Gulf Boulevard, St Petersburg, features priceless treasures recovered from shipwrecked vessels around the world. Open: daily 10am-7pm ☎ (813) 360-4141.

Railroad Historical Museum, Main Street, Dunedin, was originally a station for the Orange Belt Railroad built in 1889. It now features the area's strong Scottish heritage. Open: Wednesday and Saturday 10am-12noon ☎ (813) 733-4151.

shopping
St Petersberg
& Clearwater

Malls

Bay Area Outlet Mall
Roosevelt Blvd, Clearwater

Clearwater Mall
US19 & Gulf to Bay Blvd,
Clearwater

Countryside Mall
US19 & SR580, Clearwater

Gateway Mall
Nine Street North,
St Petersburg

Largo Mall
Ulmerton & Seminole Blvd,
Largo

Pinellas Square Mall
US19 & Park Blvd,
Pinellas Park

Seminole Mall
Seminole & Park Blvd,
Seminole

Sunshine Mall
Missouri Ave, Clearwater

Tyrone Square Mall
22nd Ave & Tyrone Blvd,
St Petersburg

Shopping Villages

Boatyard Village
Fairchild Drive, Clearwater
Restaurants, boutiques and
galleries. Open: Monday to
Saturday 10am-6pm,
Sunday 10am-5pm.

Hamilin's Landing
2nd Street East,
Indian Rocks Beach
Waterfront shopping and
dining complex.
Open: daily.

**John's Pass Village and
Boardwalk**
Gulf Boulevard,
Madeira Beach
Quaint shopping district
with galleries and
boutiques.
Open: daily.

Silas Bayside Market
Gulf Boulevard,
St Petersburg
Unique shopping village in
tropical setting, speciality
shops and food court.
Open: daily.

Ruth Eckerd Hall on McMullen Booth Road, Clearwater, is a performing arts center presenting music, dance and educational programmes for all ages. Visual arts exhibits are regularly displayed in the spacious galleries. The hall is also the home of the Florida Orchestra and offers performances by the Florida Opera ☎ (813) 791-7400 for further details.

Salvador Dali Museum to the south of the pier, on 3rd Street, St Petersburg, houses the world's most comprehensive collection of the Spanish artist's work. The collection was built up by industrialist A Reynolds Morse and his wife Eleanor, who became close friends of the artist. They donated their huge collection to a charitable trust so that people could understand and appreciate the work of Dali. There are regular tours of the museum. Open: 10am-5pm Tuesday to Saturday, 12noon-5pm Sunday and Monday ☎ (813) 823-3767.

St Nicholas Greek Orthodox Church, North Pinellas Avenue, Tarpon Springs, a replica of St Sophia's in Constantinople, and an example of New Byzantine architecture with an elaborate interior of sculpted marble, ornate icons and stained glass. Open: daily ☎ (813) 937-3540.

St Petersburg Historical and Flight One Museum, 2nd Avenue NE St Petersburg, features a permanent interactive exhibition chronicling the city's history. The **Benoist Pavilion** houses a replica of the world's first commercial airliner which made the first commercial flight from St Petersburg to Tampa on 1 January 1914. ☎ (813) 894-1052.

St Petersburg's Pier is big in every sense. It is as long as an airport runway and has a road running the entire length with masses of parking on either side. At the end of the pier is a five storey building, housing shops, restaurants, bars, aquarium and an observation deck. Open: daily 10am-9pm. Admission free ☎ (813) 821-6164.

At the beach end of the pier, there is a museum run by the St Petersburg Historical Society. Open: 10am-5pm Monday to Saturday 1-5pm Sunday ☎ (813) 894-1052.

Sawgrass Lake Park, St Petersburg, is a 360-acre (144-hectare) park with 1 mile (2km) of elevated boardwalks through a maple swamp with an observation tower. There is a selfguide booklet for the nature trails.

Spongeorama, Dodecanese Boulevard, Tarpon Springs, tells the story of the sponge industry and Greek settlers to the area. It includes a small museum and theater. Open: 10am-5pm daily ☎ (813) 942-3771.

Sea Screamer which operates from Kingfish Wharf, Treasure Island, claims to be the world's largest speedboat, and it offers daily bird and marine life trips around nearby islands and then out into the Gulf.

Suncoast Botanical Gardens, 125th Street North, Largo, cover 60 acres (24 hectares) and specializes in local plants but also features those from other parts of the world, particularly cacti. Open: daily ☎ (813) 595-7218.

Suncoast Seabird Sanctuary, Gulf Boulevard, Indian Shores, is a world-famous, non profit making bird hospital and often has 500 patients under treatment. A good place to see at close hand the region's birdlife. Open: daily ☎ (813) 391-6211.

Sunken Gardens, on 4th Street, St Petersburg, is a collection of more than 50,000 tropical plants many of which bloom year round. There is a walk-though aviary featuring exotic birds and thousands of rare and fragrant orchids. Open: 9am-5.30pm daily ☎ (813) 896-3186.

Sunshine Speedway, Ulmerton Road, Clearwater, features drag and stock car racing. Open: drag racing Friday, March to November. Stock car racing Saturday, February to November ☎ (813) 573-4598.

Sunshine Skyway Bridge is an attraction in its own right. The bridge was modelled on the Brotonne Bridge which spans the River Seine in France, and was Florida's first suspension bridge. It is 4.1 miles (6.6km) long and in places the road soars 183ft (56m) above Tampa Bay to allow shipping to sail below.

South of Tampa Bay

You can explore further south by taking Highway 41 from Tampa or take the spectacular causeway, the **Sunshine Skyway**, from St Petersburg across Tampa Bay to Bradenton. It is a glorious roller coaster of a ride with spectacular views over the bay, pelicans soaring overhead, and, if you are lucky, with glimpses of dolphins swimming in the warm waters.

Manatee County is the area south of Tampa and there are lots of little beaches to be discovered if you have the time.

Worth visiting is the **Gamble Plantation State Historic Site**, once the home of Major Robert Gamble, who owned a 3,500-acre (1,400-hectare) sugar plantation. Judah P Benjamin, the Confederate Secretary of State, hid in the massive house, built of oyster shells and molasses in the late 1840s, before escaping to Britain after the Civil War. The house was saved from demolition by the United Daughters of the Confederacy because of its historical significance, and they then donated it to the State. There are tours

191

of the house which is full of period antiques. Open: daily 9am-5pm (tours every hour) ☎ 813 722 1017.

Most visitors drive through this area on their way to Sarasota and other resorts further south and so do not get the chance to explore. There are small beach-hugging communities like **Apollo Beach** and **Sun City.**

Bradenton is the largest population center along this stretch of coast. Here you can explore the **South Florida Museum** on 10th Street, with its prehistoric Indian artifacts, planetarium and spectacular laser light shows. Star of the show is Snooty, a West Indian manatee, the oldest surviving manatee born in captivity. The museum complex includes the Spanish Courtyard with replicas of a sixteenth-century Spanish church and the home of Hernando De Soto. Open: 10am-5pm Tuesday to Saturday, 1-5pm Sunday ☎ 941-746-4131.

The **De Soto National Monument**, 75th Street, is staffed by rangers who re-enact the lifestyle of De Soto's troops. They even wear heavy armour, but only during the cooler months. The interpretative center is open year round 6am-5.30pm and displays in graphic detail how De Soto and his 500 troops

travelled more than 4,000 miles (6,440km) exploring what was then a totally unknown continent ☎ 941-792-0458.

You can then take highway 64 or 684 west on to **Anna Maria Key** with its fine beaches. This is the beach for Bradenton and has excellent seafood restaurants. A chain of keys connects Bradenton and Sarasota to the south. The next island is **Longboat Key,** where De Soto's scout is said to have come ashore in a longboat. The key has some exclusive shops and many luxury homes which you can see as you motor along the **Gulf of Mexico Drive.**

Further Information

Clearwater/Pinellas Suncoast Welcome Center: 3550 Gult to Bay Boulevard, Clearwater FL 34619 ☎ (813) 461-0011.

Clearwater Beach Welcome Center: 41 Causeway Boulevard, Clearwater Beach, FL 34630 ☎ (813) 461-0011.

Pinellas Suncoast Welcome Center: 2001 Ulmerton Road, Clearwater FL 34662 ☎ (813) 573-1449.

St Petersburg-Clearwater Area Convention and Visitor's Bureau: Florida Sunset Dome, 1 Stadium Drive, Suite A, St Petersburg FL 33705-1706 ☎ (813) 464-7200.

STATE NATIONAL PARKS, HISTORIC SITES & RECREATION AREAS

The map for this section can be found on page 159

Tarpon Springs to Crystal River

Highway 19 runs north from Tarpon Springs along the Gulf. Port Ritchey and New Port Ritchey are fast growing communities attracting many overseas residents who love the weather and the relaxed way of life. There are other small communities along the Gulf and a lot of out of the way beaches to be discovered, but you should find time to visit Weeki Wachee and Homosassa Springs.

Weeki Wachee Springs off US19, Brooksville, is a combined theme and nature park built around some of the many natural springs found in the area. The attraction is most famous for its 'mermaids' who put on several acrobatic-ballet shows a day in the unique underwater theater. There are river cruises, a large number of animals on display and a petting zoo. Open: 9am-late (closing times vary according to season) ☎ 352-596-2062.

The six mound complex over 14 acres (5 hectares) was the home of a group known as the Pre-Columbian mound builders, and for 1,600 years the site was an important ceremonial and burial center. As many as 7,500 Native Americans are thought to have visited the site annually, many travelling long distances to trade or bury their dead.

Finally, **Crystal River** marks the most northerly point of this section. It is an area of great archaeological interest and one of the oldest and longest inhabited Indian sites in Florida. Excavations have revealed settlements dating back to prehistoric times and signs of a remarkably advanced civilisation. One grave contained a complicated astronomical calendar. There is a small museum at the **Crystal River Archaeological Site** containing Indian artifacts dating back to 150BC.

It is worth climbing the highest temple mound because of the views it offers across the river. Crystal River is also an area noted because of the large number of manatees that congregate there attracted by the warm springs, especially over the winter.

Anclote Keys

Three miles (5km) off Tarpon Springs. Accessible only by private boat.

Four miles (6km) of beautiful Gulf coastline dominated in the south by a federal lighthouse built in 1887. Ospreys nest in the tall pines found throughout the island. Ideal for swimming or nature watching. The island is divided into six separate fauna zones, and is home to scores of bird species, including bald eagle and the rare piping plover. All water and supplies have to be taken on to the island, and all litter removed.

Caladesi Island State Park

Situated off Dunedin. One of the few remaining large undeveloped barrier islands on Florida's Gulf Coast. The island is only accessible by private boat or the passenger ferry which runs from nearby Honeymoon Island State Recreation Area and from Clearwater. It is a great place for boating, fishing, swimming, shell hunting and wildlife. There are many unspoiled island trails. There is a small marina and off shore anchorage for boats between March and Labor Day at the beginning of September. Overnight visitors must register before sundown.

Dade Battlefield State Historic Site

The site at Bushness commemorates the battle fought on 28 December 1835, which marked the beginning of the Second Seminole Indian War, one of the great landmark events in Florida's history. Of the troop of 108 men under the command of Major Francis L. Dade, only three survived the ferocious 8 hour long battle. The site is open daily from 8am to sunset 7 days a week, and the story of the battle is recounted in the visitor center, open from 9am-4pm. The battle is re-enacted every December.

Egmont Key State Park

At the mouth of Tampa Bay south-west of Fort De Soto Beach.

A 440-acre (176-hectare) island, wildlife refuge, and home of the only manned lighthouse in the USA. Formerly a camp for captured Seminoles during the Third Seminole War, and then a base for the Union Navy during the Civil War, the park is now jointly managed by the Florida Department of Natural Resources, the US Fish and Wildlife Service and the US Coast Guard. Good for swimming, fishing and boating. Accessible by private boat only.

Fort Cooper State Park

Two miles (3km) south-east of Inverness.

The park's main attraction is the spring-fed **Lake Hola-thikaha**, but it is popular because of its wide range of habitats — swamp, marsh, hardwood stands and sand-hills. There are 10 miles (16km) of self-guided trails which allow you to observe the plentiful wildlife. It is also a good place for swimming, fishing, boating and picnics.

At **Homosassa Springs State Wildlife Park** you can see Florida's wildlife in their natural surroundings: **above left:** *Sheena, the cougar;* **above right:** *a manatee;* **below:** *feeding Lucifer the hippo*

195

Canoes, paddleboats and pedalos can be rented in the park and for those who want to get away from the crowds, wilderness camping is permitted. Horses can be rented locally and there are horse trails through the park.

Hillsborough River State Park

Twelve miles (19km) north of Tampa at Thonotosassa.

This 2,990-acre (1,196-hectare) park was created by the Civilian Conservation Corps in 1936 and opened to the public 2 years later. Facilities include camping, picnicking, swimming and boating with canoes for rental. There are about 8 miles (13km) of nature trails through the woodland oaks, sabal palms, magnolias and hickories which border the Hillsborough River. Fort Foster is located in the park and you can see what fort life was like in the 1830s. Park guides, dressed in replica uniforms of the US Second Artillery, act out what life was like in the camp more than 160 years ago.

Homosassa Springs State Wildlife Park

Homosassa Springs, about 75 miles (121km) north of Tampa.

A chance to see Florida's gentle giants, the manatees in their natural surroundings, as well as much of Florida's other wildlife. You can walk along transparent tunnels under the water watching the manatees and the thousands of fish which are attracted by the spring waters. On land, you can see black bear, bobcats, alligators and a large collection of wild birds. The **Animal Encounters Arena** features Florida snakes and other local wildlife, and you can watch alligators being fed at **Gator Lagoon**. There are walking trails and boat trips. Open: daily 9am-5pm
☎ 352-628-5343.

Honeymoon Island State Recreation Area

At the western end of SR586, north of Dunedin.

Originally known as Hog Island, the name was changed in 1939 when a New York developer built 50 palm-thatched honeymoon bungalows. There are magnificent beaches, safe swimming, good fishing and lots of wildlife to be seen from the nature trails through the mangrove swamps and tidal flats. Open: daily 8am-sunset
☎ (813) 469-5942.

Lake Louisa State Park

Clermont. The 1,790-acre (716-hectare) park stretches round the shores of Lake

Louisa in the north-east corner of the Green Swamp. It is one of a chain of thirteen lakes connected by the Palatlakaha River, which has been designated as an Outstanding Florida Water. Good for picnics, swimming, fishing, canoeing and wildlife.

Little Manatee River State Recreation Area

Four miles (6km) south of Sun City, off US301.

The river has been designated as an Outstanding Florida Water and is formed in a swampy area near Fort Lonesome before running 40 miles (64km) into Tampa Bay. It is part of **Cockroach Bay Aquatic Preserve**, and the river flows for 4.5 miles (7km) through the recreation area which covers 1,638 acres (655 hectares), offering camping, canoeing, fishing, boating, walking and horse-riding trails.

Lake Manatee State Recreation Area

15 miles (24km) east of Bradenton on SR64.

A 556-acre (222-hectare) recreation area stretching 3 miles (5km) along the southern shores of the lake. It is an excellent place for camping, picnicking, swimming, fishing and boating.

Weedon Island State Preserve

Off Gandy Boulevard, just south of Gandy Bridge.

A former 1,000-acre (400-hectare) citrus grove, the park is now one of the few remaining mangrove swamps and green spaces in Florida's most densely populated county. In the 1920s, the citrus grove was uprooted and the island became home to a roaring 1920s nightclub, a motion picture studio, and one of Florida's first airports. During this development, one of Florida's most important archaeological finds was unearthed, providing evidence of settlement dating back to AD300. Today, the park offers a wealth of wildlife and opportunities for hiking, canoeing, fishing and picknicking.

Yulee Sugar Mill Ruins State Historic Site

On SR490, west of US19 in Homosassa.

The 5,100-acre (2,040-hectare) park was once part of a prosperous sugar plantation owned by David Levy Yulee and employing 1,000 slaves. The mill operated for 13 years and supplied sugar to southern troops during the Civil War. Open: daily 8am dusk ☎ 352-795-3817.

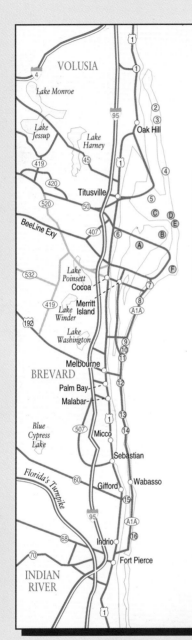

CENTRAL FLORIDA'S SPACE COAST

KEY TO KENNEDY SPACE CENTER

- Ⓐ Kennedy Space Visitors Complex
- Ⓑ Vehicle Assembly Building
- Ⓒ Shuttle Landing Facility
- Ⓓ Launch Area B
- Ⓔ Launch Area A
- Ⓕ Cape Canaveral Air Force Station

KEY TO BEACH AREAS

- ① New Smyrna Beach
- ② Canaveral National Seashore
- ③ Turtle Mound
- ④ Playalinda Beach
- ⑤ Merritt Island National Wildlife Refuge
- ⑥ US Space Camp/US Astronaut Hall of Fame
- ⑦ Port Canaveral
- ⑧ Cocoa Beach
- ⑨ Satellite Beach
- ⑩ Indian Harbour Beach
- ⑪ Canova Beach
- ⑫ Melbourne Beach
- ⑬ Melbourne Shores
- ⑭ Floridana Beach
- ⑮ Vero Beach
- ⑯ Pepper Beach

7 THE SPACE COAST

For most visitors the main attraction is the Kennedy Space Visitor Complex, but there are excellent unspoiled beaches along this 72 miles (116km) of beautiful sandy coastline on the Space Coast, and lots of interesting seaside towns to explore. Many of the town beaches are patrolled by lifeguards, and you must take note of the warning flags as the sea can be rough with strong undertows. While the Space Coast officially ends at the Sebastion Inlet State Park, we have continued a little further south to Fort Pierce in this chapter, taking in Vero Beach and Indian River County.

From Orlando and Central Florida the **Bee Line Expressway** is the fastest route to the Space Coast. It is a toll road but the modest charges are worth paying. It takes about an hour to get from Orlando/Kissimmee to the Atlantic. If you do not want to pay, take Highway 50 which runs east to the coast.

Above: *The new Apollo/Saturn V Center at KSVC*

During the summer, you have to wear sandals on the beach because the sand gets so hot, and you must take care not to get too much sun. The reflection of the sun from the sand and water can cause you to burn very quickly although you may not appreciate this until it is too late because of the water and any cooling breezes.

Kennedy Space Visitor Complex

The Visitor Complex is one of the USA's top attractions and well worth a visit. There are now approximately 3 million visitors a year, and if you are really interested in space, there is too much to pack into a single trip. On launch days, all roads around the Space Center are packed, and even as far away as Orlando, you can usually hear the sonic booms as the space shuttle blasts skywards.

The Kennedy Space Visitor Complex is often billed as Florida's best visitor value because so many exhibits, films and demonstrations are free. **A family of four can enjoy everything here for less than the cost of one admission to other major Central Florida attractions.** It is open from 9am to dusk except Christmas Day and certain launch days.

The Space Center is the home launch base of America's Space Shuttle or **Orbiter** and all missions begin at **Launch Complex 39**. The first launch from Kennedy Space Center was **Apollo 4** on 9 November 1967. Eleven subsequent Apollo missions and all Shuttle flights have taken off from here. The Kennedy Space Visitor Complex (formerly Spaceport USA) was opened in 1966 as the visitor center for Kennedy. It now co-ordinates all visitor activities within the Space Center situated on the north end of Merritt Island. All approaches are well signposted.

To see what it really must be like to hurtle into space, visit the IMAX movies in the **Galaxy Theaters**. The three sight and sound spectaculars are presented on massive screens, five and a half storeys tall and 70ft (21m) wide.

The first film *The Dream is Alive*, which lasts 37 minutes, is so realistic that astronauts say it is as close to the real thing as you can get without riding in the Space Shuttle. The presentations cover pre-flight training, boarding procedures, and breathtaking blast off and landing.

The new presentations are "*Mission to Mir*", and "*L5, First City in Space*" a new 3-D space movie depicting a future space settlement and using real NASA footage and data. The Visitor Complex is the only place in the world with two IMAX theaters.

You only have to pay for the bus tours and the IMAX

HOT TIP

Parking is free, and plan to arrive as early as possible in order to be able to see as much as possible. Set aside 6-8 hours at least to see everything. Weekends tend to be less busy than weekdays.

---

presentations; the rest of the Visitor Complex is free. Book your tours early, and try to fit in the IMAX screenings before the rush.

Visit **Information Central** in the main complex building for advice on how best to plan your visit, and for free use of cameras and wheelchairs.

For further information on the Visitor Complex ☎ (407) 452-2121. For information about launch days when in Florida ☎ 800-KSC-INFO. This line is available in Florida only. If you are calling from outside Florida ☎ (407) 867-4636.

Afterwards, visit the **Rocket Garden** and outdoor exhibits featuring rockets, lunar modules and other space equipment. The enormous **Saturn V** rocket, which burnt 150,000 gallons of fuel a second, is now housed in a new exhibit.

The 45 minute *Satellites and You* audiovisual and anima-tronics exhibit provides an enjoyable and informative look at how satellites affect our daily lives, and visit the **Astronauts Memorial**, a 42ft by 50ft (13m by 15m) space mirror, honouring the courage and spirit of the sixteen US astronauts who gave their lives for space and exploration. The monument, on a computerised rotating base, uses the sunlight to illuminate the names of the astronauts inscribed on it. There are alligators and turtles in the lake below the Astronauts' Memorial.

Other things to see include movies and live demonstrations in the Spaceport Theater, each lasting between 15 and 30 minutes. The award-winning movie *The Boy From Mars*, is shown continuously in the Galaxy Theater, and the NASA Art Gallery features paintings and sculptures commissioned by the NASA Art programme.

The **Gallery of Manned Spaceflight** features moon rocks, spacecraft and other exhibits, including the Apollo capsule which docked with the Russian Soyuz spacecraft. Find time to take in the **Wildlife Exhibit** which highlights the wealth of flora and fauna found on the 140,000-acre (56,000-hectare) Kennedy Space Center site.

Latest developments have included the replacement of the Space Shuttle Orbiter *Ambassador* with a permanent lifesize

If you are visiting in the week before a scheduled launch, you may be able to buy one of the 1,500 special tickets to view it. The tour buses ferry observers to the causeway linking the Space Center with the mainland, which is 6 miles (10km) from the launch pads, the closest anyone can get during a launch. Tickets have to be picked up in person, on a first come first served basis.

The Visitor Complex is usually closed on launch days until 2 hours after lift-off. Best views can be obtained from along US Highway 1 around Titusville and along Highway A1A around Cape Canaveral and Cocoa. There are also views from Port Canaveral at Jetty Park although this gets very crowded. Much of the seashore is closed to the public the day before the launch for security. The Orbiter takes only 8 seconds to clear the tower and uses half a million gallons of fuel during the lift-off.

NASA has four Orbiters (not Shuttles) currently in use — *Atlantis*, *Columbia*, *Discovery* and *Endeavour* (which replaced the ill fated *Challenger*). Missions are frequent; in fact the historic one which carried the first Russian (on 3 February 1994) was the sixtieth flight. So there is a reasonable chance that there might be a launch during your stay in Florida. For up to date information on launches ☎ 1-800-KSC-INFO when in Florida or (407) 867 4636 if calling from outside the state.

A lot of people try to see the lift off from a distance too far away to make it worthwhile. Why not do it properly? Buy one of the 1,500 inexpensive tickets at the Visitor Complex. You will be admitted to as close as any spectators are allowed, 6 miles (10km) away. You can listen to the launch countdown on the public address system and there is limited food available from a mobile snack bar. If it is an early morning launch, you can get a good breakfast afterwards at the Visitor Complex (it opens 30 minutes after the launch).

There is a lot of congestion from visitors without tickets and gates open 4 hours prior to the launch. It is recommended that you arrive at least 2 hours prior to launch time. If you are coming down the Bee Line Expressway, you can avoid much of the traffic by turning north up I-95 to exit 79 (Highway 50). Turn east to US Highway 1 and then right (south) to SR405, where you will be directed to Gate 3. Entry is limited to ticket holders only.

As elsewhere on a visit to the Visitor Complex, cameras are welcome. Take note that gates close about 1 hour before launch time.

You will be directed to a point on the Banana River 3 miles (5km) beyond the Visitor Complex. The two lanes will become choked with traffic. The left lane moves the fastest as it eventually merges with the right one. If you are one of the last to arrive, you may be told to park at the road side. This may preclude you from seeing the actual lift off (because of trees) from your vehicle.

You can listen to, and watch, the press conference which follows a launch in the Spaceworld Theater. It is quieter there than in the main lobby where it is relayed onto TV screens.

Atlantis clearing the tower on a night-time launch

replica. **The Explorer** enables visitors to climb aboard and see the environment NASA astronauts work in while in space. Wheelchair access is available.

Also impressive is the 365ft (111m) long Saturn V Moon Rocket housed in the new **Apollo/Saturn V Center** and the new **International Space Station** exhibit.

A 'must' visit is to the 60ft (18m) observation gantry in the heart of **Launch Complex 39**. The air-conditioned observation gantry, with surrounding open air walkway, offers 360 degree panoramic views.

New Attraction — International Space Station Center

The largest and most ambitious space program since the Apollo moon landings, the International Space Station (ISS) is the subject of another new interactive attraction. In the Kennedy Space Center Industrial Area, the International Space Station Center (ISSC) is located adjacent to the Space Station Processing Facility.

Visitors learn the purpose and importance of a space station, how it will be constructed, and what benefits it will contribute to mankind. The highlight of the attraction will fascinate guests. Visitors get an up-close glimpse inside the actual facility where NASA is processing the real components of the ISS. An elevated walkway brings guests to a viewing gallery actually looking into the bay where each space station module is checked out, processed and readied for its trip into orbit.

Upon leaving the theater, visitors can discover several incredibly detailed full-scale mock-ups of space station modules. These walk-through space station components include the Habitation Module, which is where crew members live, sleep and work; the Laboratory Module, where science experiments are conducted and maintained; the Mini Pressurized Logistics Module, where racks and supplies are transported back and forth from KSC to space; and "Node 1," which functions as a major connector piece between modules of the space station.

Touring KSC

To get the most out of your visit, take one or both of the guided double-decker bus tours. The tours start at 9.30am and the last leaves 2 hours before dark. The buses make frequent camera stops, although it is advisable to book up for these tours as early in the day as possible as they are very popular. The tours last 2 hours and run throughout the day. Everything at the Visitor Complex runs to precision timing, so do not be late turning up for your tour.

204

Red Tour

You experience a simulated launch countdown from the site where all the Apollo astronauts trained, inspect a **Saturn V** rocket which is over 330ft (100m) long and visit the gigantic **VAB** (Vehicle Assembly Building), one of the world's largest buildings enclosing 129 million cubic feet (158.5 million cubic metres). The VAB is 520ft (837m) high. It is 52 storeys high and equivalent to 51 storeys wide and 71 storeys long. It covers 8 acres (3 hectares) and could house the Empire State Building 3.75 times. The statistics are endless and the bus drivers know them all.

You will also see the monster **Crawler Transporters** — weighing in at more than 6 million pounds — which carry the Space Shuttles to the launch pad at 1 mile (2km) an hour. They can carry loads of up to 14.4 million pounds. You are also able to inspect one of the launch pads where they blast off. The **Space Shuttles** are usually hauled out to the launch pad about a month before launch.

The tour is centerd on **Launch Complex 39** which includes all the massive buildings and shuttle launch pads A and B, where today's shuttles are launched, and the drivers are expert at pointing out wildlife highlights along the way such as lounging alligators and perching bald eagles.

Blue Tour

You visit **Cape Canaveral Air Force Station**, discover how the early space age developed, see the sites where the first astronauts were launched in the *Mercury* and *Gemini* flights, visit a number of launch pads currently in use for various scientific, commercial and military missions, and tour the **Air Force Space Museum** with its unique collection of missiles and space memorabilia.

US Space Camp

The **US Space Camp**, east of the intersection of Highway 405 and US1, has got to be one of the ultimate summer camps for children. The children use astronaut training simulators from the Mercury and Apollo training programmes, and are taken through a 5 day hands-on educational and fun program learning about America's space program. The course even teaches the children to design, build and launch their own model rockets. The Camp is also the home of the **US Astronaut Hall of Fame** which tells the story of the first days in space, as told by the original seven astronauts. You can climb inside the cargo bay of a full sized Shuttle Orbiter, and take part in a simulated Space Shuttle flight of the future. Open: 9am-6pm with seasonal variations ☎ (407) 269-6100.

Canaveral National Seashore & Merritt Island National Wildlife Refuge

All the land not actually used operationally by the Space Center is managed in cooperation with the Merritt Island National Wildlife Refuge and Canaveral National Seashore. More species of endangered wildlife can be found within the 220-sq mile (570-sq km) boundary than anywhere else in the continental US. It is the home of manatees, bald eagles and ospreys, and over 4,000 alligators flourish within the reserve area. By walking the trails, you can also see great blue herons, egrets, woodstorks and 310 other species of birds, as well as 25 mammals, 65 species of amphibians and reptiles, 117 fishes and 23 species of migratory waterfowl. There are four types of poisonous snakes including the diamond backed rattlesnake, bobcats, wild pigs, four kinds of turtle and plenty of armadillos munching away beside the road. There are auto trails for those who do not want to get out of their cars.

Cape Canaveral Air Force Station was selected for the site of a US missile testing range in 1947 and the first missile, a German V2 rocket with an Army WAC Corporal second stage, was launched on 24 July 1950. It was at Cape Canaveral that the Americans developed the facilities that led to the

Titusville

Titusville has a bustling marina and an historic Main Street boasting many fine buildings from the late 1800s and early 1900s. Worth visiting are St Gabriel's Episcopal Church in Palm Avenue which dates from 1887, and the Pritchard House built in 1891 on Washington Avenue, the city's finest example of Queen Anne architecture. The Wager House on Indian River Avenue is one of the oldest buildings in town and a fine example of the Colonial Revival Style, while Judge George Robbins house on Indian River Avenue, built in 1892, is the only remaining example of the Dutch Colonial Revival style in Titusville.

A revitalisation scheme has created a charming area of antique shops, restaurants, stores and a theater. The North Brevard Historical Museum is housed in a former storefront in old downtown, now part of Main Street.

The Valiant Air Command and Aviation Warbird Museum in Titusville is dedicated to the preservation of American's aviation heritage and features 350 military aircraft from World War I onwards. It is located on Tico Road at the Space Center Executive Airport. Open: 10am-6pm daily ☎ (407) 268-1941.

Mercury, *Gemini* and *Apollo* manned space flights.

The **Cape Canaveral Lighthouse** was built in 1843 of brick and relocated to its present site in 1893. From 1847 until 1952, when it was taken over by the US Coast Guard, it was operated by descendants of the first lighthouse keeper Captain M O Burnham.

You have to drive via Titusville or New Smyrna Beach to gain access to the Canaveral National Seashore as roads within the Space Center are not open to the public, but it is worth it.

South of Titusville is the **Windover Archaeological Site**. In 1982 a plough unearthed a number of bones and subsequent excavations have revealed a wealth of artifacts and textiles dating back between 4,000 and 6,000BC. Because the skeletons were buried in peat, even some brain tissue was preserved, and valuable information has been gathered about the biology, diet and environment of this period.

There are park information centers along Apollo Beach and there are drives which take you close to the wildlife without having to get out of your vehicles. For thousands of years sea turtles have been coming ashore along this beach to lay their eggs

Right: *Look for the southern bald eagles' enormous nests on Kennedy Parkway North*

Below: *The VAB and launch complex at KSC with pods 39A & B in the distance where the shuttles lift off*

Visitor Information

Canaveral National Seashore
308 Julia Street, Titusville
☎ (407) 267-1110
Open: 8am-sunset, except when there are launches.

Florida's Space Coast Office of Tourism
2725 St Johns Street, Melbourne FL 32940
☎ (407) 633-2110 or US only 800-USA-1969

Brevard County Tourist Development Council
2235 North Courtenay Parkway,
Merritt Island FL 32953
☎ (407) 453-2211 or US only 800-USA-1969

Indian River Tourist Council
1216 21st Street, Vero Beach FL 32961
☎ (407) 567-3491 or USA only 800-338-2678

Melbourne-Palm Bay Visitors Bureau
1005 E Strawbridge Ave FL 32901
☎ (407) 724-5400

Kennedy Space Center
Kennedy Space Visitor Complex,
Kennedy Space Center, FL 32899
☎ (407) 452-2121 (Visitor Complex), launch information while
in Florida ☎ 800 KSC Info or (407) 867 4636 if calling from
outside Florida.
Open: daily 9am-sunset, except Christmas Day

St Lucie County/Fort Pierce Tourist Development Council
2300 Virginia Avenue,
Fort Pierce, FL 34982
☎ (407) 468-1535

Titusville Area Chamber of Commerce
PO Drawer 2767, FL 32781
☎ (407) 267-3036

(early May to late August), and **Turtle Mound**, on the sands south of New Smyrna Beach gives a good indication of just how many turtles and other shellfish were killed for food over the years by the Timucuan Indians. A boardwalk leads to the mound from the car park. It shows the diversity of the dense local vegetation. Look for the smooth barked naked skin tree, which is at its northern limit here. The boardwalk climbs to the top of the shell mound which gives a good vantage point.

Look for the prickly pear cactus which fruits at the beginning of the year. The fruit is edible, but best used as jelly because of its small spines. The mound is now a State protected archaeological site. The beach here is also excellent for swimming and sunbathing, although if you plan to spend the day, you must take everything you need, including lots of water and soft drinks. You must also check the tides, as the sands are very narrow in places and in very high tides you might risk being cut off.

The areas undeveloped by NASA are managed by the Merritt Island National Wildlife Refuge and the Canaveral National Seashore. This section of coast is the last significant natural coastline on the eastern seaboard of the USA. It is recommended that you pick up the free official map and guide at the information centers on Highway 402 and the park road south of Highway AIA (on Apollo Beach). It gives a lot of information on the refuge.

In the winter, the **Indian River Lagoon** and **Merritt Island** supports populations of 50,000 to 70,000 ducks and 100,000 coots. However the endangered species which live here also attract much attention from naturalists. They include for instance, the Atlantic Salt Marsh snake which is now found nowhere else beyond this refuge.

Apollo Beach can be reached by a few boardwalks and parking is free. The beach between here and Playalinda Beach further south can only be reached on foot. The area is cleared during launches and NASA takes security very seriously. A warship and submarine are positioned offshore, a SWAT team is on standby and nature helps with 4,000 alligators, let alone the snakes, so if the beach is off-limits, accept it graciously.

At the southern end of Canaveral National Shoreline **Playalinda Beach** is a further stretch of undeveloped, secluded natural shoreline. Free parking and boardwalk crossovers allow access without damaging the dune vegetation. Hundreds of giant turtles still haul themselves ashore here every year to lay their eggs. There is a self-guided nature trail for motorists through the undeveloped area inland from the beach.

Port Canaveral is a busy port and marina, and the third largest cruise port in the USA, home of Premier Cruise Lines and their "Big Red Boat", Disney's new cruise line, Europa Cruise Lines and Carnival Cruise Lines. Many of the cruises are of 3 or 4 days duration to the Bahamas, but there are even half-day and all-day mini cruises as well. Natural and artificial reefs attract shoals of fish and fishermen.

The Space Coast has two Visitor Information Centers — at the Kennedy Space Visitor Complex and at the Melbourne

Regional Airport. Both open every day except Christmas Day.

For information on Canaveral National Seashore contact 308 Julia Street, Titusville, F1 32796 ☎ (407) 267-1110. Open: 8am-sunset, except when there are launches.

The **Indian River Lagoon**, which separates Merritt Island from the mainland, is a mixture of salt and fresh water, which runs for 160 miles (258km) along Florida's east coast and, at the southern tip of Merritt Island is the Merritt Island Dragon. The 100ft (30m) dragon was built in 1970 using more than 20 tons of concrete and steel, and is the work of Tampa sculptor Lewis Vandercar. In 1982 four smaller dragons were added. According to Indian legend, a dragon rose out of the river hundreds of years ago to chase away mainland enemies that were attacking the island Indians.

Cocoa Beach and Beyond

Driving south along the coast takes you to Cocoa Beach, a bustling seaside town with good beaches and popular with day trippers from the Orlando area. **Cocoa Beach Pier**, stretching 840ft (256m) into the Atlantic Ocean, is the most famous landmark and open 365 days a year offering food, drink, shopping and live entertainment and

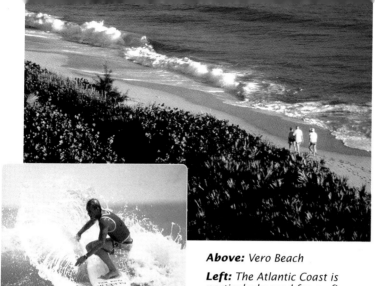

Above: *Vero Beach*

Left: *The Atlantic Coast is particularly good for surfing*

Opposite page: *A bobcat caught by a remote activated camera. Merritt Island is a huge wildlife refuge surrounding KSC, with its own Visitor Center.*

incredible views of the ocean and beaches. It is also a terrific place to fish from. Ron Jon's Surf Shop has to be one of the most advertised establishments in Florida and it is open 24 hours a day all year long.

Brevard Museum of History and Natural Science is in Michigan Avenue, Cocoa. It traces the history of the area from the earliest days with artifacts from the native Indians who first lived there, then the fifteenth-century Spaniards and finally, the pioneers who were largely responsible for developing the area as it is today. Next to the museum are 22 acres (9 hectares) of nature trails, some of which have wheelchair access. The museum

is open: 10am-4pm Tuesday to Saturday, 1-4pm Sunday, closed Monday ☎ (407) 632-1830.

The **Astronaut Memorial Hall and Planetarium** are on the Brevard Community College Campus, Clearlake Road, Cocoa. The **Planetarium** provides multi-media shows on its 360 degree domed ceiling. The Hall contains astronaut and space memorabilia while a giant telescope in the observatory next door gives an astronaut's-eye view of the stars. For more information ☎ (407) 631-7889.

South of Cocoa Beach is the sprawling **Patrick Air Force Base** and a number of beach areas, such as Satellite Beach,

Cocoa Village

Cocoa Village is another historic district worth visiting. The old down town area has been faithfully recreated. The **Porcher House**, originally the home of a prominent citrus grower, is open to the public. It was the grandest home in Cocoa at the time of its construction in 1916 and is a unique example of twentieth-century Classic Revival Style interpreted in local coquina rock. There are many interesting stores and craft shops around the museum. **The Cocoa Village Playhouse**, originally a Vaudeville theater, now features a wide range of entertainment, as well as being the home of the Children's Community Theater.

Indian Harbour Beach and Canova Beach. There is public access to the beaches along the whole length of the Space Coast. Make sure you leave your car in a road zoned for parking, because several of the beach access roads are tow-away areas.

Inland from Patrick is **Rock-ledge** with a number of historic buildings, and a 5,000 seat Olympic size skating rink — the third largest in the USA. Then drive down to Melbourne or return to the coast and head south for Melbourne Beach, Sebastion, Vero Beach and Fort Pierce.

Apart from the space center and the beaches, the area offers a host of sports and recreations. Almost any type of water sport is available, from airboating on the St John's River to water-skiing, surfing and swimming. There is excellent fishing, both freshwater and saltwater, and no shortage of boats available for charter to take you to the best angling grounds. There is golf, tennis, hiking and biking trails, or enjoy the arts and cultural activities on offer.

There are three major shopping malls along the Space Coast, many other smaller shopping areas, often in historic districts, and the Frontenac Flea Market, the largest on the east coast. There are more than 1,400 restaurants to choose from. There is also a good selection of night life to choose from if you still have the energy with clubs, dancing, movies and live entertainment.

Melbourne

Melbourne is a quiet community with many of the houses hidden from the road by gardens of lush vegetation, and the area to the south is largely undeveloped.

Downtown Melbourne nestles along the banks of Crane Creek and is another historic district which has managed to maintain its air of nostalgia with galleries, restaurants, boutiques, theaters and antique stores, housed in fine examples of turn-of-the-century architecture. Of particular interest are the Brevard Symphony Orchestra House built in the late 1890s in Highland Avenue, and a fine example of Florida 'cracker' frame style, and James Wadsworth Rossetter House, also in Highland Avenue, and believed to have been originally built before the Civil War although much altered since.

Visit the **Brevard Art Center and Museum**, 1463 Highland Avenue, which stages touring art exhibitions as well as having its own permanent show. Open: gallery tours 2-4pm Tuesday to Saturday, 12noon-4pm Sunday ☎ (407) 242-0737. Enjoy classical musical or theater at the Maxwell C. King Center for the Performing Arts, or Henegar Center. The Brevard Symphony Orchestra, which celebrated its fortieth anniversary in 1994, frequently performs at the King Center, while the Melbourne Municipal Band provides several free concerts during the year, especially on Sunday afternoons in the park during the summer.

The **Space Coast Science Center**, 1510 Highland Avenue, combines education, entertainment and exploration. There are hands-on exhibits and games, and you can gain a fascinating insight into native plants, reptiles and sea life in the Nature Discovery Room. Open: 10am-5pm Thursday to Saturday, 12noon-5pm Sunday. Closed Monday ☎ (407) 259-5572.

For those who want something different, **Melbourne Greyhound Park** opened in 1991 offering nightly parimutuel betting, and the Florida Marlins now have an 8,000 seat training facility at Viera, just outside Melbourne, although it will be used for other things beside baseball. Melbourne Regional Airport serves all the Space Coast and is served by six major airlines and three commuter air carriers.

Melbourne Beach Pier was built between 1888 and 1889 by the Melbourne and Atlantic Railroad Company who founded the settlement at Melbourne Beach. It provided the most practical access to the island, and the community's first post office opened on the pier in 1894.

South of Melbourne Beach is **Palm Bay** and **Turkey Creek Sanctuary**, offering three very distinct Florida plant communities and the opportunity to see a number of endangered species, including manatees, in their natural habitat via a 4,000ft (1,219m) long path of boardwalks.

Other good manatee-watching areas are: Indian River Lagoon, Archie Carr National Wildlife Refuge, Melbourne Beach, Banana River Aquatic Reserve, Turkey Creek Sanctuary and Crane Creek.

Sebastian

You can view authentic shipwreck artifacts, Spanish treasure and fine jewelry at the **Mel Fisher Treasure Museum** in Sebastian. Open: Monday to Saturday 10am-5pm, Sunday 12noon-5pm. The Sebastian waterfront has undergone some dramatic changes in the last year or so, and has now taken on a 'fishing village' atmosphere, with more opportunities for water sports, river cruises and fishing charters. The State operates a visitor information center and museum at the McLarty Center in the Sebastian Inlet area.

Indian River County

Further south, Indian River County has a population of around 92,000, of whom 18,000 live in Vero Beach. The area is a center for citrus growing where you can visit a citrus packing plant and, of course, buy the produce.

Vero Beach

Vero Beach has the dual distinction of being where the tropics begin in Florida, and of being Florida's best 'little town', combining sun, sea, sand and uncrowded beaches — all 26 miles (42km) of them. It boasts an average year-round temperature of 73.3°F (23°C). There are hotels, motels, campgrounds and RV parks to suit all pockets, fine restaurants and nightly entertainment, as well as arts and cultural activities and year-round sports and recreation, including the famous **Windsor Polo Club** which attracts world class polo teams.

Many of Vero Beach's shops are located in attractive beachside sites where parking is easy, and you can stroll along landscaped walkways wafted by sea breezes. There are also excellent restaurants for lunch or dinner. Ocean and Cardinal Drives also offer interesting boutiques, gift and curiosity stores.

Vero Beach is the winter home of the **Los Angeles Dodgers**, and home of the world-famous Indian River Citrus.

There is an art museum in the **Center for the Arts** in Riverside Park (open: Monday to Sunday 10am-4.30pm, Thursday until 8pm ☎ (407) 231-0707) and the **Indian River Citrus Museum**, housed in the

calendar
Space Coast

FEBRUARY

- Seafood Festival (3rd week).

MARCH

- Valiant Air Command Warbird Airshow (2nd week).
- Port Canaveral Seafood Festival (4th weekend).

APRIL

- Easter Surfing Festival Cocoa Beach (Easter weekend).
- Indian River Festival, Titusville (4th weekend).
- Melbourne Arts Festival (4th weekend).

MAY

- Bluegrass Festival, Titusville (1st weekend).
- Cocoa Beach Fest (3rd weekend).

JUNE

- Aquafest, Melbourne (3rd weekend).

JULY

- Firecracker Festival, Melbourne (4th of July).

AUGUST

- Family Festival, Titusville (2nd weekend).

SEPTEMBER

- All Star Jazz Festival, Cocoa Beach (Labor Day weekend).
- Pro-Am Surfing Contest, Cocoa Beach (Labor Day weekend).
- Port Weekend, Cocoa Beach (3rd weekend).

OCTOBER

- Cocoa Village Autumn Art Festival (1st weekend).
- Titusville Oktoberfest (2nd weekend).
- Seminole Indian and Florida Pioneer Festival, Brevard Community College (2nd weekend).
- Melbourne Oktoberfest (3rd weekend).

NOVEMBER

- Brevard County Fair, Cocoa (2nd and 3rd weekends).
- Space Coast Art Festival, Cocoa Beach (Thanksgiving weekend).

Heritage Center in historic downtown, open daily.

The **Indian River County Historical Society**, open on weekends only, has restored an old Florida East Coast Railway depot on 14th Avenue, into a museum displaying railroad artifacts and historical exhibits of local interest. Historical walking tours are also available by appointment.

Vero Beach is also home of the first Disney resort constructed off-site from its theme parks. The first phase of the complex includes a 120-room inn and 60 villas, restaurant, shops, a 6-acre (2-hectare) lake, swimming pools and other recreational amenities.

If you are interested in wildlife, it is worth visiting the **Environmental Learning Center,** open daily ☎ (589) 5050, a 51-acre (20-hectare) island reserve south from the Wabasso bridge on country road 510 and north of Vero Beach. It is a series of indoor and outdoor laboratories and classrooms, exhibit area and auditorium surrounded by a variety of wetland habitats rich in wildlife.

Fort Pierce

The **St Lucie County Historical Museum** in Fort Pierce, 414 Seaway Drive, includes exhibits salvaged from the sunken Spanish treasure ships in 1715, and the history of the area, particularly the citrus industry and

> ### Best Beaches
>
> Best local beaches are Sebastian Inlet State Recreation Area, Golden Sands Park Beach on Orchid Island (the newest public access beach), Wabasso Beach Park on A1A and SR510, Jaycee Beach Park on Ocean Drive and Mango Road, Humiston Beach Park on South Ocean Drive, South Beach Park, South Ocean Drive, and Riverside Park, east of the Barber Bridge on Orchard Island.

fishing, is well told using old photographs. Open: 10am-4pm Tuesday to Saturday, 12noon-4pm Sunday ☎ (407) 468-1785.

The **UDT-SEAL Museum** in Fort Pierce, 3300 North A1A, is devoted to the work of the US Navy's Underwater Demolition Teams and the SEALS (Sea, Air and Land forces), a cross between the British SAS and SBS (Special Boat Squadron). You will learn that it was navy frogmen who trained the first astronauts, and how scuba equipment developed. Open: 10am-4pm Tuesday to Saturday, 12noon-4pm Sunday except holidays.

STATE NATIONAL PARKS, HISTORIC SITES AND RECREATION AREAS

Fort Pierce Inlet State Recreation Area 4 miles (6km) east of Fort Pierce via North Causeway.

A 340-acre (136-hectare) park offering group camping, fishing, swimming, surfing, cycling and picnicking. An area of dunes and coastal hammocks teeming with birdlife, as is nearby Jack Island which has nature and hiking trails ☎ (407) 468-3985.

New Smyrna Sugar Mill Ruins State Historic Site

New Smyrna Beach.

Once the heart of a flourishing sugar plantation owned by two New York merchants and manned by slaves. There used to be ten sugar mills operating along this stretch of coast in the early 1800s. The sugar mill was attacked and burned down by Seminole Indians during the Second Seminole War in 1835 ☎ (904) 428-2126.

Sebastian Inlet State Recreation Area

Melbourne Beach.

One of the best saltwater fishing locations on Florida's east coast. From the jetties one can catch snook, redfish, bluefish and Spanish mackerel. You can also camp, swim, go boating and scuba diving (for qualified divers). There is a boat ramp and a beach area for sunbathing. The McLarty Treasure Museum is on the site of the Spanish sailors' salvage camp ☎ (407) 984-4852.

The **McLarty Museum** is part of the Sebastian Inlet State Recreation Area, and traces the turbulent history of the coast which has seen many wrecks. In 1715, around 1,500 survivors from a wrecked Spanish treasure fleet struggled ashore. They built a camp and then set about recovering the treasure. No-one knows how much of the treasure was salvaged, but about half found its way back to Spain. The wrecks of the fleet were not rediscovered until 1926.

The recreation area is reputed to have the best surfing on the Florida coast and the surfing and swimming beaches are kept apart.

Hotels and Motels

Central Florida must boast more hotel and motel accommodation than any other tourist destination in the world. Not only are there literally thousands of hotels and motels

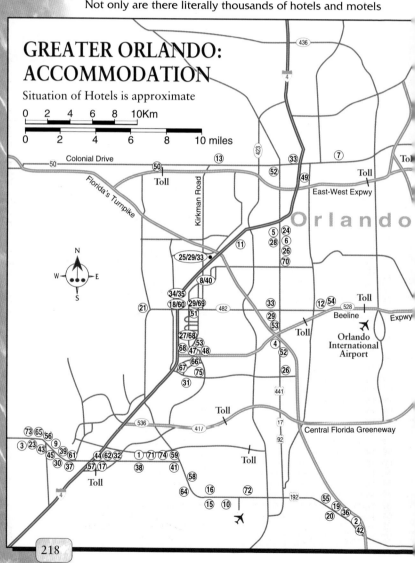

GREATER ORLANDO: ACCOMMODATION

Situation of Hotels is approximate

Fact File

to choose from, but there is a huge choice of categories, from luxury to basic, to suit all tastes and pockets.

Most modern hotels and motels usually offer two double beds in each room, and as you pay for the room, this can work out very reasonably if you are travelling as a family or with friends. As rooms tend to be large, an extra single bed or cot can also usually be obtained for a small additional fee, provided the management receive adequate notice. Most rooms have en suite bathroom and telephone, air-conditioning and cable/satellite television is standard. Older hotels often offer rooms with just a single or double bed.

KEY TO MAIN ACCOMMODATION

① Best Western Eastgate
② Best Western Kissimmee
③ Best Western Maingate
④ Budgetel
⑤ Budget Lodge Midtown
⑥ Choice Inn
⑦ Colonial Plaza Inn
⑧ Comfort Inn
⑨ Comfort Inn Maingate
⑩ Comfort Suites Hotel
⑪ Days Inn
⑫ Days Inn Airport
⑬ Days Inn Central
⑭ Days Inn Civic Center
⑮ Days Inn Downtown Kissimmee
⑯ Days Inn Downtown North
⑰ Days Inn East
⑱ Days Inn International Drive
⑲ Days Inn Kissimmee East
⑳ Days Inn Kissimmee Turnpike
㉑ Days Inn Lakeside
㉒ Days Inn/Lodge
㉓ Days Inn Maingate West
㉔ Days Inn South
㉕ Days Inn Universal
㉖ Econo Lodge
㉖ Fairfield Inn
㉗ Gold Key Inn
㉘ Hampton Inn
㉙ Hilton Inn Gateway
㉚ Hilton Grand Vacation
㉛ Hojo Inn Maingate East
㉜ Holiday Inn
㉝ Holiday Inn Express
㉞ Holiday Inn International Drive
㉟ Holiday Inn Kissimmee East
㊱ Holiday Inn Maingate
㊲ Holiday Inn Maingate East

㊳ Holiday Inn Maingate West
㊴ Howard Johnson
㊵ Howard Johnson Fountain Park Plaza Hotel
㊶ Howard Johnson Kissimmee Lodge
㊷ Howard Johnson Maingate Hotel
㊸ Hyatt Orlando
㊹ Inns of America
㊺ Marriott Courtyard
㊻ Omni Rosen
㊼ Orlando Heritage Inn
㊽ Orlando Plantation Manor Youth Hostel
㊾ Orlando Motel
㊿ Orlando Marriott
51 Palm Court Hotel
52 Peabody Hotel
53 Quality Inn Airport
54 Quality Inn East
55 Quality Inn Maingate
56 Quality Suites Maingate East
57 Ramada Inn
58 Ramada Limited
59 Ramada Resort
60 Ramada Resort Maingate
61 Ramada Inn Maingate Parkway
62 Rodeway Inn
63 Sevilla Inn
64 Sheraton Lakeside Inn
65 Sheraton World
66 Stoffer Resort
67 Summerfield Suites
68 The Floridian
69 Travelodge
70 Travelodge Hotel Maingate East
71 Travelodge Kissimmee Flags
72 Travelodge Maingate West
73 Travelodge Suites East Gate
74 Wynfield Inn

Fact File

Because competition is so intense prices are generally much lower than comparable accommodation elsewhere and there are usually added incentives to tempt you. These can range from free breakfasts to free shuttle buses to take you to and from the attractions.

Prices vary according to season and standard of service offered. Most hotel chains offer vouchers which, if pre-paid, offer substantial discounts, so it is worth checking with your travel company. Before buying vouchers, however, make sure the hotel offers the standard of service you require. There are also substantial discounts for senior citizens, and members of the American Automobile Association.

If you are visiting during peak seasons, around Christmas, Easter or during the summer, it is advisable to book accommodation. At other times, you may want to cruise around and hunt out the best bargains. All hotels and motels clearly advertise their room rates as well as other perks on offer, and you can always pop in and check the room out before deciding. If you feel up to it, you can always haggle over the price and see if you can get a few extra dollars knocked off for staying several nights, paying cash or whatever.

Many restaurants and motels have their own restaurants, and will usually offer American Plan (full board) or Modified American Board (half-board). If the establishment has no restaurant, there is usually coffee available in the lobby at most times, with free doughnuts often available in lieu of breakfast. Ice machines and soft drinks dispensers are generally available.

Many hotels and motels also provide cooking facilities in rooms, and these establishments are advertised as 'efficiences'. The cooking facilities provided, however, can vary from a single hot plate to a fully-fitted kitchen, so if you plan to do a lot of cooking, check out the facilities on offer before agreeing to take the room.

Most hotel and motel chains have toll-free numbers to ring from within the US for information and reservations. Always check to see what discounts are available and if there are any restrictions concerning children and pets.

Best Inns	☎ 800-237-8466
Best Western	☎ 800-528-1234
Budgetel Inns	☎ 800-4-BUDGET
Budget Host Inns	☎ 800-BUD-HOST
Clarion-Choice Hotels:	
Comfort Inns	☎ 800-228-5150
Clarion Inns	☎ 800-CLARION
Econo Lodges	☎ 800-55-ECONO
Friendship Inns	☎ 800-453-4511
Quality Inns	☎ 800-228-5151
Rodeway Inns	☎ 800-229-2000
Sleep Inns	☎ 800-62-SLEEP
Days Inns	☎ 800-325-2525
Economy Inns of America	☎ 800-423-3018
Embassy Suites	☎ 800-528-1100
Hilton Hotels	☎ 800-HILTONS
Holiday Inn	☎ 800-HOLIDAY
Hospitality	
International Inns	☎ 800-251-1962
Howard Johnson	☎ 800-654-2000
Hyatt Hotels International	☎ 800-228-9000
Marriott Hotels	☎ 800-228-2800
Ramada Inns	☎ 800-2-RAMADA
Sheraton Hotels,	
Motor Inns and Resorts	☎ 800-325-3535
Super 8 Motels	☎ 800-800-8000
Travelodge	☎ 800-255-3050

Condominiums

A condominium or condo is an apartment of several rooms. There may be just a few condos in the building or hundreds in a high-rise tower block. Many people from out of state buy a condo as an investment, and a place for their summer holidays, and rent them out through agents when they are not there. They can be available to rent from a week up to a year. They offer more space and privacy than a hotel or motel room, and for larger groups, work out much cheaper.

Resorts

These usually consist of a hotel or group of hotels built around a specific development offering first-class accommodation, food and entertainment. The Walt Disney World Resort hotels, for instance, not only offer almost on-the-spot access to the theme park, but a variety of other attractions as well. Many of the resorts are built around golf courses or man made lakes offering swimming and a variety of water sports.

Bed and Breakfast/Guesthouses

Worth hunting out if you want a taste of real Florida living. They are often more expensive than a cheap motel or hotel, but they do allow you to stay in a family home. Local tourist offices have lists of homes offering bed and breakfast accommodation, and guest houses, otherwise known as boarding houses. For details contact:

The Director, Tourist House Association of America
PO Box 355-AA, Greentown
Pennsylvania 18426

Rental Homes

Thousands of holidaymakers who have visited Florida have fallen in love with the State and bought a second home there. Many of these homes are rented out in their owner's absence and they make excellent bases. Most homes are furnished to a very high standard, have air-conditioning and their own swimming pool, often heated over the winter months. Rental homes are usually advertised by their owners, or are booked by holiday companies who then offer combined packages including rental, air fares and car rental. For larger families and groups of friends, the cost of renting a three or four bedroom house is significantly cheaper than comparable hotel accommodation, and you have the added bonus of more space, privacy and your own pool. For listings contact tourist offices.

YMCA and Youth Hostels

For inexpensive accommodation, these make ideal bases, although advance booking is essential for both during peak periods. If travelling from abroad and wanting to stay in a youth hostel, you must be a member of your own country's hostelling association. For further information:

American Youth Hostels Inc, 1332 Eye Street NW, Washington DC 20013-7613

YMCA via The Y's Way, 356 West 34th Street, New York, NY 10001, ☎ 212-769-5856

Hostelling International—Orlando at Plantation Manor overlooks beautiful Lake Eola at 227 North Eola Drive, Orlando, FL 32801. Those staying in the lovely Spanish-style hostel, located in Downtown Orlando, can swim, jog and play basketball at the nearby YMCA or go on hostel-sponsored van trips. ☎ (407) 843-8888

Hostelling International — American Youth Hostels (HI-AYH) has recently opened its first 'resort style' hostel in Kissimmee, 5 miles from Disney World. On the shores of Lake Cecile, it offers 200 beds in small dormitories with en-suite bathrooms and private double rooms ☎ (407) 396-8282. 4840 West Irlo Bronson Highway (Highway 192).

Babysitting

Most hotels and resorts offer baby sitting facilities, and there are a number of registered companies that will send baby sitters to your hotel room or villa, or take the children off your hands by escorting them to the attractions. Most hotels and resorts also have special events and areas for children, from infants to teens, with trained staff to supervise them.

BICYCLES

On the road cycling in built up areas can be hazardous, but cycling in rural areas and on cycle trails can be very rewarding. Many state parks offer cycle trails and the Florida Park Service is committed to expanding park-to-park bike routes. It is currently developing three cycle tours ranging in length from 101 miles (163km) to 327 miles (526km). The state is also converting many former railroad routes into cycling, hiking trails. There are bike trails at Rock Springs Run State Reserve (12 miles/19km), Lower Wekiva River State Reserve, Seminole State Forest, Tosohatchee State Reserve (40 miles/64km), Lake Wales, Haines City and Sugarloaf Mountain.

CANOEING

Canoe rentals are available in several locations, including many State Parks, and provide an excellent way of seeing the real Florida, as you gently paddle down backwaters inaccessible in any other way. Even within a couple of miles of Walt Disney World, it is possible to rent a canoe for an hour or two, and within minutes the noise of traffic has vanished and you are alone with nature. Always use an effective insect repellent and a good sun screen.

For more serious canoeists there are hundreds of miles to be paddled in the State Parks. There are thirty-six canoe trails within the Florida Recreational Trails System, often using publicly-owned waterways to link State Parks and forests.

CARAVANS/CAMPING

Caravans and RVs* also make excellent bases. Caravan and RV parks are usually equipped to a high standard, and apart from electricity and water hook-up, usually have on-site shop, restaurant, bar and club house, as well as many other facilities. Most parks rent out mobile homes, and if you want to travel about you can rent a car and caravan, or an RV. (* For overseas visitors RVs are recreational vehicles and trailers are motorised caravans and caravans.)

Camping and backpacking is popular, but it is advisable only in official campsites or in the National or State Parks. Facilities are generally excellent, but always check first that tents are allowed, and if so, where they can be pitched. In many parks, camping is free in the remoter areas but you will have to hike in, and you may require a wilderness permit. These are usually obtained locally from the information centre. Always check first. If moving on foot in remote areas always try to travel in groups of at least three. In that way if someone is hurt, one person can stay and look after the injured, and another can go for help.

A word of warning — off-road camping, even when permitted, is not recommended.

CLIMATE

Florida's year-round good weather is the main reason people flock to the Sunshine State in their millions, both on holiday and to live. Central Florida has two seasons — hot, humid and wet summer months (June to September), and warm and mostly dry for the rest of the year.

During the summer months there can be spectacular electrical storms, thus Orlando's title as the lightning capital of the world, and torrential downpours, usually accompanied by thunder, and often in the late afternoon or early evening. Rain lasting all day, however, is not common. These summer deluges rarely last for long, and can often be over in a few minutes. They can also be incredibly localised. You can be in one part of town which is dry all day, yet just a few hundred yards away, they have had torrential rain.

When it does rain, it really pours. It is why houses in Central Florida do not have gutters, because they just would not be able to cope. If you are caught out in one of these downpours, seek shelter at once. You normally get a little warning, but you will usually notice the temperature dropping. As soon as the rain stops, however, the temperature and humidity rises again, and the water quickly evaporates.

If you are driving when it starts to rain, turn on your headlights and windscreen wipers, and reduce your speed. Exercise the greatest caution because the roads often flood, there can be blinding spray and the risk of aquaplaning.

There is the risk of hurricanes any time betwen June and November, with September the most at-risk month, but having said this, the risk of one actually hitting central Florida is not great. Hurricane Andrew with winds of 164mph (264kph), which devastated an area south of Miami in August 1992, was the most severe storm to hit Florida for decades.

Hurricane Georges, which hit the Keys in September 1998, caused $250 million of damage but all

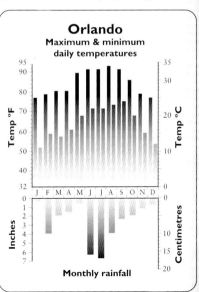

Orlando
Maximum & minimum daily temperatures

Monthly rainfall

tourist facilities were re-opened within 10 days.

On average, a hurricane can be expected to hit Florida about once every 5 years, and the vast majority of these cause minimal damage. Florida can expect to be affected by an offshore hurricane about once every 2 years.

Apart from fierce high winds and towering seas, heavy rainfall is another feature associated with hurricanes. Florida's wettest day was in September, 1950 during hurricane activity, when 38.5 inches of rain fell during a 24 hour period close to Cedar Key on the Central Gulf Coast.

In Central Florida, summer temperatures top 90°F (32°C) two days in three inland, although they may be a degree or two lower on the coast. Temperatures above 100°F (38°C) are very unusual.

Early morning fog can be a problem during early spring and late autumn, and March and April are the windiest months of the year.

During the winter sustained cold spells are rare as is snow, although overnight frosts do occur infrequently in Central Florida. Temperatures quickly rise, however, and even in the 'coldest' months of December and January maximum temperatures are usually in the high 70s.

DISABLED FACILITIES

Florida leads the world in the provision of facilities for the handicapped. By law, all public buildings, National and State Parks must provide access facilities for the handicapped, and most hotels and attractions mirror this with superb access and facilities. The major attractions have also made special provision for the totally or partially blind or deaf.

Many of the major car rental companies can provide specially adapted cars and vehicles with special controls, if given advance notice.

For those who do not want to drive there are options of joining organised tours, or staying in one of the many resorts which can provide self contained holidays without the need for lots of travelling.

One of the major problems for handicapped people is moving around urban areas and especially crossing streets because of the risk of meeting motor traffic even when the lights are red. The danger is because of the highway code which allows motorists to turn right from a side road onto the main road if safe to do so, even when the lights are red.

EATING OUT

Central Florida has restaurants and eateries to suit every taste and pocket, from gourmet establishments to eat-all-you-can buffets, and a huge range of ethnic cuisines to choose from. Most of the upmarket hotels have very good, if sometimes pricey restaurants, and many of these also operate a dress code, one of the very few occasions in Florida when what you wear matters.

The quality of food is excellent as is the speed and level of service. Most waiters and waitresses rely on tips to pad out their low basic wages so they are going to be polite, but almost all seem genuinely interested in making sure you have a good time.

In the height of the season you may have to wait to be seated if you choose to eat at busy times, but once at the table your order is taken quickly and your meal delivered not too long after that. First time visitors to 24 hour restaurants like Dennys are amazed when a stop watch is put on the table as soon as the order is taken, and even more surprised when told that the meal is on the house if it is not served within 10 minutes.

For Overseas Visitors

Traditional American menus concentrate on steaks, ribs and seafood, followed by mouthwatering desserts, especially local specialities like Key Lime Pie. The beef is generally excellent and the portions large. There is no shortage of choice, however, and some of the buffet restaurants where you can eat all you can for a few dollars, offer more than 100 different dishes for you to try. These establishments are a great idea if you have growing children with healthy appetites. Many table service menus offer soup or salad and dessert free with the main course. Most restaurants subscribe to the many discount coupon magazines freely available, so collect these and hand them in to cut down on your eating costs, and many restaurants actually give a range of ready-prepared meals, cooked on the premises, which can be eaten cold or warmed up when you get home.

Eating out is cheap. A family of four with two young children can expect to spend $10 to $12 for a meal at a burger bar, $25 to $35 for a light lunch, and $30 to $40 for a family restaurant dinner. Of course if you splash out, the cost will be that much higher.

The following is a selection of restaurants graded as follows:

$ — dinner for one under $10
$$ — dinner for one between $10-$20
$$$ — dinner for one $20

All telephone numbers: code is 407, except where indicated.

AMERICAN RESTAURANTS

Bennigan's $-$$
6109 Westwood Blvd,
Orlando ☎ 352-5657

Black-Eyed Pea $
5305 W Irlo Bronson
Highway, Kissimmee
☎ 397-1500

Cafe Terrace $$
2950 Reedy Creek Blvd,
Kissimmee ☎ 396-4466

Calico Jack's $
11726 E. Colonial Drive,
Orlando ☎ 249-2526

Friday's $-$$
5034 W. Irlo Bronson Hy.,
Kissimmee ☎ 397-2200

Hard Rock Cafe $
Universal Studios (admission
to park not necessary)
☎ 351-7625

Hollywood Diner $
☎ 351-7625

Hooters $
5300 South Kirkman Road,
Orlando
☎ 354-5350

Jungle Jim's $$
12501 SR 535,
Lake Buena Vista
☎ 827-1257

Kettle Restaurant $
7777 W. Irlo Bronson
Highway/5351 W. US 192,
Kissimmee ☎ 847-7709

**Lombard's Landing
Restaurant $$**
Universal Studios
☎ 224-7000

Magic Mining Co. $-$$$
7763 W. Highway 192
☎ 396-8986

**The Mill Bakery Eatery
Brewery $$**
5905 Kirkman Road,
Orlando ☎ 282-9772

Morrison's Cafeteria $
Osceola Square Mall,
Kissimmee ☎ 896-2091

Pebbles Cityside Restaurant $$ 17 W. Church
Street, Orlando
☎ 839-0892

Pebbles Restaurant $$
12551 SR 535,
Lake Buena Vista
☎ 827-1111

Shooters Waterfront Cafe $$
4315 North Orange Blossom
Trail, Orlando. No phone.

TGI Friday's $-$$
6424 Carrier Drive,
Orlando ☎ 345-8822

Victoria and Albert's $$$
WDW Grand Floridian Resort
☎ 939-3463

Westerly's At Metro West $$
2100 South Hiawassee
Road, Orlando. No phone.

Wolfgang Puck Cafe $$$
Downtown Disney
West Side ☎ 938-9653

BARBECUE

**Cheyenne Saloon and
Opera House**
129 West Church Street,
Orlando ☎ 422-2434

Damon's The Place for Ribs
$$ 8445 International Drive,
Orlando ☎ 352-5984

The Fireworks Factory $$
Pleasure Island,
Lake Buena Vista
☎ 934-8989

Lazybone Ribs $-$$
4738 W Irlo Bronson
Highway, Kissimmee.
No phone.

**Tony Roma's –
A Place for Ribs $-$$**
3415 W. Vine Street,
Kissimmee ☎ 870-9299

BUFFET-STYLE RESTAURANTS

Billy The Kid's Buffet $
on Highway 192 half a mile
(1km) west of SR 535
☎ 396-4009

Stacey's Smorgasbord $
4118 W. Vine St Kissimmee.
No phone.

Western Steer Steakhouse
$-$$ 6315 International
Drive, Orlando ☎ 363-0677

CHINESE

China Pearl $-$$
2959 Vineland Rd,
Kissimmee ☎ 397-4448

The Forbidden City $-$$
948 N. Mills Ave, Orlando
☎ 894-5005

Ming Court $$
9188 International Drive,
Orlando ☎ 351-9988

Pagoda Garden $-$$$
5737 W. Highway 192
☎ 396-0669

**Szechuan Chinese
Restaurant $-$$**
5489 W. Irlo Bronson
Highway, Kissimmee
☎ 396-1885

CUBAN

**Rolando's Cuban
Restaurant $-$$**
870 Semoran Boulevard,
Casselberry ☎ 767-9677

ENGLISH

Harry Ramsbottom's $-$$
'Sunday Roast everyday'

5260 W. Irlo Bronson
Highway ☎ 396-4114

Rose and Crown $-$$
World Showcase,
Epcot ☎ 824-4321

There are a number of
English pubs serving food
along Highway 192 in Kissi-
mmee including **Rovers
Return Pubs**, 3620 W. Vine
Street and at West 192,
Kissimmee. English food
and beers ☎ 870-1535.

FRENCH

**Chalet Suzanne
Restaurant & Inn $$$**
3800 Chalet Suzanne Drive,
Lake Wales
☎ (941) 676-6011

La Normandie $$-$$$
2021 Colonial Drive,
Orlando ☎ 896-9976

Maison & Jardin $$$
430 South Wymore Road,
Altamonte Springs
☎ 862-4410

Park Plaza Gardens $$$
Park Avenue South,
Winter Park ☎ 645-2475

INDIAN

Bombay Chapati $
7400 Southland Boulevard,
Orlando ☎ 649-4884

**New Punjab Indian
Restaurant $-$$**
7451 International Drive
☎ 352-7887

Passage to India $$
5532 International Drive
☎ 351-3456

ITALIAN

**Bergamo's Italian
Restaurant $$-$$$**
8445 International Drive
☎ 352-3805

Christini's $$$
7600 Dr Phillips Boulevard,
Orlando ☎ 345-8770

Enzo's Restaurant $$$
1130 S. US 17-92,
Longwood ☎ 834-9872

Flippers Pizza $
6125 Westwood Boulevard/
7480 Republic Drive,
Orlando ☎ 345-0113

Gina's On The Water
309 N. Lake Blvd,
Altamonte Springs
☎ 834-5880

**Milano's Italian
Eatery & Pizza $**
6807 B & C Visitors Circle,
Orlando ☎ 382-9004

**Olive Garden
Restaurant $-$$**
branches throughout area

**Pacini's Italian
Ristorante $-$$**
5795 W. Highway 192
☎ 396-8022

Palio $$
World Swan Hotel, Lake
Buena Vista ☎ 934-3000

Roma's $$
730 S. Orange Blossom
Trail, Apopka ☎ 886-2360

**Rosario's Italian
Ristorante & Pizzeria $$**
4838 W. Highway 192,
Kissimmee ☎ 239-0118

JAPANESE

Benihana Restaurant $$
Hilton Walt Disney World
☎ 827-4865

Kobe $-$$
2901 Parkway Boulevard,
Kissimmee ☎ 396-8088

**Osaka Japanese
Steak House $-$$**
3155 W. Vine Street,
Kissimmee ☎ 847-8822

Ran-Getsu of Tokyo $$
8400 International Drive
☎ 345-0044

**Shogun Japanese
Steak House $$**
6327 International Drive
☎ 352-1607

MEDITERRANEAN

Kiko's Cuisine $
6911 Municipal Drive,
Orlando. No phone.

**Phoenician
Restaurant $-$$**
2920 Vineland Rd,
Kissimmee ☎ 397-2230

NIGHTCLUBS

Pleasure Island
Lake Buena Vista
☎ 934-7781

SEAFOOD

Atlantic Bay Seafood $$-$$$
2901 Parkway Boulevard,
Kissimmee ☎ 396-7736

Boston Lobster Feast $-$$
branches in Orlando and
Kissimmee

Cap't Nemo's $-$$
5469 Highway 192 West,
Kissimmee ☎ 396-6911

Charlie's Lobster House $$
8445 International Drive
☎ 352-6929

Crabhouse Seafood $$
8496 Palm Parkway, Lake
Buena Vista ☎ 239-1888

Cracker's Oyster Bar $$
129 West Church Street,
Orlando ☎ 422-2434

**Larry's Cedar River
Seafood & Oyster Bar**
7107 S. Orange Blossom
Trail ☎ 858-0525

Ocean Grill $$
6432 International Drive
☎ 352-9993

Red Lobster $$
branches throughout
the area

STEAK & SEAFOOD

**Barney's Steak and
Seafood $$**
1615 E. Colonial Drive,
Orlando ☎ 896-6864

Black Angus $-$$
2001 W. Vine St,
Kissimmee
☎ 846-7117

**The Butcher Shop
Steak House $$**
8445 International Drive
☎ 363-9727

**Cattleman's Steak
House $$-$$$**
2948 Vineland Road,
Kissimmee ☎ 397-1888

Charley's Steakhouse $$
6107 S. Orange Blossom
Trail, Orlando ☎ 851-7130

Del Frisco's $$$
729 Lee Rd, Orlando
☎ 645-4443

**Key W. Kool's
Restaurant $$**
7725 W. Highway 192,
Kissimmee ☎ 396-1166

**Lili Marlene's Aviator's
Pub and Restaurant $$**
129 W. Church St, Orlando
☎ 422-2434

Sizzler $
branches throughout
Orlando and Kissimmee

**Western Sizzlin
Steak House $-$$**
5073 W. Highway 192
☎ 397-1900

TEX-MEX

Fajita Grill $-$$
4941 Sunward Drive,
Kissimmee. No phone.

Rio Bravo Cantina $-$$
3770 Colonial Dr, Orlando
☎ 896-2167

THAI

**Siam Orchid
Restaurant $-$$$**
7575 Republic Drive,
Orlando ☎ 351-0821

WEST INDIAN

The Spicy Hot $-$$
2141 W. Colonial Dr,
Orlando ☎ 843-2251

WORTH VISITING

Planet Hollywood is a
movie and TV-themed
restaurant filled with movie
memorabilia and holograms
of stars, plus a private
screening room.
☎ 827-7827

DINNER SHOWS

Arabian Nights
6225 W Irlo Bronson
Highway, Kissimmee
☎ 239-9223

Asian Adventure
5225 International Drive
☎ 351-5655

Capone's Dinner and Show
4740 W. Highway 192,
Kissimmee
☎ 397-BEST

Hilarities Comedy Theater
5251 International Drive
☎ 352-7161

King Henry's Feast
8984 International Drive
☎ 351-5151

Mai Tiki Polynesian Luau
464 W. Highway 436,
Altamonte Springs
☎ 682-1688

Mardi Gras
8445 International Drive
☎ 351-5151

Medieval Times
4510 W. Irlo Bronson
Highway, Kissimmee
☎ 239-0214

Pacino's Italian Ristorante
5795 Irlo Bronson Highway, Kissimmee,
☎ 239-4141

Sleuth's Mystery Dinner Show
Republic Square, Orlando
☎ 363-1985

Wild Bill's Wild West Dinner Show
Fort Liberty, 5260 W. Irlo Bronson Highway, Kissimmee
☎ 351-5151

LIVE ENTERTAINMENT AND NIGHT CLUBS

Baja Beach Club
Vista Center, 3 miles (5km) off I-4 at exit 27. Disco.
☎ 239-6996

Big D's Lounge & Package
1221 11th Street, St. Cloud. Live rock & roll.
Friday & Saturday
☎ 892-8879

Branding Iron Bar Grill
4509 S. Orange Blossom Trail, Kissimmee.
Country Rock Bank.
☎ 846-4533

Church Street Station
124 W. Church St, Orlando. Dixieland and cancan at Rosie O'Grady's, folk music and bluegrass at Apple Annie's, Phineas Phogg's disco, and Cheyenne Saloon and Opera House.
☎ 422-2434

Club Juana
Highway 17-92 and SR436 in Casselberry
☎ 831-7717

Empress Lilly
Lake Buena Vista Village.
Jazz. ☎ 828-3900

Hollywood Nites
5715 Major Boulevard, Orlando. Dancing nightly.
☎ 351-3340

J.J. Whispers
5100 Adamson St, Orlando. Nightclub and disco.
☎ 629-4779

Laughing Kookaburra
Buena Vista Palace Hotel, Buena Vista Dr.
☎ 827-2727

Langford Hotel
Winter Park.
Jazz. ☎ 644-3400

Litle Darlin's Rock & Roll Palace
5770 W. Irlo Bronson Highway, Kissimmee.
☎ 396-6499

Pleasure Island
Entertainment complex with six night clubs, including country-western theme club, comedy club, nightly New Year's Eve celebrations, jazz.
Lake Buena Vista.
☎ 934-7781

Shooter's
4315 N. Orange Blossom Trail, Winter Park.
Nightly dancing.
☎ 298-2855

Sullivan's Trailway Lounge
1108 S. Orange Blossom
Trail, Orlando.
Nightly dancing to
local and touring bands.
☎ 843-2934

Top of the World Restaurant
WDW Contemporary Resort.
Dancing.
☎ 824-3611

FISHING

Fishing is almost a way of life in Florida. People fish for
both food and sport. Florida saltwater and freshwater
fishing licenses are needed for all anglers aged 16 and
older. All fees collected are used specifically for improving
and restoring fish habitats, building artificial reefs,
researching marine life and habitats, enforcement and
education.

Licenses are obtained from county tax collectors and
local fishing and bait shops. Fishing charters and cruises
are available throughout the area, both on inland lakes and
sailing out from the Atlantic and Gulf Coasts. It is usually
best to go in a group or be prepared to join others as this
cuts the cost down. Most charters include the cost of boat,
equipment, bait and guides. There are also a number of
fishing camps, some of the best found on Lake
Tohopekaliga. For information on fishing, size and species,
contact:

Department of Natural Resources, Office of Fisheries
Management & Assistance Services, Mail Station #240,
3900 Commonwealth Boulevard, Tallahassee FL 32399-
3000 ☎ (904) 922-4340.

GOLF

More than 55 million rounds of golf are played every year
on Florida's 1,100 courses. There are more than one
hundred 18-hole courses in the Greater Orlando area
alone, and every year Florida hosts around twenty professional golf tournaments. It is the home of the PGA Tour,
PGA of America, the Ladies PGA, Senior PGA Tour and the
Ben Hogan Tour.

Fact File

HORSE RIDING

There are many opportunities for horse riding. Many State/
National Parks have horse riding trails, ie Fort Cooper/Little
Manatee River, Highlands Hammock/Lower Wekiva River,
Rock Springs Run/Wekiwa. You can hire horses at Fort
Wilderness Campground (☎ (407) 824-2803), Flying
Unicorn Ranch, Sanford (☎ (407) 322-5501), Grand
Cypress Equestrian Centre, Grand Cypress Resort (☎ (407)
239-4608), and Poinciana Riding Stables, Kissimmee
(☎ (407) 847-4343).

INFORMATION FOR OVERSEAS VISITORS

CLOTHING

Central Florida is one of the few destinations where you
can get away with a single piece of carry-on luggage for
all your clothes if you are flying. Unless you are staying in
a very smart resort and like dressing up, T-shirts and
shorts suit most people during the day, with slacks or
jeans and a casual shirt or blouse, ideal for the balmy
evenings.

Sandals are fine for around the pool and beach (they are
sometimes essential because the sand can literally get too
hot to walk on with bare feet). If you plan to spend a lot of
time visiting the attractions, a comfortable pair of shoes or
trainers is advisable.

Although the temperature drops a few degrees during
the winter months, most visitors still find it very warm,
although a light jumper may be needed for evening wear,
if only to cope with the icy-blast from the air conditioning.
You will need bathing costumes, sunglasses and hat. The
sun is deceptively strong and sunglasses not only help you
see better in the glare, they will protect your eyes from
harmful rays. You only have to spend a little time in Florida
to appreciate how useful a baseball cap is.

It really is important to acclimatize to the Florida sun
before spending too long exposed to it. It is even more
important for children to take things carefully at first by
covering up, especially their heads. A sun screen, with a
screen protection factor of at least 15+ is essential.

Fact File

CRIME

Some years ago there were some disturbing attacks on tourists, but there is no evidence to show that holiday-makers face any greater risk in Florida than they do in many other places worldwide. While each incident is hugely regrettable, it has to be said that tens of millions of visitors travel to Florida every year and never see any signs of trouble. If basic sensible precautions are taken, there is no reason why you should.

Do not wave money about, wear as little jewelry as possible and keep money, credit cards and passport separate.

Before leaving the airport, make sure you know where you are going and how to get there. If it is very late and you are tired, take a taxi to an airport hotel and stay overnight so that you can continue your journey the next day refreshed and in daylight.

If you are staying in a hotel or motel, use their safe for valuables such as passports, tickets etc. Carry a photocopy of your passport in case you are officially asked for identification.

When travelling in a car keep the doors locked and the windows up, and when leaving the car parked, make sure there is nothing visible that might tempt a thief. Never sleep in the car overnight, find a cheap motel or hotel.

Ask the hotel staff or your courier if there are any areas to avoid, and make sure you do not stray into them, especially at night.

In Central Florida, it is quite safe to walk around during the day, but there is always the outside chance of a bag snatcher, or someone trying to grab your video camera, so be careful.

If you are stopped and threatened, do not resist. Most thieves only want cash or easily disposable items, and most will make their getaway as soon as you hand them over.

If you are robbed, report it to the police immediately. Report the theft of credit cards and traveller's cheques to the appropriate organisations, and if your passport is stolen, report it as soon as possible to your Embassy or Consulate.

Fact File

THEFT AND LOST PROPERTY

If luggage or property is lost or stolen report it to the
police and the relevant authority (airport, car rental company, hotel) as soon as possible. Try and contact your
insurance company for permission to replace stolen items
and keep all receipts.

CURRENCY AND CREDIT CARDS

The American dollar comes in denominations of $1, $2
(rare), $5, $10, $20, $50 and $100. In practice, it is not a
good idea to have higher denomination bills and some
establishments refuse to accept $50 and $100 dollar bills
because there are forgeries about. Always keep a few $1
bills in your wallet for tips.

It is easy to confuse the various denominations because
they are all the same size and colour, the only difference is
their face value. Always check that you are handing over
the right note, and check your change. The dollar is divided into cents with the following coins: 1c (penny), 5c
(nickel), 10c (dime) and 25c (quarter). There are 50c and
$1 dollar coins but these are rarely found in circulation.

Most major credit cards are widely accepted, particularly
American Express, Diners Club, Visa and Mastercard. There
may be problems occasionally in submitting foreign Access cards, but these are usually overcome if you point out
that it is part of the Mastercard network.

There is little point in taking all your credit cards with
you so pick one or two that will be most useful, and leave
the others in a secure place at home. If taking traveller's
cheques, make sure they are dollar cheques, which can be
handed over in lieu of cash in most places.

CUSTOMS

There are strict Customs and Department of Agriculture
laws governing what can and cannot be imported into the
United States. Drugs, dangerous substances, firearms and
ammunition are banned, as are a wide range of foods,
such as meat, dairy products, fruit and vegetables in order
to maintain the disease-free state of Florida's agriculture.
Florida has rabies and pets being brought into the State
should be vaccinated against the disease.

While there are no restrictions on how much cash you can take into the USA, all amounts over $10,000 must be listed on your customs declaration form. This is part of the authorities' fight against drug trafficking.

All gifts taken into the country and their value, should be listed on the declaration, and should not be wrapped so they are available for inspection if required.

You are allowed to import duty-free into the USA, 200 cigarettes, 50 cigars, 2kg of tobacco, or proportionate amounts of each; 1 litre of alcoholic drinks (if aged 21 or over), and gifts up to the value of $100. If arriving by air from outside the US, you will have to hand in your customs declaration after clearing immigration.

You can buy duty-free goods at the airport before leaving the USA, but you cannot pick up your purchases until just before you board the plane. After paying for your goods you will be given a receipt, and you must remember to collect your goods from the duty-free staff who will be somewhere in the tunnel between the exit gate and plane.

DOCUMENTS

All visitors to the USA must have a valid passport with at least 6 months to run from the day they are scheduled to return home.

Under the Visa Waiver Program, visitors from the UK, most EC countries and Japan, arriving by air or sea aboard a carrier participating in the programme, do not require a waiver, provided they do not plan to stay for more than 90 days. If travelling under this programme, you must complete a green 'visa waiver' form, which is handed in to immigration on arrival.

Visitors making frequent trips to the USA or planning to stay for more than 3 months should have a valid visa. You obtain a US visa by filling in the application form (obtainable from Embassies and some travel companies) and sending it, together with your passport and other documents required, to the visa section of the United States Embassy in your country. Allow at least 21 days for processing, although the visa is often returned earlier than this. Some travel companies, because of special arrangements with the US Embassy, can get the visa within 48 or 72 hours. In emergencies, it may be possible to visit the visa section personally, but always check first.

Fact
File

The normal tourist visa allows multiple entries to the US and is valid indefinitely. Even if you have to renew your passport, the visa is still valid in the cancelled passport, provided you present both at immigration. Further information can be obtained by writing to The United States Consulate General, Visa Branch at the United States Embassy in your country (see Embassies p 243).

DRIVING

A valid UK driving licence is needed if you want to rent a car in Florida, and you must be 21 years of age or over. If you plan to spend a lot of time in the State it may well pay you to get a Florida driving licence, which is valid throughout the USA.

Many overseas automobile clubs are affiliated with the American Automobile Association (AAA) and proof of membership of one of these, entitles you to a range of services, including breakdown assistance, free maps and discounts for car rental, hotels and attractions.

Driving in Florida is a pleasure once you have got used to driving on the right hand side of the road and familiarised yourself with traffic signs and so on.

Because of the lower speed limits and generally good lane discipline, you should not have any problems driving. It also helps if you can remember that even numbered roads generally run east to west, while highways with an odd number usually run north to south.

If you want to get from A to B in a hurry, take an interstate road or a turnpike. Interstate roads are multi-lane highways with a maximum speed limit of 55mph (88kph), except in some rural areas where it increases to 65mph (104kph) and occasionally 70mph (112kph). Interstates also often have minimum speed limits, usually 40mph (64kph).

While no charge is levied for travelling on interstate highways, a toll is due if you travel on turnpikes. These roads are privately maintained and you either pay a toll to go on to a particular stretch of road, or you take a ticket and pay when you turn off the toll based on how far you have travelled. The same speed limits apply as for interstates. On both turnpikes and interstates there are frequent pull in areas for food and fuel.

US Highways are slower, often running through towns where delays can occur at traffic lights and because of lower

Fact File

urban speed limits. You will find, however, far more road-side cafés, restaurants, and overnight accommodation and other services along US Highways. Speed limits vary between 45mph (72kph) and 65mph (104kph) in rural areas to 15-40mph (24-64kph) in urban areas. The lowest speed limits are usually found in areas around schools.

A freeway is a road running through the heart of an urban area, designed to get traffic quickly through the built up area.

Accidents

If you are involved in any road accident, exchange particulars with other drivers and get the names and addresses of any witnesses. You must report to the police any accident that involves personal injury, or significant damage (anything other than a minor bump). Never admit liability or even say 'I'm sorry'. Some insurance companies will not honour a policy if a driver has admitted liability. If you are driving a rented car, notify the rental company as soon as possible. If people are injured, no matter how hard it seems, leave medical assistance to those who are qualified to administer it. If you try and help and something goes wrong, you could face a massive bill for damages.

Car Rental

It is usually cheaper to arrange this through your travel company or as part of a fly-drive package. Although it is optional, you are strongly advised to have collision damage waiver (CDW) and it is often cheaper to pre-pay this as well.

The car rental companies are either situated on the airport or a short drive away. If off the airport, courtesy buses shuttle to and from the car pick-up point.

You will need a valid driving licence and be 21 years old or over. You will need to give the address at which you will be staying in Central Florida and a telephone number, and you may be asked to produce your passport and return airline ticket. If paying by pre-paid voucher, you will also be asked for a credit card to pay for incidentals such as airport tax, additional drivers and so on.

When you check in to collect your car, the clerks will try to persuade you to upgrade or take out extra insurance. Be sure you understand what they are trying to sell you and decide if you need it. Cars available range from economy

models to limousines, and some rental companies will urge you to upgrade simply because they have run out of vehicles in the category you ordered. If they can persuade you to upgrade they will charge you the difference, but if you refuse they must still give you a bigger car because they are obliged to provide you with a vehicle. If they have run out of models in the category you ordered, you will finish up with something bigger but at no extra cost.

Driving under the influence of alcohol or drugs

Even having an open container of alcohol in a car is illegal, and it is just not worth the risk of drinking and driving as the penalties are very severe, including imprisonment and vehicle confiscation. Driving under the influence of drugs is also a serious crime and you could end up in prison.

Emergencies

Breakdown

If you break down in a rural area, move across on to the hard shoulder, lift the bonnet (hood), and then get back into your vehicle, lock the doors and wait for help. If it is at night, you must use your emergency flashers. Police cars patrol the highways and will come to your assistance. If you are driving a rental car, contact the company at once and ask for a replacement vehicle.

Members of affiliated overseas automobile associations can also contact the American Automobile Association. You can find the AAA number in the telephone directory,or in the event of a breakdown, you can ring toll-free ☎ 1-800-AAA-HELP.

Getting Lost

If you get lost in the Central Florida area you can use more than 2,500 Sprint/United Telephone pay phones to get directions. Dial ☎ 1-800-414-LOST and then enter the telephone number of your destination. The 24-hour computer controlled service will then work out the fastest, safest way to get you there and give you directions. The system takes into account one-way street systems, speed restrictions and traffic conditions and is constantly up-dated. At some locations, you will even get the directions printed out by fax. There is a small fee for each request which can be billed to any major credit card.

Fact File

Maps

For pre-trip planning, the Rand McNally Road Atlas (United States, Canada and Mexico) has state and city maps, distances between major cities, scenic routes and major sites of interest. Free maps are available from car rental companies, tourist information offices and the American Automobile Association (AAA) if you belong to an affiliated association or club. Before setting out on a journey plan your route and allow plenty of time to reach your destination without speeding. If arriving in Florida by air for the first time, ask your car rental company to indicate on their free map, the best route to take to reach your destination.

Parking

When parking at night, choose a spot that is well lit and ideally in a busy area. Lock all doors and make sure that no luggage is visible.

Gas (Petrol)

Most new cars take unleaded fuel, but always check before filling up.

Getting fuel can be confusing because pumps operate in a number of different ways. Usually the nozzle has to be removed and then the bracket it rests on, moved into an upright position to activate the pump.

Some filling stations require pre-payment and smaller stations will often not take credit cards, while others may charge a fee if a credit card is offered.

Rules of the Road

1. Drive on the right and pass on the left.
2. Observe the posted speed limits: 55-70mph (88-112kph) on highways, 25-40mph (40-64kph) in urban areas, and 15mph (24kph) in school zones.
3. All traffic accidents must be reported.
4. School buses. If a school bus has stopped to board or unload passengers traffic in both directions must stop. The only exception is when oncoming traffic is separated from the bus by a central reservation.
5. Do not park near a fire hydrant. If you do you will be fined and your vehicle may be towed away.
6. Always give way to emergency vehicles.

Speeding

Police in Central Florida impose on the spot fines for speeding, and you can even spend a night in jail for going too fast. Be careful on turnpikes as your ticket is time-stamped and if you get to a payment booth too fast, you can also be fined for speeding.

Traffic Signals

Red light	—	you must stop
Amber light	—	signal is about to change, or it is a warning light
Green	—	go
Green arrow	—	follow the direction of the arrow
Flashing red light	—	you must stop but may then proceed with care
Flashing yellow light	—	slow down and then proceed with care

ELECTRICITY

Electrical appliances in Florida operate on a 110 volt alternating current.

EMBASSIES

UK
5 Upper Grosvenor Street
London
W1A 2JB
☎ 071 499-7010

Canada
1155 Saint Alexandra
Montreal
Quebec H22 122
☎ 514-398-9695

Australia
36th floor, Electricity House
Park & Elizabeth Streets
Sydney NSW 2000
☎ 02-261-9200

New Zealand
4th floor, Yorkshire General
Building
CNR Shortland & O'Connell
Auckland
☎ 09-303-2724

EMERGENCIES

The emergency telephone number is 911, and if that fails, dial 0 for the operator who will put you through to the appropriate service.

ILLNESS AND INJURY

It is absolutely essential to have adequate insurance cover if travelling to Florida. It is a good idea to carry a photo-copy of your insurance policy with you, and keep the original in your room. While medical service is first rate, it is expensive.

If you need to seek a doctor while staying in a hotel, motel or rental home, the staff will normally be able to recommend someone to call. If you are injured away from your base, there are emergency clinics and hospitals. Procedures for payment vary but you will most probably be asked to pay by credit card or cash, so make sure you get all receipts so that you can reclaim on your insurance. If you need a dentist, you will find a list of the names in the telephone directory, and again expect to have to pay on the spot and reclaim for treatment later.

In an emergency dial 911, keep calm, explain the prob-lem and help will be sent.

If bitten by an animal, wild or domestic, seek medical help as rabies is endemic in Florida. There are also poison-ous snakes and spiders but their bites are rarely dangerous if treated promptly, and such bites are, in any case, un-common.

It is always worth travelling with a small first aid kit, and you will need sun screen and insect repellant, although these are best bought locally. If you are taking medication, make sure you have enough to last throughout the trip, and a letter from your doctor explaining why the medica-tion was prescribed, may prevent a difficult situation if questioned about the drugs.

IMMIGRATION

If flying from abroad to Florida you will have to clear US Immigration and Naturalisation formalities. You must have a valid passport and appropriate visa or visa waiver docu-ment. You will be directed to an immigration line (queue) once you enter the terminal building. When you are called by the immigration officer, present your passport and other necessary forms which you will have been given to fill in on the plane. Provided you have a return ticket, you should have no problems and your passport will be stamped with a date in the future allowing you time to complete your holiday or business. You must leave the country by this date, or seek an extension from an immigration office. A portion of your immigration form is stapled to your passport, and this is surrendered when you leave the country, so do not lose it. This portion is used to tell the computer that you have left the country, and without it, you may be classified as an illegal alien, and have a lot of explaining to do next time you try to go back into the USA.

INSURANCE

It is essential to take out insurance before travelling to Florida. Make sure that the cover is adequate to meet any claims that might have to be submitted in the event of an accident or health problem. Remember that medical care and hospital bills are likely to be much higher in Florida than in many other parts of the world, and awards in the court for damages as a result of an accident can be astronomic.

Make sure the insurance covers you against third party law suits, and carry a copy of your insurance cover with you.

It is always worth shopping round for holiday insurance because cost and cover can vary enormously.

NATIONAL AND STATE PARKS

Take advantage of the State and National Parks. They offer an exciting view of the 'real' Florida and a chance to see at first hand wildlife, historic sites and monuments. A modest charge is usually made for the driver and slightly less for passengers. Florida has more than 110 park areas where you can usually swim, camp, hike, fish, canoe or watch the wildlife. Every year, around 13 million people visit the parks, although most are so large, that even on a busy day, you will never feel you are one of a crowd.

State Parks open from 8am to sunset every day of the year, although opening times of visitors centres, historic sites and museums vary. Most of the State Parks are accessible to disabled visitors.

A recent study of the best beaches in the USA found that nine in the top twenty were in Florida's State Parks.

It is important to keep them that way, so follow the out-back rule: take nothing but pictures, leave nothing but footprints.

For further information contact:
Department of Natural Resources Park Information
Mail Station #535, 3900 Commonwealth Boulevard,
Tallahassee FL 32399-3000☎ (904) 488-9872

PHOTOGRAPHY

All types of film are freely available in Florida and often cheaper than at home. Always ask for a discount if buying large quantities of film because you can normally get a reduction, especially if paying by cash.

One hour developing is also widely available but it costs more than the normal turn round for film processing. Many of the main attractions have cameras for hire, and video cameras are also available for hire from a number of out-lets.

Because of the intense sunshine, it is best to use high speed film, and if your camera permits, it is worth buying a suitable filter to reduce glare.

It is important to prevent your camera from getting too hot because the film may be damaged.

POST OFFICES/MAIL

Many shops sell stamps but it is often advisable to avoid stamp machines which can work out more expensive. Post offices can handle all your mailing requirements and will hold letters sent to you for up to 30 days provided they are clearly marked with your name and the words 'c/o General Delivery'. You will be asked for identification before any letters are handed over.

American Express card holders can also have mail sent to them c/o the local AMEX office. Again, it is usually held for 30 days. Mail should be clearly addressed with the recipient's name and marked 'Client Mail'.

US Mail boxes are not always immediately obvious but can be found in most shopping areas, and there are usu-ally facilities in hotels and so on, for posting mail.

Fact File

SALES TAX

Sales tax causes a lot of confusion among foreign visitors who find that they are asked to pay more for goods than the amount printed on the price tag. State sales tax is added automatically when you pay and in Central Florida it is either 6 or 7 per cent, depending which county you are in. Most goods are subject to the sales tax but groceries and medicines are exempt, as are legal and accounting services, and other services 'that do not involve the sale of a tangible item.'

TELEPHONES

The emergency code is 911, and if that fails, dial 0 for Operator.

All American (and Canadian) telephones have a three-digit area code, and a seven-digit phone number. Area codes are only used when calling between areas. The area code 800 is reserved for toll free calls, usually valid only from America or Canada. Major airlines, hotels and car rental companies have toll free numbers listed in the Yellow Pages. Long distance and toll free calls are normally preceded with 1.

Direct dialling of calls, even international ones, are possible from most hotels and public pay phones. The international code 011 and the country code is followed by the phone number, minus the leading zero. To telephone 0171-784-9659, a ficticious London number, dial 011 (International Direct Dialling Access), 44 (the United Kingdom Country Code), 171-784-9659 (the London Number, less the leading zero).

Not all pay-phones are operated by AT&T, and rules for long distance dialling vary, but most phones provide instructions. International direct dialling from a public phone box requires a fistful of quarters, up to $10 worth for a short call. BT, AT&T and others make calling home easier with their phone cards. Collect or telephone credit card calls may be made to the United Kingdom by dialling 1-800-445-5667. It is cheaper to make long distance and international calls between 5-11pm and at weekends.

For directory enquiries, dial 411 for local numbers, or the area code and 555-1212 for long distance numbers.

To find the toll free number of an airline, hotel, or car rental firm, dial 1-800-555-1212 and ask for their number.

TIME AND DATES

Central Florida is in the Eastern Time Zone, which is 5 hours behind Greenwich Mean Time (ie when it is 12noon in London, it is 7am in Orlando). Daylight Savings Time comes into effect in the first Sunday of April when the clocks go forward one hour, and they go back one hour to standard time on the last Sunday in October.

Americans write their dates in the format: month, day, year. Thus Christmas Day in 1999 is December 25, 1999 or in shorthand 12/25/1999.

TIPPING

Generally tip $1 to porters for each piece of luggage carried. Elsewhere tips of 15 per cent are considered normal in bars, restaurants, taxis and so on. Wages in the catering sector are low and staff aim to boost their take home pay by tips. For exceptional service you may be inspired to tip 20 per cent. If dining in a restaurant which adds an automatic service charge, this is normally paid in lieu of tips. If the service was not up to expectations, however, complain and refuse to pay the service charge.

TOILET FACILITIES

Better known in Florida as the rest room, bathroom, men's room or lady's room. Public toilets are found almost everywhere. There are frequent rest areas with toilets along major highways, and you will find them in most shopping malls, attractions and so on. You will even find them in stores. If you need the toilet, ask for the men's or lady's room or the restroom.

TOURIST OFFICES

Main American tourist offices are at the following addresses. For those countries not listed, contact the American Embassy.

**United States Travel &
Tourism Administration
United States Department
of Commerce**
Washington, DC 20230
USA
☎ 0101-202-659-6000

**United States Travel &
Tourism Administration**
PO Box 1EN
London W1A 1EN
United Kingdom
☎ 071 495 4466

**United States Travel &
Tourism Administration**
Suite 602, 480 University
Avenue
Toronto, Ontario M5G 1V2
Canada
☎ 416-595-5082

**United States Travel &
Tourism Administration**
Suite 6106, MLC Centre
King & Castlereagh Streets
Sydney, NSW 2000
Australia
☎ 02-233-4055

TRAVEL

Air

Most foreign visitors arrive by air at either Orlando, Tampa or Miami airports. They may fly direct into one of these airports from abroad, or clear immigration at another USA destination before catching a Florida flight, depending on the carrier. Competition on Florida routes is intense and pricing is very competitive. Air fares are highest at peak times — Christmas, Easter and the summer holidays. At other times of the year, however, there are usually bargain air tickets to be found if you look around for them but check the details. The fare might sound cheap but it might mean long stopovers between connecting flights and a very late arrival into Orlando, which could be a problem with young children. Package deals generally afford the best value. If you want the freedom to roam or pick your accommodation, go for fly-drive. Always check with your travel agent what special offers, hotel discounts and so on are available.

If you fly on a regular basis, it is worth joining the free 'frequent flyer' schemes operated by most airlines.

Buses

The Greyhound service is almost legendary, and a Greyhound Ameripass is a very cheap and interesting way to travel around, especially city to city, and to meet a lot of people. The scheme incorporates Greyhound and a number of other private bus and coach companies, and is fine for medium and long distance travel. Problems can occur when you get off the Greyhound bus and then have to find public transport to take you to your final destination. Local bus services are infrequent at best.

Land

The only way into Florida by land is from the north through Georgia or Alabama. Interstate 95 runs all the way down the Atlantic seaboard, while Interstate 10, which starts in Los Angeles, enters Florida just west of Pensacola on the Gulf. There are 'Welcome Centres' on all the main roads entering the State. Interstate 75 heads south from I-10 to the Central Gulf Coast. If you leave I-74 for the I-4 just beyond Wildwood, you will drive down into the Greater Orlando area.

Taxis

Local public transport is erratic in Central Florida, and rental cars or taxis are the best ways of getting around. Taxis are not expensive and offer a safe way of travelling around.

Train

If you like train travel, get an Amtrak USA Rail pass, which offers unlimited travel and as many stopovers as you like, for 45 days. Some routes carry restrictions and you will have to pay extra for sleeping car accommodation. For further details ask your travel agent, or write to Amtrak at 60 Massachusetts Ave NE, Washington DC 20002, or ☎ US (202) 383-3000 from outside North America, or use freephone 800-USA-RAIL from within the USA or Canada.

WEIGHTS AND MEASURES

Americans still use the Imperial system of weights and measures, although metric measures are becoming more common. Road distances are always in miles while gas (petrol) can be in either gallons or litres, or both.

Liquid measure differs between America and Britain. 1 US Gallon = 0.833 Imperial Gallons = 3.8 litres.

Women's clothes sizes in the US are two sizes less than the UK equivalent (ie a size 12 dress in the UK would be labelled size 10 in the US), while women's shoe sizes in the US are labelled two sizes larger (ie a size 6 in the UK would be size 8 in the US).

CREDITS

A Day in the Park with Barney™, Adventure Island™, Audio-Animatronics®, Back To The Future®... The Ride℠, Beauty & the Beast®, Beetlejuice's™ Graveyard Revue, Bermuda Triangle℠, Disney's Animal Kingdom® Theme Park, Epcot®, Busch Gardens®, Congo River Rapids™, Cypress Gardens®, Earthquake® – The Big One, ET Adventure®, Fievel's Playland®, Gatorland®, Ghostbusters®, Goosebumps™ Fright Show, Hercules & Xena: Wizards of the Screeen℠, IMAX®, Indiana Jones™, Jaws®, Jurassic Park®, Kongfrontation®, Kumba℠, Lucy: A Tribute℠, Manatees: The Last Generation℠, Marvel Super Hero Island℠, Murder She Wrote® Mystery Theater, Nickelodeon Studios Tour®, Pacific Point Reserve℠, Penguin Encounter℠, Pleasure Island®, Python™, Scorpion™, Seuss Landing℠, Star Wars™, Tanganyika Tidal Wave™, Teenage Mutant Ninja Turtles®, Terminator 2: 3D Battle across time™, Terrors of the Deep®, The Adventures of Rocky and Bullwinkle™, The Funtastic World of Hanna-Barbera™, The Magic Kingdom® Park, The Twilight Zone™ Tower of Terror, Toon Lagoon℠, Walt Disney World® Resort, Walt Disney World® Village, Wild, Wild, Wild, West Stunt Show™, Universal Studios Florida®, Universal Studios Escape℠, Universal Studios Islands of Adventure℠, Universal Studios Citywalk℠, Universal Studios Escape℠ Resorts

Index

A

Anclote Keys   194

B

Blue Spring
  State Park   152
Bok Tower
  Gardens   138
BUSCH GARDENS 160
  Crown Colony   164
  Edge of Africa   164
  Egypt   163
  Lorikeet Landing   167
  Morocco   163
  Myombe Reserve   164
  Nairobi   164
  Stanleyville   165
  The Bird Gardens   166
  The Congo   165
  The Serengeti
    Plain   165
  Timbuktu   165

C

Caladesi Island
  State Park   194
Canaveral National
  Seashore   206
Clearwater   180
Cocoa Beach   210
Cypress Gardens   139
  Southern Belles   140

D

Dade Battlefield State
  Historic Site   194
De Leon Springs State
  Recreation Area   152
Disney's Animal
  Kingdom®
  Theme Park   68
Disney's-MGM

Studios   75

E

Egmont Key
  State Park   194
Epcot®   48

F

Flora and Fauna   7
Fort Cooper
  State Park   195
Fort Pierce   216
Fort Pierce Inlet State
  Recreation Area   217

G

Getting Around   15

H

Heart And Soul
  Of Tampa   172
Highlands Hammock
  State Park   152
Hillsborough
  County   158
Hillsborough River
  State Park   196
Homosassa
  Springs State
  Wildlife Park   196
Honeymoon
  Island State
  Recreation Area   196
Hontoon Island State
  Park   152

I

Indian River
  County   214
International Space
  Station Center   204

K

Kennedy Space
  Center   200
Kissimmee and
  St Cloud   130

L

Lake County   147
Lake Kissimmee
  State Park   153
Lake Louisa
  State Park   196
Lake Manatee State
  Recreation Area   197
Little Manatee
  River State
  Recreation Area   197
Loch Haven Park   129
Lower Wekiva River
  State Reserve   153

M

Major Attractions
  Price Guide   10
Melbourne   212
Merritt Island National
  Wildlife Refuge   206

N

New Smyrna Sugar
  Mill Ruins State
  Historic Site   217

O

Orlando   119

P

Paynes Creek State
  Historic Site   153
Pinellas Suncoast   182
Planning Your
  Holiday   12

Q

Questions and
  Answers   17

R

Rock Springs Run
  State Reserve   154

S

Sanford   145
SEA WORLD
  OF FLORIDA   90
  Anheuser-Busch
    Hospitality
    Center   100
  Bayside Water Ski
    Stadium   101
  Clydesdale
    Hamlet   100
  Journey to Atlantis   97
  Key West at
    Sea World   96
  Manatees: The Last
    Generation   97
  Pacific Point
    Reserve   99
  Penguin Encounter   99
  Sea Lion and Otter
    Stadium   99
  Sea Turtle Exhibit   97
  Sea World Theatre   99
  Shamu Stadium   100
  Shamu: Close Up!   100
  Shamu's Happy
    Harbor   101
  Stingray Lagoon   97
  Tide Pool   96
  Tropical Rain Forest   96
  Tropical Reef and
    Flamingo Exhibit   96
  Whale and Dolphin
    Stadium   97
  Wild Arctic   101

Sebastian   214
Sebastian Inlet State
  Recreation Area   217
Seminole County   143
Silver Springs   141
South of
  Tampa Bay   191
Space Coast   199
SPLENDID CHINA   114
  Terra Cotta Warriors
    and Horses   118
  The Ancient Star
    Observatory   118
  The Forbidden City
    and
    Imperial Palace   117
  The Great Wall   117
  The Mausoleum of
    Genghis Khan   118
  The Potala Palace   117
St Petersburg   180

T

Tampa   155
Tampa Adventure   177
Tarpon Springs   182
Tenoroc Recreation
  Area   154
The Magic
  Kingdom® Park   29
Tosohatchee State
  Reserve   154

U

Universal Studios
  Escape   113
  Universal Studios
    CityWalk   113
  Universal Studios
    Islands of
    Adventure   113
Universal Studios
  Escape Resorts   113

UNIVERSAL
STUDIOS
FLORIDA   104
  A Day in the Park
    With Barney   111
  Back to the Future…
    The Ride   111
  Beetlejuice's
    Graveyard Revue   109
  E.T. Adventure   112
  Earthquake —
    The Big One   109
  Fievel's Playland   112
  Hercules and Xena:
    Wizards of the
    Screen   108
  Hitchcock's 3-D
    Theatre   108
  Jaws   111
  Kongfrontation   109
  Lagoon   113
  Lucy: A Tribute   108
  New York   109
  Nickelodeon
    Studios and Tour   108
  Production
    Tram Tour   106
  Terminator 2: 3-D   113
  The Boneyard   112
  The Funtastic
    World of Hanna-
    Barbera   108
  The Gory, Gruesome
    & Grotesque Horror
    Make-Up   112
  The Hi-Tones   113
  Twister   109
  Wild, Wild, Wild West
    Stunt Show   111

V

Vero Beach   214

Index

W

Walt Disney World®
Hotels 24

WALT DISNEY WORLD® RESORT 18

DISNEY-MGM
STUDIOS 75
ABC Sound Studio
1 Saturday
Morning 80
"Beauty and the
Beast" Live on
Stage 81
Disney's: The
Hunchback of
Notre Dame —
A Musical 84
Goosebumps™
Fright Show 81
Honey I Shrunk the
Kids Movie Set
Adventure 81
Indiana Jones™
Stunt
Spectacular 80
Jim Henson's
Muppet™ Vision
3D 4D 81
Mulan: The Parade 85
New York Street 81
Star Tours 80
Sunset Boulevard 85
The American
Film Institute
Showcase 81
The Great
Movie Ride 84
The Magic of Disney
Animation 84
The Twilight Zone™
Tower of Terror 85
Voyage of the
Little Mermaid 84

Disney's All-Star
Movies Resort 87
Disney's All-Star
Music Resort 87
Disney's All-Star
Sports Resort 87
DISNEY'S ANIMAL
KINGDOM®
THEME PARK 68
Africa 72
Animal Kingdom
Shows 73
Asia 73
Camp
Minnie-Mickey 72
Conservation
Station 72
DinoLand USA 73
Safari Village 69
The Oasis 69
Disney's Blizzard
Beach Water Park 86
Disney's
BoardWalk 88
Disney's
Discovery Island 23
Disney's Typhoon
Lagoon Water
Park 22
Disney's Wide
World of Sports 87
Downtown
Disney Area 88
EPCOT® 48
Future World 51
GM Test Track 58
Honey, I Shrunk
The Audience 58
Horizons 58
Innoventions 52
Spaceship Earth 51
The Land 58
The Living Seas 59
Wonders of Life 57
World Showcase 60

THE MAGIC
KINGDOM®
PARK 29
Adventureland 34
Cinderella Castle 33
Fantasyland 41
Frontierland 35
Liberty Square 37
Main Street, USA 31
Mickey's
Toontown Fair 43
Tomorrowland 44
River Country 23

Water Lovers 178
Weedon Island
State Preserve 197
Wekiwa Springs
State Park 154
Winter Park 128

Y

Ybor City 171
Yulee Sugar Mill
Ruins State
Historic Site 197

LANDMARK
Publishing Ltd ● ● ● ●
VISITORS GUIDES

* Practical guides for the independent traveller
* Written in the form of touring itineraries
* Full colour illustrations and maps
* Detailed Landmark FactFile of practical information
* Landmark Visitors Guides highlight all the interesting places you will want to see, so ensuring that you make the most of your visit

1. *Britain*

Cornwall
Cotswolds &
 Shakespeare Country*
Devon
Dorset
East Anglia
Guernsey
Hampshire

Jersey
Kent
Lake District*
Peak District
Scotland*
Somerset
Yorkshire Dales & York

2. *Europe*

Bruges
Cracow
Italian Lakes*
Madeira

Provence*
Riga
Tallinn

3. *Other*

Dominican Republic
India: Goa
India: Kerala & The South
The Gambia
St Lucia*

Florida Keys*
Florida: Gulf Coast*
Orlando & Central Florida*
New Zealand*

Landmark Publishing
Waterloo House, 12 Compton,
Ashbourne, Derbyshire
DE6 IDA England
Tel: 01335 347349
Fax: 01335 347303
e-mail: landmark@clara.net
Catalogue sent on request

*In the USA order from:
Hunter Publishing Inc,
130 Campus Drive,
Edison NJ 08818
Tel: (732) 225 1900
or (800) 255 0343
Fax: (732) 417 0482
www.hunterpublishing.com

Published by
Landmark Publishing Ltd,
Waterloo House, 12 Compton, Ashbourne, Derbyshire DE6 1DA England
Tel: 01335 347349 Fax: 01335 347303 e-mail: landmark@clara.net

Published in the USA by
Hunter Publishing Inc,
130 Campus Drive, Edison NJ 08818
Tel: (732) 225 1900, (800) 255 0343 Fax: (732) 417 0482
Web site: www.hunterpublishing.com

2nd Edition
ISBN 1 901 522 22 9

British Library Cataloguing in Publication Data: a catalogue record for this
book is available from the British Library.

Print: UIC Printing & Packaging Pte Ltd, Singapore
Cartography: James Allsopp
Design: Samantha Witham

Picture Credits:
© **Disney Enterprises:** Chapter 2 all;
Sea World® of Florida: 3, 94/95, 98, 103 all;
© **Universal Studios Florida:** back cover top, 6, 90, 110 all, 111;
Don Philpott: back cover B, 138, 142T, 147 both, 151, 182, 183;
Florida's Pinellas Suncoast TB: 186;
Florida Department of Environmental Protection: 142BL,154, 195 all;
Kennedy Space VC: back cover bottom, 14M, 199, 203, 207B;
NASA: 207T, 210; **Tampa/Hillsborough C&VA:** 170T,
170B (HM Stewart III), 171 both, 175, 178 (Jeff Greenberg), 179 both;
© **Busch Entertainment Corp:** 14T, 14B, 155, 163 both,166 both;
Church Street Station: 123;
Orlando/Orange County C&VB: 126, 131T (Mark Englert), 134;
Kissimmee/St Cloud C&VB: 114 both, 119,135 both;
Gatorland: 131B; **Geiger Asoc:** 142M, 142BR;
St Petersburg Clearwater Area CVB: 187 both;
Vero Beach Tourism Council: 211T; **St Lucie TB:** 211B